Lecture Notes in Business Information Processing 434

More information about this series at http://www.springer.com/series/7911

Xiaofeng Wang · Antonio Martini ·
Anh Nguyen-Duc · Viktoria Stray (Eds.)

Software Business

12th International Conference, ICSOB 2021
Drammen, Norway, December 2–3, 2021
Proceedings

Springer

Editors
Xiaofeng Wang
Free University of Bozen-Bolzano
Bolzano, Italy

Antonio Martini
University of Oslo
Oslo, Norway

Anh Nguyen-Duc
University of South Eastern Norway
Bø, Norway

Viktoria Stray
University of Oslo and SINTEF
Oslo, Norway

ISSN 1865-1348 ISSN 1865-1356 (electronic)
Lecture Notes in Business Information Processing
ISBN 978-3-030-91982-5 ISBN 978-3-030-91983-2 (eBook)
https://doi.org/10.1007/978-3-030-91983-2

This Springer imprint is published by the registered company Springer Nature Switzerland AG
The registered company address is: Gewerbestrasse 11, 6330 Cham, Switzerland

Preface

Welcome to the proceedings of the 12th International Conference on Software Business (ICSOB 2021). This edition of the conference was hosted by the School of Business at the University of South-Eastern Norway (USN) and the Department of Informatics at the University of Oslo (UiO), Norway. USN has 88 undergraduate programs, 44 master's degree programs, and eight PhD programs. Measured in terms of the number of students, USN is among the largest providers in higher education in Norway. UiO is Norway's oldest institution for research and higher education and celebrated its 200th anniversary in 2011. UiO has 28,000 students and 7,000 employees and offers 40 master's degree programs. In 2020, a total of 497 students completed their doctoral degree. UiO has eight faculties, two museums, and numerous research centers including 10 Norwegian Centres of Excellence. UiO is one of the world's top 100 universities, according to the Shanghai Ranking. Five Nobel laureates have been employed at the UiO.

The special theme of ICSOB 2021 was 'Software Sustainability'. Sustainability is derived from the concept of sustainable development and is defined by the World Commission on Environment and Development as "a process of change in which the exploitation of resources, the direction of investments, the orientation of technological development, and institutional change are made consistent with future as well as present needs". Research about software sustainability addresses sustainability concerns regarding aspects such as software products, software development processes, strategy and policy, people, partnerships, ecosystems, and business models.

For ICSOB 2021, we received 39 submissions covering a wide range of research topics. Each submission was reviewed by three to five independent expert reviewers. After a round of discussion among reviewers and program chairs, the Program Committee accepted 13 full papers and five short papers. The papers were primarily selected for the quality of the presented work and their relevance to the community. The conference covered a range of topics including software sustainability, Agile development, DevOps, software startups, prototyping, software ecosystems, crowdsourcing platforms, technical debts, and risk management. The authors of the selected papers came from Finland, Germany, Sweden, Denmark, Norway, Estonia, Brazil, the UK, and Spain.

The conference offered two interesting keynotes: the first one titled "From Software through Art to Sustainability", given by Letizia Jaccheri from Norwegian University of Science and Technology, and the second one titled "Software Sustainability: Wake-Up Call for Taking Responsibility", given by Jutta Eckstein.

As a part of the conference this year, the ICSOB community collaborated with the Founder Institute to organize two events that connected researchers, practitioners, and startup founders. The first one was "Lightning Talks on Sustainability in Software Startups" bringing together researchers seeking to connect with software startups about particular phenomena and software startups seeking to explain their business model and traction. The second one was a workshop on "Bridging the Gap: Entrepreneurial Theory and Practice in Software Businesses". The events were hosted by Bruno Pešec and Dimitris Polychronopoulos.

On the behalf of the organization team, we would like to thank the members of the Program Committee and the additional reviewers for their efforts in evaluating the submissions and ensuring the high quality of the conference. The efforts of the Steering and Organizing Committees and all the chairs were of enormous value in building a successful conference. We extend our gratitude to all the scholars who submitted papers to the conference, all the authors who presented papers, the various audiences who participated in very inspirational discussions during the conference, and the practitioners who shared their experiences and thoughts during the workshops.

October 2021

Xiaofeng Wang
Antonio Martini
Anh Nguyen-Duc
Viktoria Stray

Organization

Conference Chair

Anh Nguyen-Duc	University of South-Eastern Norway, Norway

Program Co-chairs

Xiaofeng Wang	Free University of Bozen-Bolzano, Italy
Antonio Martini	University of Oslo, Norway

Proceedings Chair

Viktoria Stray	University of Oslo and SINTEF, Norway

Publicity Co-chairs

Kryzstof Wnuk	Blekinge Institute of Technology, Sweden
Sonja Hyrynsalmi	LUT University, Finland

Startup Community Co-chairs

Dimitris Polychronopoulos	Founder Institute, Norway
Orges Cico	NTNU, Norway

Program Committee

Pekka Abrahamsson	University of Jyväskylä, Finland
Jan Bosch	Chalmers University of Technology, Sweden
Sjaak Brinkkemper	Utrecht University, The Netherlands
Henry Edison	The Maersk Mc-Kinney Moller Institute, Denmark
João M. Fernandes	University of Minho, Portugal
John Mcgregor	Clemson University, USA
Awdren Fontão	Federal University of Mato Grosso do Sul, Brazil
Juan Garbajosa	Universidad Politécnica de Madrid, Spain
Javier Gonzalez-Huerta	Blekinge Institute of Technology, Sweden
Des Greer	Queen's University Belfast, UK
Paul Grünbacher	Johannes Kepler University Linz, Austria
Eduardo Guerra	Free University of Bolzen-Bolzano, Italy
Georg Herzwurm	University of Stuttgart, Germany
Helena Holmström Olsson	Malmö University, Sweden
Sami Hyrynsalmi	LUT University, Finland
Slinger Jansen	Utrecht University, The Netherlands

Dron Khanna	Free University of Bozen-Bolzano, Italy
Eriks Klotins	Blekinge Institute of Technology, Sweden
Johan Linåker	Lund University, Sweden
John Mcgregor	Clemson University, USA
Jorge Melegati	Free University of Bozen-Bolzano, Italy
Tommi Mikkonen	University of Jyväskylä, Finland
Juergen Muench	Reutlingen University, Germany
Dimitri Petrik	University of Stuttgart, Germany
Emil Numminen	Blekinge Institute of Technology, Sweden
Jari Porras	LUT University, Finland
Marcin Ocieszak	Kozminski University, Poland
Usman Rafiq	Free University of Bozen-Bolzano, Italy
Narayan Ramasubbu	University of Pittsburgh, USA
Rodrigo Rebouças de Almeida	Federal University of Paraíba, Brazil
Dirk Riehle	Friedrich-Alexander University Erlangen-Nürnberg, Germany
Guenther Ruhe	University of Calgary, Canada
Andrey Saltan	LUT University, Finland
Rodrigo Santos	UNIRIO, Brazil
Marko Seppänen	Tampere University, Finland
Kari Smolander	Lappeenranta University of Technology, Finland
Gero Strobel	University of Duisburg-Essen, Germany
Pasi Tyrväinen	University of Jyväskylä, Finland
Michael Unterkalmsteiner	Blekinge Institute of Technology, Sweden
Erno Vanhala	LUT University, Finland
Karl Werder	University of Cologne, Germany
Ehsan Zabardast	Blekinge Institute of Technology, Sweden

Sponsoring Organizations

The Research Council of Norway Founder Institute

Contents

Software Sustainability

Elements of Sustainability for Public Sector Software – Mosaic Enterprise Architecture, Macroservices, and Low-Code

Manu Setälä[1], Pekka Abrahamsson[2], and Tommi Mikkonen[2,3(✉)]

[1] Solita, Tampere, Finland
manu.setala@solita.fi
[2] University of Jyväskylä, Jyväskylä, Finland
{pekka.abrahamsson,tommi.j.mikkonen}@jyu.fi
[3] University of Helsinki, Helsinki, Finland
tommi.mikkonen@helsinki.fi

Abstract. Public sector is a large consumer for software. In countries such as Finland, many of the systems are made to order by consultancy companies that participate in public tenders. These tenders initiated by the state, cities, and other public sector organizations. Furthermore, as public sector tasks are often decomposed to various actors, each and every one of them makes their purchase based on their own needs. In this paper, we argue that to maintain software sustainability in this context, there is a need for three key elements. Firstly, there is a need for an enterprise architecture where independent services from various vendors are can be easily deployed and integrated. Secondly, these services are build in a such manner that they can interact via well-defined APIs, but need no direct access to other services. Finally, techniques that support systematic, rapid development and deployment are needed.

Keywords: Public sector software · Mosaic architecture · Macroservices · Software sustainability

1 Introduction

Public sector is a large consumer for software that public sector has multiple, conflicting, and often intangible goals [2]. In countries such as Finland, many of these systems are made to order by consultancy companies that participate in public tenders, initiated by the state, cities, and other public sector organizations. Furthermore, as public sector tasks are often decomposed to various actors, each and every one makes their purchase based on their own needs.

This approach has led to surplus of information systems. For instance, a recent study on information systems at a city of Kerava, Finland, with 35.000 inhabitants found out that here were 93 information systems that interacted in

X. Wang et al. (Eds.): ICSOB 2021, LNBIP 434, pp. 3–9, 2021.
https://doi.org/10.1007/978-3-030-91983-2_1

one way or another [13]. Extrapolating from this, as there are over one hundred cities in Finland, one can conclude that there are thousands of information systems, many of which made to order. Furthermore, while designing systems to order based on a public tender arguably fosters competition, the model has also been considered time consuming and error-prone [7].

While software is (almost) free to copy, there is no point in copying a piece of software that is specifically crafted for single client, solving a single problem that no-one else has. Since all software needs maintenance, this model leads to overly expensive use of software, and replacing it is next to impossible, because the replacement should be done following the same model – public tender and bidding for contracts. In other words, vendor lock-in forces municipalities to use a certain product or service, regardless of its quality, because switching away from it can be challenging, and the switching costs may be substantial [14].

To understand the scale of the public sector software we are talking about, let us consider software company Gofore[1] as a representative consultancy company operating with public sector based on public information[2]. It is pointed out that year 2019, 70% of the revenues of the company, totalling 64Me, resulted from public sector. In addition, it is pointed out that during years 2017–2019, public sector has increased on average 45%, whereas private sector only reached 24% at the same time. With several other companies similar to Gofore in the Finnish ICT ecosystem, public sector software has huge potential for exports as well. In total, the state of Finland only made a procurement worth over 1000Me [8] in the field of ICT. Much of the associated software is made to order, and focuses on problems of a single organization only.

In this paper, we argue that to maintain software sustainability in this context, three core elements must be considered:

- mosaic-like enterprise architecture – Mosaic EA for short – for public sector that allows integrating services from various vendors;
- ability to deploy subsystems in a fashion where they can liberally interact, but need no direct access; and
- systematic, affordable way to build subsystems that meet stakeholders' requirements.

The paper is based on observing public sector projects and related tenders as well as on bidding for such projects. The three authors have jointly more than 75 years of experience in practice and in academia. The experiences are drawn mostly from Finland. However, Finland is a good representative of a Northern European highly digitalized welfare state inside the European Union. Importantly, we consider the export possibility as a mechanism to foster sustainability.

2 Background and Motivation

While in many businesses, IT forms the core of all operations, the public sector often needs to outsource the whole solution. For instance, resources are often

[1] https://gofore.com/en/.
[2] https://gofore.com/vuosi-2020-julkisen-sektorin-kumppanina/.

allocated such that the organization can run its operations but not design and implement new solutions. To foster competition, public sector information system projects are often based on public tenders. Typically, these are formal, structured procedures for generating competing offers from different potential suppliers or contractors, who seek to win a service contracts. The contract can involve several phases of software development and operations. For instance, specification phase can be a separate contract, separated from implementation. Similarly, the contract can also include running daily operations [6].

Upon placing an open tender for the development, organisations often seek to avoid vendor lock-in. However, this is not always successful. Since tendering is only the beginning of the implementation process, chances are that it takes a considerable amount of time before the new system is operational, and during this time, the situation might change. Furthermore, those that loose in the tendering process can slow this even more with claims of unfair tendering. Hence, public sector actors by necessity must provide their services with various systems, some of which are new and some of which may have a long history. This, with the growing tendency to build systems that rely on other systems – for instance using AWS for certain routines via a well-defined API – adds complexity to managing public sector software.

Oftentimes, these tenders are based on a organization-centric view, simply because the acquiring organization focuses the tendering process to its own needs. For an end user citizen that needs such service, the result is that she needs to access the particular information system, and the service cannot be easily linked to other, related services. Hence, the end user needs to access the different systems independently, and ensure that her data in the different systems are in sync.

Based on the above, we argue that to manage its information systems a transition is needed from organization-centric to a citizen-centric model. To implement such, public sector organizations need an enterprise architecture (EA) that fosters open competition for tenders as well as supports multi-vendor operations. Furthermore, this EA must be defined and under the control of the organization in question, as otherwise it no longer can operate independently. We call such model Mosaic EA, since each party can provide individual pieces to the mosaic, whereas the public sector actor(s) fundamentally control and maintain the system as a whole.

3 Proposed Architecture and Approach

Today, there is a common tendency to acquire information systems such that one vendor delivers the whole solution. That way, the development is under the control of the single vendor, who can decide on many of the technical details. However, these systems do not constitute a coherent enterprise for public sector, but each one of them is a separate entity, with minimal interaction with other systems. To improve, we propose that systems are acquired in a fashion where their interfaces enables interaction across the different systems. Based on our

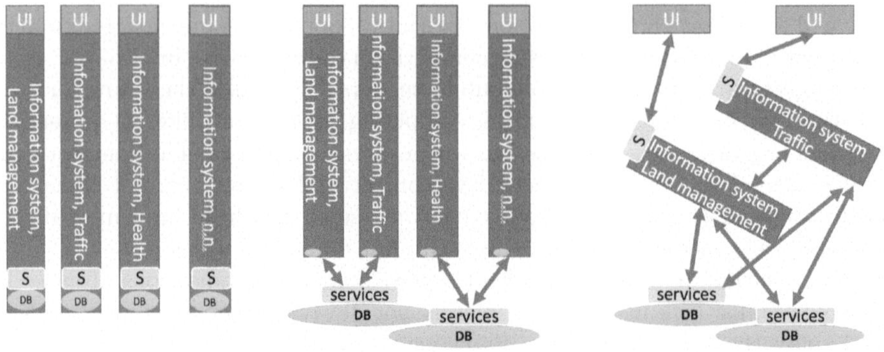

Fig. 1. Mosaic EA illustrated. Left: traditional software subcontracting model: each domain has own solutions, and nothing is shared. Center: Situation in Finland today: mix of shared and private databases, applications made to order. Right: true Mosaic EA, where databases and services are shared, based on open APIs.

view, this calls for reconsidering the role of each vendor and the public stakeholders, so that data and services can be shared across different applications. This is illustrated in Fig. 1.

Mosaic Enterprise Architecture. Echoing the findings of [14], the development of a unified enterprise architecture is critical to the success of public sector software systems. The fashion we propose implementing this uses a mosaic as a metaphor. In a true Mosaic EA, the system consists of independent services that can originate from various vendors. A Mosaic EA defines common guidelines that are needed for monitoring and updating the services. Furthermore, openness, transparency and the ability to connect to other systems are at the core of Mosaic EA. In addition, Mosaic EA is used to define APIs for different services. These APIs are the only way to interact with other services, and each API can be implemented by several vendors. Therefore, services can be replaced with new, updated ones, given that the APIs remain unchanged.

Macro-service Decomposition. The services defined by Mosaic EA have been inspired by micro-services and micro-service architecture [10], but they are of coarser granularity. Hence we call them macro-services. While a micro-service is something that a team of developers can single-handedly design and deploy, macro-services are of size and complexity that can be easily covered by a single public tender. Furthermore, a common requirement is that the macro-service API remains well-defined and maintained, so that it can evolve over time, and they can be replaced without major complications. Furthermore, with well-defined and maintained API, also reusing testware is possible. Hence, macro-services are a tool for the public sector when considering acquiring new information systems. While not an advocated practice in general, real-life examples of such systems are numerous, already when considering only Finland. These include regulatory and legal principles – such as registry legislation or taxation and anti-corruption regulation, as well as national registries, digital health care services, and digital authorization and mandates. In more detail, the Digital Fact Sheet 2019 Finland [3] lists the following services we characterise as macro-services: (i) the eAuthorisations service verifies a person's or organisation's authorisation to use digital services; (ii) a semantic interoperability workbench was implemented; (iii) Two new important registers have been created, incomes register and register of housing company shares. In general, the report presents a number of potential macro-services that seem like ready-made components for Mosaic EA. Obviously, these are just the tip of the iceberg, and there are several candidates when digging deeper in the existing services.

Low-Code Development. The final piece in the proposal is relying on low-code development model, where tools enable rapid development of new systems. The model has been found helpful in automating processes in e.g. manufacturing [12,16]. A recent Gartner report [15] proposes certain essential use cases for the technology, where productivity gains are identified for professional and citizen development. In addition, considerable benefits are also seen in as speed of delivery. At present, tools for low-code development are plentiful. Often, they support rapid application development, one-step deployment and execution, and management using declarative, high-level programming abstractions. Model-driven development and metadata often play an important role. In parallel, also new development practices, such as opportunistic reuse [4], is opening doors to faster development and deployment, although arguably with a higher risk rate [9]. Both approaches offer faster development and deployment as ever before, to the extent that the whole public sector is at a brink of a potential disruption. At the core of this disruption is true openness at interface level, which combines macro-services and low-code development in the proposed model.

4 Discussion

Our key assumption is that no organization is interested in purchasing and managing small subsystems. Hence, to avoid large, vendor specific subsystems, a supporting enterprise architecture is needed, which we call Mosaic EA. This EA enables managing and operating the system, so that several vendors can participate in the development. In addition, since the organization operating the system needs assume its control, this liberates public organizations from vendors that aim at taking control over the systems. However, the public sector players have to have their own technical expertise to define and maintain the Mosaic EA. Currently, they continue relying on vendor's technical expertise [14], which needs to be changed for the new approach to work.

With this approach, if and when the public sector wants to buy complete systems, any vendor can be the lead in the process, as long as there is a healthy ecosystem producing and operating subsystems for the MEA. This consists of API economy based on clouds [11], reliance on open source [5], and strategic decision for a public actor to avoid vendor lock-in. The main foreseen negative consequence concerns large companies as this lowers the barrier of entry to the field. Indeed, one does not need to be a Global giant to serve governments.

The new model can also catalyst new income in terms of exports, which can be based on the same model. So far, the most focused approach is EU's Gaia-X initiative [1]. At present, the initiative is not yet at the level of Mosaic EA, but it is under active development, aiming to shape the whole EU software industry. We expect that this will inspire new types of software ecosystems, where smaller actors can participate in projects in a key role.

Supporting the proposed more generic approach requires a change in business processes as well. Current business models favor the large vendors and the large subsystems. Moreover, interoperability issues with completely closed, single-vendor systems traditionally introduce problems related to reuse or replacing the system, which the proposed model is trying to eliminate. Similarly, parallel use of several systems, which address the same issue but are designed by different vendors, is often complicated.

Finally, from the technical perspective, it is important to notice that macro-services represent a level of abstraction that can be conveniently specified at a contractual level, not necessarily something that is convenient to implement as such. Instead, macro-services' practical implementation requires their decomposition into smaller entities. Some of these can be new, but interfacing with existing macro-services is also possible. Furthermore, many of the existing implementations rely on open source components, which can be implemented by some other actors than the company that delivers the service to the public sector. In addition, in certain cases relying on AI requires a related approach, where AI related features are separated from the rest of the system, to avoid potential problems related to confidentiality, for instance.

5 Conclusions

In conclusion, when public sector acquires software systems, the requirements are often based on the intermediate needs at hand. This leads to an architecture model, where each system is tailored for a particular actor, and offers little opportunities for reuse. In this paper, we clam that this model is not sustainable for public sector in the long run, but a more ecosystem centric view is needed. As the technical solution that is inline with such ecosystems, we propose following a mosaic-like approach called Mosaic EA as the starting point of both the development and tendering process to initiate it.

With this framework in place, the development of functions can advance from one tendering process at a time. However, tendering and development needs to follow the ideology defined by the Mosaic EA, with guidelines how to deal with open APIs in the technical sense and ecosystem formation guidelines and operations in the process and organizational view. Moreover, since there are several open source projects as well as new methodologies such as low-code development, we expect that the new model will decrease IT costs, due to the increased competition and the ability to select the services in smaller, more understandable, upgradeable pieces, instead of acquiring a single system that must also be upgraded as such.

Achieving this, however, requires a new mindset, where public sector organizations assume responsibility over their information systems. This calls for increased IT and EA competence in the public organizations.

References

1. Braud, A., Fromentoux, G., Radier, B., Le Grand, O.: The road to European digital sovereignty with Gaia-X and IDSA. IEEE Netw. **35**(2), 4–5 (2021)
2. Caudle, S.L., Gorr, W.L., Newcomer, K.E.: Key information systems management issues for the public sector. MIS Q. 171–188 (1991)
3. European Commission: Digital Government Factsheet 2019: Finland (2019)
4. Hartmann, B., Doorley, S., Klemmer, S.R.: Hacking, mashing, gluing: understanding opportunistic design. IEEE Pervasive Comput. **7**(3), 46–54 (2008)
5. Jokonya, O.: Investigating open source software benefits in public sector. In: 2015 48th Hawaii International Conference on System Sciences, pp. 2242–2251. IEEE (2015)
6. Koski, A., Mikkonen, T.: On the windy road to become a service provider: reflections from designing a mission critical information system provided as a service. In: 2016 International Conference on Information Systems Engineering (ICISE), pp. 51–56. IEEE (2016)
7. Koski, A., Mikkonen, T.: What we say we want and what we really need: experiences on the barriers to communicate information system needs. In: Ramachandran, M., Mahmood, Z. (eds.) Requirements Engineering for Service and Cloud Computing, pp. 3–21. Springer, Cham (2017). https://doi.org/10.1007/978-3-319-51310-2_1
8. Kähkönen, H.: Growth in government ICT procurement slowed - We list the top 20 suppliers. TIVI, 12 March 2021 (2021). (in Finnish). https://www.tivi.fi/uutiset/valtion-ict-hankintojen-kasvu-hidastui-listasimme-top-20-toimittajat/0b7d7b29-6250-4c8d-aaa3-b21da75ff785
9. Mäkitalo, N., Taivalsaari, A., Kiviluoto, A., Mikkonen, T., Capilla, R.: On opportunistic software reuse. Computing **102**(11), 2385–2408 (2020)
10. Nadareishvili, I., Mitra, R., McLarty, M., Amundsen, M.: Microservice Architecture: Aligning Principles, Practices, and Culture. O'Reilly Media, Inc. (2016)
11. Sallehudin, H., Razak, R.C., Ismail, M.: Factors influencing cloud computing adoption in the public sector: an empirical analysis. J. Entrepreneurship Bus. (JEB) **3**(2), 30–45 (2015)
12. Sanchis, R., García-Perales, Ó., Fraile, F., Poler, R.: Low-code as enabler of digital transformation in manufacturing industry. Appl. Sci. **10**(1), 12 (2020)
13. Vilpponen, H., Grundström, M., Abrahamsson, P.: Combining social service and healthcare as the first country in the world: exploring the impacts on information systems. J. Adv. Inf. Technol. **9**(4), 84–88 (2018)
14. Vilpponen, H., Grundström, M., Abrahamsson, P.: Exploring the critical success factors in social and health care information systems project procurement. In: Goel, A.K. (ed.) Recent Developments in Engineering Research, vol. 8. Book Publisher International (2020)
15. Vincent, P., Iijima, K., Driver, M., Wong, J., Natis, Y.: Magic quadrant for enterprise low-code application platforms. Gartner report (2019)
16. Waszkowski, R.: Low-code platform for automating business processes in manufacturing. IFAC-PapersOnLine **52**(10), 376–381 (2019)

How Could We Have Known? Anticipating Sustainability Effects of a Software Product

Jari Porras[1(✉)], Colin C. Venters[2], Birgit Penzenstadler[1,3], Leticia Duboc[4], Stefanie Betz[5], Norbert Seyff[6], Saeid Heshmatisafa[1], and Shola Oyedeji[1]

[1] Lappeenranta-Lahti University of Technology LUT, Lappeenranta, Finland
Jari.Porras@lut.fi
[2] University of Huddersfield, Huddersfield, UK
[3] Chalmers University of Technology, Gothenburg, Sweden
[4] La Salle University Ramon Llull, Barcelona, Spain
[5] Hochschule Furtwangen, Furtwangen, Germany
[6] FHNW and University of Zurich, Windisch, Switzerland

Abstract. Companies are required to think of ways to address their sustainability responsibilities and impacts. Although they commonly present some of their activities and impacts at a high-level of abstraction in their sustainability strategies, the impacts of their products and services may remain unclear in such reporting. This is partly due to the lack of suitable tools to increase their awareness regarding the potential effects of these products and services on different sustainability dimensions. Using a case study, this paper shows how the Sustainability Awareness Framework (SusAF) can be applied to identify such potential effects of an IT company's (software) product and how such identified effects could be linked to the company focus.

Keywords: Software product · Sustainability effects · SusAF

1 Introduction

Evidence suggests that the planet's average surface temperature has risen by approximately 0.9 °C since the late 19th century as a result of increased carbon dioxide and other human-made emissions in the Earth's atmosphere. This rise in temperature has led to a range of environmental issues including warming oceans, shrinking ice sheets, etc. It is argued that climate change is inevitable, and the consequences are potentially irreversible in the absence of major action to reduce emissions by all stakeholders [12]. Complying with the requirements set by both governments, as well as users, is a very high priority, especially in the business community [14].

Corporate responsibility (CR) is concerned with the longevity of an organisation and aims to ensure organisational activities have a positive impact on

X. Wang et al. (Eds.): ICSOB 2021, LNBIP 434, pp. 10–17, 2021.
https://doi.org/10.1007/978-3-030-91983-2_2

society, the environment, and the economy [8]. However, the environmental challenges facing planet Earth require a dramatic transformation in the way in which companies of all sizes address their corporate responsibilities [1]. Low [11] argues that corporate responsibility is not only about running a profitable business but also about caring for the social and physical environment within which the company operates. A responsible and sustainable business is one that takes account of the positive and negative environmental, social and economic effects it has on society. As a result, responsible and sustainable activities need to be adopted as an integral part of all business actions and decisions.

This paper presents a case study with one company in the IT field, providing financial management services to other companies. Within this case study, we have anticipated potential effects of one of the company's products with the help of the Sustainability Awareness Framework (SusAF) [6] and link these potential effects to the sustainability goals (and actions) presented by the company. Our research question for this study is "How can the existing products and services of the company be studied to find possibly new sustainability effects and how can these effects then be connected to the sustainability goals of the company?".

2 Sustainability

Society's high dependency on software systems has resulted in the emergence of sustainability as a growing area of interest in the field of system science [15]. In the context of this paper, sustainability is defined as the capacity of a socio-technical system to endure [2]. Two important and closely related concepts which extend the basic definition of sustainability are *sustainable use* and *sustainable development*. Sustainable use of a system **S** is defined with regard to a function **F** and a time horizon **T**, which in essence means to "use **S** in a way that does not compromise its ability to fulfil **F** for a period of **T**" [10]. The impacts of sustainability actions are typically mapped to different sustainability dimensions, i.e. the three pillars of the Brundtland report [4] (economic, environmental protection, and social) or more recently added technical [13] and individual [9] dimensions. Consensus on what sustainability means in the field of software systems engineering is still emerging despite a number of attempts to formalise a definition [15]. To address this, the Karlskrona Manifesto for Sustainability Design [2] provides a focal point for establishing a common ground for the software systems engineering community to engage with sustainability by advocating a set of fundamental principles and commitments that underpin sustainability design. The principles stress the importance of recognising that sustainability is an explicit consideration, even if the primary focus of the system under design is not sustainability. The concept of sustainability has been discussed extensively in a number of publications and readers are directed to these for an in-depth treatment of this topic [3,5].

3 Sustainability Awareness Framework

The Sustainability Awareness Framework (SusAF) was proposed by the Sustainability Alliance for Sustainability Design as an approach that provides companies (or any other interested stakeholders) a process to think about and extend their perception on possible sustainability-related effects of their technological-based products and services. SusAF adopts the five above mentioned sustainability dimensions (read more how they are considered in SusAF from [6]).

SusAF is based on the ideas presented by Becker et al. [3] and can be used in different formats, such as a means to self-reflection, to guide conversations with experts or in workshops with several stakeholders. The latter is its most common application, which consists of a **process** that helps stakeholders to discuss how an organisation's products and services may affect the different sustainability dimensions and produce, as an outcome, a broader perception of the possible effects of products and services. The workshop has different phases. The **scoping phase** helps to uncover the participants' current understanding of the product/services' sustainability effects. The **discussion phase** uses a set of guiding questions to reveal various potential effects on different sustainability dimensions and timescales (orders of effects - direct, indirect and structural [10]). The identified effects may be positive (e.g. benefits) or negative (e.g. trade-offs or rebound effects) and may lead to other effects, thus forming chains of effects. The **analysis phase** revise, classify and summarise effects and chains of effects. It also attempts to identify the threats and opportunities that such effects may bring to the organisation, as well as define possible actions to mitigate threats and exploit opportunities. Finally, the **reporting phase** produces a short report with the main findings of the process. During the discussion, analysis and reporting, chains of effects can be captured on a Sustainability Awareness Diagram (SusAD), as shown in Fig. 1. This diagram aims to give an overview of the possible effects (notes in figure) in relation (position in figure) to sustainability dimensions and timescale of the effect (immediate, enabled and systemic), and how effects can lead to each other (arrows between notes). Openly available material for SusAF is accessible at Zenodo[1].

4 Case Study: The IT Company

SusAF has been applied to different companies and their software products during the past few years [6]. This study reports on the application of SusAF to financial management software from a large international IT company. This software automates financial management processes in real-time.

4.1 Workshop

The sustainability awareness activity with the IT company was arranged as a half a day workshop with two product owners, three experts - in social, environmental, and technical fields - and three researchers. The latter facilitated

[1] https://zenodo.org/record/3676514#.XsTgKy-ZPGI.

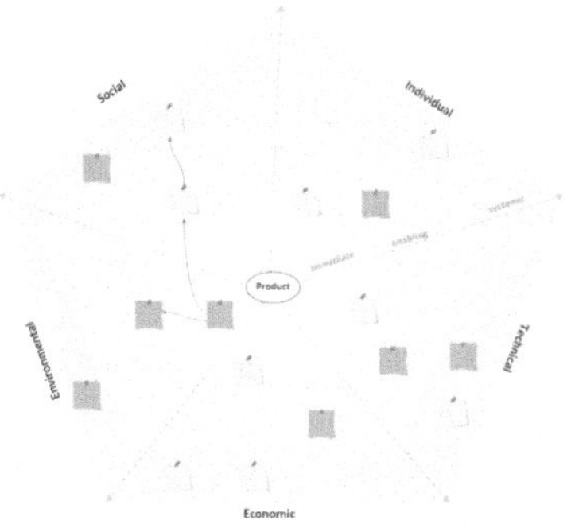

Fig. 1. Illustration of a SusAD with a set of effects and possible links between effects.

Fig. 2. Visualisation of the main effects of the case study on example category.

and recorded the workshop. The scoping and discussion phases were carried out during the workshop. The *scoping phase* was used for getting a holistic view of the IT product and its features. The product was shortly introduced and a view of the preliminary company understanding of the sustainability effects on that particular product was constructed. The *discussion phase* used the guiding questions of SusAF to discuss the various features and the potential effects of the product. All discussions were kept open in terms of following the discussion topic to other areas and cross-related impacts. Facilitators guided the discussion based on the SusAF questions, and the experts provided their viewpoints.

4.2 Analysis

The analysis of the workshop discussions was carried out by researchers after the workshop. Raw data consisted of the notes on the main points of the guided discussions carried out during the workshop. The analysis followed three steps:

Sustainability dimensions coding. Here is worth noting that the discussions followed the questions, one dimension at a time. However, effects prompted by the discussions can span across dimensions. In this first step, we coded the notes according to the questions that prompted them, not considering the dimension of the effects themselves.

Generalising and combining the effects. In the second step, effects in different dimensions were combined if they meant the same. Links between different effects were looked at.

Categorisation of the effects. In the end, the rather high number of possible effects are categorised into a few very descriptive high-level categories to summarise the outcomes.

4.3 Results

At the beginning of the workshop, the IT company recognised only three sustainability effects that its financial management software might have. Firstly, managing finances digitally clearly *reduces paper use* (ecological impact) as all invoices etc. are in a digital form. Secondly, the digitalised system *saves time* (economic impact) as many operations are or can be automated. Thirdly, the use of the financial service *forms a community* (social impact) or an ecosystem of stakeholders. This perception is based on their experience of how their customers link to each other and use the peer network to collaborate.

The discussions at the workshop revealed 28 direct (first-order) effects, approximately 100 enabling (second-order) effects and 23 structural (third-order) effects and several chains of effects. These effects were grouped into six high-level categories at the end of the analysis: Automation and digitalisation, Data and data security, Customer analytics, System improvement and training, System architecture, maintenance and interoperability and Future possibilities. For each of these categories, a set of the main effects and their chains of effects were visualised (as shown in Fig. 2 for Automation and digitalization).

5 Mapping Sustainability Focus of the Company and SusAF Results

For this study the web pages of the company under study were studied for revealing the current sustainability emphasis, sustainability values and activities of the company. This analysis revealed that according to their sustainability reporting, the company contributes to the sustainable growth and prosperity of industry, public organisations and the society in general. The company emphasises a) environmental responsibility, b) economic growth and c) support for society. These match well with the triple bottom line [7] and are used as high-level categories for measuring the company impacts.

The *environmental responsibility* of the IT company can be divided into a) minimising their footprint by using resources (energy, water, ...) efficiently and reducing waste and pollution and b) providing efficient solutions (hand-print) for their customers to reduce their footprints. The efficient solutions are fully digitalised and provide optimised workflows that reduce printing needs and provide time savings. All these were clearly reported under the environmental section of the sustainability reports, and the company seemed to have a clear vision of their impacts. *Economic growth* is tackled by providing automated solutions for companies to run their operations effectively. The solutions comply with the necessary laws and consider ethical decisions in all actions. The *support for society* includes actions on social welfare, health and education. Their passion for gender equality and social diversity helps them to support the local communities.

After the analysis of the sustainability focus and activities of the company, the results of the SusAF analysis were mapped to the high-level categories of the company activities (Environmental responsibility, Economic growth and Support for society). The purpose of this mapping is to study if critical analysis of a single product or service could help in finding new possible avenues for reinforcing positive sustainability impacts of the company and mitigating negative ones. Table 1 shows the results of this mapping. Table 1 presents the original company perceptions (bolded), and adds some positive and negative contributions from the SusAF work, that can point out possible new avenues for the company.

Digitised services like the product under study have a few clear, but not often emphasised, *environmental effects.* The use of a centralised service will optimise the infrastructure and its energy usage. However, it's important to transparently provide data concerning the energy usage of the offered service as that could provide a better vision of the footprint for the customer. Too often, we neglect to count the effects outside our own environment, e.g. energy usage of the data center used for the service. Although the original perception of the product contained only three possible effects, the company, in general, already has an understanding of its possible impacts. Digitalization and automatization of IT services can have several effects of *economic growth.* Technically, digitalization enables better scalability and optimisation of processes and, once audited, will ensure the compliance to regulations. On the other hand, automatization can have effects on the *social and individual dimensions of sustainability.* Digitalization of services will evidently change the working habits and may even change the worker roles. This may even lead to loss of certain types of roles (e.g. accountants), but at the same time may enable the more efficient use of these people and their knowledge on other tasks. Due to automatization, there is a risk that certain knowledge will vaporise over time. These kinds of structural changes

Table 1. Linking of SusAF sustainability effects to the company focus

Service effect category based on SusAF	Environmental responsibility	Economic growth	Support for society (local communities)
Automation and digitalisation	**Reduction in paper use (+)**, Optimized energy consumption (+)	**Time and money savings (+)**, Less people needed (+), Process knowledge in the system (+)	Vapourization of knowledge (−), Social inequality (−), Less interaction (−), No boring tasks (+), New working habits (+), New roles (+)
Data and data security		Potential risk of data loss (−), Accountability (+), Trust (+), Transparency (+)	Trust (+), Transparency (+), Compliance to regulations (+)
Customer analytics	Decreased need for travels (+)	Informed decisions (+), Uptodate knowledge (+)	Social exclusion (−), User satisfaction (+), Agency (+), Surveillance (−)
System improvement and training		Community testing and improvement (+), Loss of opportunities (−)	Increased participation (+), **Peer support (+)**, Reduced training cost (+), New skills (+), Less face-to-face conversation (−)
System architecture, maintenance and interoperability	Reduced infrastructure (+), Transparency on energy usage (−)	Workforce and cost savings (+), Maintenance costs (+)	
Future possibilities		Scalability (+), Optimization (+)	Inclusiveness and equity (+), Loss of roles (−)

are hard to forecast but, if seen and understood early enough, mitigations to anticipated negative effects could be engineered into the product or taken into consideration in the surrounding processes and company strategies.

6 Conclusion

The workshop with an IT company on one specific product and analysis of the gathered data revealed approximately 100 different potential sustainability effects, considerable more than the three effects mentioned by the company in the scoping phase. The analysis of the sustainability focus of the company revealed (another) three quite clear impact areas. These were supported by examples of different sustainability actions. When the outcome of the SusAF workshop (possible effects) were mapped to the company focuses it became clear that the company could utilize more of their product effects on their sustainability reporting. Thus SusAF helps the companies to increase the awareness of possible sustainability effects they have.

References

1. Annandale, D., et al.: Asian Environment Outlook 2005: Making Profits, Protecting Our Planet: Corporate Responsibility for Environmental Performance in Asia and the Pacific. Asian Development Bank, December 2005
2. Becker, C., et al.: Sustainability design and software: the Karlskrona manifesto. In: Proceedings of the 37th International Conference on Software Engineering, vol. 2, pp. 467–476. IEEE Press (2015)
3. Becker, C., et al.: Requirements: the key to sustainability. IEEE Softw. **33**(1), 56–65 (2016)
4. Brundtland, G.: Report of the World Commission on Environment and Development: Our Common Future. United Nations General Assembly Document A/42/427 (1987)
5. Chitchyan, R., et al.: Sustainability design in requirements engineering: state of practice. In: Proceedings of the 38th International Conference on Software Engineering Companion, pp. 533–542. ACM (2016)
6. Duboc, L., et al.: Do we really know what we are building? Raising awareness of potential sustainability effects of software systems in requirements engineering. In: 27th IEEE International Requirements Engineering Conference, pp. 3–12 (2019)
7. Elkington, J.: Partnerships from cannibals with forks: the triple bottom line of 21st-century business. Environ. Qual. Manag. **8**(1), 37–51 (1998)
8. Fontaine, M.: Corporate social responsibility and sustainability: the new bottom line? Int. J. Bus. Soc. Sci. **4**(4) (2013)
9. Goodland, R.: Sustainability: human, social, economic and environmental. Soc. Sci. **6**, 220–225 (2002)
10. Hilty, L.M., Aebischer, B.: ICT for sustainability: an emerging research field. In: Hilty, L.M., Aebischer, B. (eds.) ICT Innovations for Sustainability. AISC, vol. 310, pp. 3–36. Springer, Cham (2015). https://doi.org/10.1007/978-3-319-09228-7_1

11. Low, M.: Corporate social responsibility and the evolution of internal corporate social responsibility in 21st century. Asian J. Soc. Sci. Manag. Stud. **3**(1), 56–74 (2016)
12. NASA: Is it too late to prevent climate change? https://climate.nasa.gov/faq/16/is-it-too-late-to-prevent-climate-change/. Accessed 14 July 2020
13. Penzenstadler, B.: Infusing green: requirements engineering for green in and through software systems. In: CEUR Workshop Proceedings, vol. 1216, pp. 44–53 (2014)
14. Tsalis, T.A., et al.: New challenges for corporate sustainability reporting: united Nations' 2030 Agenda for sustainable development and the sustainable development goals. Corporate Social Responsibility and Environmental Management. Wiley Online Library (2020)
15. Venters, C.C., et al.: Characterising sustainability requirements: a new species red herring or just an odd fish? In: 2017 IEEE/ACM 39th International Conference on Software Engineering: Software Engineering in Society Track, pp. 3–12 (2017)

Software Sustainability: Academic Understanding and Industry Perceptions

Shola Oyedeji[1(✉)], Hatef Shamshiri[1], Jari Porras[1], and Dominic Lammert[2]

[1] LUT University, Lappeenranta, Finland
{shola.oyedeji,hatef.shamshiri,jari.porras}@lut.fi
[2] Furtwangen University, Furtwangen, Germany
lado@hs-furtwangen.de

Abstract. Sustainability is a major concern for our society today. Software acts as a catalyst to support different business activities which have an impact on sustainability. Research from software engineering and other academic disciplines have proposed various software sustainability guidelines, tools, and methods to support software sustainability design in industry. However, there are still challenges on how to design and engineer sustainability into software products by software development practitioners in industry using those proposed sustainability guidelines and tools. The goal of this research is to seek understanding on what software sustainability means for software development practitioners and identify how to properly support engineering of sustainability into software design and development through academic research. Data were gathered and analyzed using grounded theory from workshop with different software development practitioners to seek their understanding on what sustainability means in their software systems. The results show economic and technical sustainability dimensions are the most important to software development practitioners for software sustainability. While the social sustainability dimension was not considered for software sustainability. The findings from this study indicates contrast in academia where all sustainability dimensions are treated as an important element to achieve software sustainability. Therefore, there is need for better collaboration between industry and academia to improve understanding of software sustainability and support effective sustainability engineering in software systems.

Keywords: Sustainability · Software sustainability · Software engineering · Software development practitioners

1 Introduction

In a broad definition, software sustainability is the capacity of software systems to endure [1]. Sustainability is now important worldwide, reinforced through the global development goals (SDGs) with different initiatives worldwide to tackle the problem of sustainability [2]. Sustainability is the founding principle of sustainable development, which encompasses four interrelated areas ecology, economics, politics, and culture [3]. Sustainable development has been reported as one of the top three challenges for humans

X. Wang et al. (Eds.): ICSOB 2021, LNBIP 434, pp. 18–34, 2021.
https://doi.org/10.1007/978-3-030-91983-2_3

today and tomorrow. The world is faced with challenges in all dimensions of sustainable development - economic, social, and environmental [4].

Sustainability is becoming an important factor in business today. As reported by Bonini et al. [5] sustainability is a crucial element in the agenda of many companies but their environmental, social and governance activities are disconnected from sustainability in their core strategies. According to Nielsen's global online study [6], the percentage of consumers willing to pay extra for products and services from companies dedicated to positive environmental and social impact increased from 55% in 2014 to 72% in 2015. McKinsey [5] estimates that the clean-tech product market will reach $1.6 trillion by 2020, up from $670 billion in 2010. Bonini et al. [5] research finds that a handful of companies are capturing significant value of sustainability by systematically pursuing the opportunities sustainability offers. Most companies creating value through sustainability look first to improving returns on capital, which often means reducing operating costs through optimized natural-resource management (such as energy use and waste).

One major catalyst at the core of Information and Communication Technology (ICT) for companies in optimizing resources usage is a software system to support different activities within companies. This means software is a major driver of social and economic activity [7] and the backbone for ICT. Studies have shown that the global environmental impact of ICT itself is roughly 2% and ICT can reduce the global footprint of other sectors by up to 16% [8]. This shows the importance of software as a driving force. However, Software development practitioners lack the knowledge, experience and methodological support that can enable discussion about sustainability effects in software design [9]. This research investigates the gap in understanding what software sustainability means between academia and industry. The goal is to identify the differences that will facilitate future research efforts on how to support engineering of sustainability into software design and development between academia and industry. The remaining part of this paper is structured as follows: background studies are detailed in Sect. 2. Section 3 covers the study design. Results and discussion are in Sect. 4 and Concluding remarks is in Sect. 5.

2 Background

Sustainability as a concept was created from forestry meaning "*never harvesting more than what the forest yields in new growth* [10]". The word "Sustainability" was first used in 1713 by authors German forester and scientist Hans Carl von Carlowitz in a book called Sylvicultura Oeconomica [11, 12]. Sustainability from a broad perspective is a vision for the world in which current and future humans are reasonably healthy; communities and nations are secure, peaceful and thriving; there is economic opportunity for all; and the integrity of the life-supporting biosphere is restored and sustained at a level necessary to make these goals possible [13]. Sustainability is also a process that helps create a vibrant economy and a high quality of life, while respecting the need to sustain natural resources and protect the environment [14].

2.1 Sustainability and Software Engineering

Relating sustainability to software, Giovannoni et al. [15], Rondeau et al. [16] and Kuhlman et al. [12] classified sustainability for software into three pillars; Planet (environmental sustainability), People (Social Sustainability) and Profit (Economic sustainability). Sustainability in software engineering (SE) can be viewed from four perceptions [17]:

- Sustainability in software development (Design): the processes that take place within software design and development (software development life cycle).
- Software for sustainability (Usage): how software systems are used to support sustainability (embedded software for energy efficiency in fridge).
- Green software systems (Focused impact): dedicated to software systems that consume less energy resources and generate environmental awareness.
- Sustainability of software ecosystems (Net effect) addresses the overall impact of the entire software ecosystem (systems of system).

In SE, software sustainability is now classified into five dimensions [18]:

- **Technical sustainability** covers the fundamental goal of long-time usage of systems and their suitable evolution along with changing user requirements and environments. For Software Engineering (SE), the question is 'How can software/service be designed and developed for easy evolution, maintainability, adaptability to changes in the future'?
- **Environmental sustainability** refers to the use and maintenance of natural resources, such as water, land, air, minerals. For SE, the question is 'How does software/service impact and affect the environment during/after development and maintenance?'
- **Social sustainability** is about the relationship between individuals, groups and maintaining social capital; the mutual trust structure in the societal communities. For SE, the main question is, 'What are the impacts of software systems and services on the society?' (Example: communication, sense of belonging, interaction, and equality).
- **Individual sustainability** refers to the maintenance of individual human capital, health, education, equal access to services, ability to thrive, exercise their rights, and develop freely. For SE, how does software/service support the individual endeavor towards the goals of that person (end user)?" software should be created to support adaptation and personalization (end user). For software developers this individual sustainability may also mean their own satisfaction of their product.
- **Economic sustainability** is about maintaining financial capital, assets and added value towards financial growth. For SE, the focus is on how to design and develop software systems and services in a cost-effective manner.

Some researchers also suggested some specific definitions regarding sustainability as it is understood and perceived in the software engineering community for software systems. Among the most cited definitions are the following in Table 1:

Table 1. Software sustainability definitions from academia

Software sustainability definition from research	Interpretation	Identified sustainability dimension
"Ability to modify a software system based on customer needs and deploy these modifications" Seacord et al. [19]	Software sustainability based on this definition means the ease at which user requirements can be implemented in a software which corresponds to modifiability	**Individual:** Satisfying user requirements **Technical:** Implementing user requirements in the software
"Software you use today that will be available and continue to be improved and supported in the future" Software Sustainability Institute [20]	Software sustainability requires qualities such as availability, extensibility, and maintainability	**Technical:** Degree to which a software is available, extensible, and can be maintained
"Long living system that should last for more than 15 years and can be cost efficiently maintained and evolved over its entire life cycle." Heiko Koziolek [21]	This means how well a software can exist while been economical to maintain. The definition suggests maintainability, evolution and extensibility over time (longevity). Also, this view is supported in research by Venters et al. [22] stating that longevity and maintenance are the two most important factors for understanding software sustainability	**Technical:** Maintainability, extensibility **Economic:** How cost efficient is the maintenance of the software over time
"Software whose direct and indirect negative impacts on economy, society, human beings, and environment that result from development, deployment, and usage of the software are minimal and/or which has a positive effect on sustainable development." Naumann et al. [23]	This definition points at the need for developers and organizations to be aware of how to minimize negative impacts of software development and usage on economy, society and people. Also, the impacts from such software development and usage should positively support sustainable development	**Environment:** Reduce impacts such as pollution and resource usage during software development and usage **Individual:** Reduce the negative impacts software can have on user **Economic:** Ensure software is designed and developed in a way that ensures economic values are not wasted
"From the sustainable development and climate change point of view, good software helps to reduce greenhouse gases, waste, and resource requirements while bad software increases them. Sometimes software can be downright ugly: badly written, difficult to use, and resource intensive. On the other hand, we can have elegantly beautiful software that not only reduces resource use but also affects how people see sustainable development" [24]	The definition categorizes software into good and bad from a sustainable development lens. The author perceives a good software as software that aids in decreasing greenhouse gases, wastes, and resource requirements. This means software that is designed to aid in reduction of harmful environmental impacts promote sustainable development	**Environment:** Reduce environmental negative impacts such as greenhouse gases and wastes **Social:** Impact how people perceive sustainable development

(*continued*)

Table 1. (*continued*)

Software sustainability definition from research	Interpretation	Identified sustainability dimension
"The term Sustainable Software can be interpreted in two ways: (1) the software code being sustainable, agnostic of purpose, or (2) the software purpose being to support sustainability goals, i.e., improving the sustainability of humankind on our planet" [25]	The author interprets sustainable software from two perspectives: clean code that can be maintained (sustainable) and software for sustainability	**Technical:** Maintainable code **Environment:** sustainability of the planet **Social:** sustainability of humankind (people) on the planet; helping the people to enhance sustainability of the planet

2.2 Sustainability and Software Engineering Practice

Sustainability in software engineering is centred around building trustable, durable software that fulfills users' demands and decreases environmental effects at the same time [26]. Therefore, it is important to integrate sustainability in software engineering to make software development processes and products sustainable. In 2014, the authors of the Karlskrona Manifesto established a broad comprehension of sustainability in software engineering. The signatories call for the establishment of a software engineering process based on sustainability that will profoundly change the role of software engineers. Software engineers are to share responsibility for the impacts of their products and services. Software engineers usually refer to sustainability in only one dimension, namely the environmental one. It ignores the fact that the concept of sustainability can be applied to five other dimensions: social, individual, environmental, economic, and technical [27]. The impacts of software are to be located on three-time scales: immediate, enabling, and structural effects. Sustainability Awareness Framework (SusAF) was created to support evaluation of software system sustainability impacts on these three different time scale covering the five software sustainability dimensions [7]. Furthermore, in an interview study, Chitchyan et al. [28] conclude that software engineers cannot adequately address sustainability. There is a lack of tools and techniques in practice as well as the necessary knowledge in education on this topic. The 13 interviewees in this study conclude that organizations should invest in vision building and training to benefit from sustainability in software engineering. This requires standards that assign tasks, obligations, and responsibilities to software developers. Lammert et al. [29] also published an interview study which shows that the current state (practice in industry) does not correspond to the target state (theory in education) when it comes to integrating sustainability aspects into software development. The 13 interviewees (Software Engineers and Developers) are insufficiently involved in all software design process instead largely fixated on technical implementation assign to their role. As a result, there are communication difficulties with teammates from other areas. The authors conclude that one of the main reasons preventing change is role separation. SEs are limited to individual topics such as data security but fall short of a broader concept of sustainability. The link between sustainability and software development is a growing field for which a variety of definitions and perspectives exist. In addition, the understanding of software sustainability is always linked to the respective software product or service. Thus, both academia and industry are forced to search for individually adapted solutions to meet the demand for sustainability in software development.

3 Study Design

The meaning of sustainability can be quantified when associated to a particular context, according to Tainter [30] to define sustainability in a specific context, the question should be "to sustain what", "for whom", "how long", and "at what cost". This research work frames sustainability from the context of software sustainability for software companies to identify the current perceptions of software sustainability from software development practitioners in industry. Grounded theory [31] was applied in this research to identify gaps between academia and industry on software sustainability. Data were collected through two days online interview in a workshop from software development practitioners within Europe. The first workshop was with entry level to junior-level software development practitioners (1–3 years of work experience) and the second day was for mid-level to managerial (senior) level software development practitioners (4 years and above of work experience). The workshop participants (software development practitioners in industry) were asked the following questions to get demographics as detailed in Table 2:

- What is your job title?
- What is your education level?
- How many years of experience do you have in software development and management?
- Company size categorized based on EU definition for business enterprises Large (>250 staff) Medium (<250 staff), Small (<50 staff), Macro (<10) [32]
- Which industry best describe your company activities? The classification of industry is based on statistical classification of economic activities in the European Community [33]: Information and Communication Technology, Finance and insurance, Public administration, Real Estate, Transportation and Storage, Health and Social work, Manufacturing.

This was followed by the main research question to the workshop participants:

What is Software Sustainability? The goal of this question is to find out the perception and understanding of software sustainability from the workshop participants.

After collating the answers from the workshop participants, a presentation of software sustainability definition and software sustainability dimensions (see Table 1) from academia was done by the researchers (authors). After that, the workshop participants were asked the main research question and one sub question:

What is Software Sustainability? The goal was to identify differences in the workshop participants responses from the first time they were asked the same question. This is to check if their perspective changed after the presentation on software sustainability definition from academia.

Table 2. Background of workshop participants

No	Job role	Education	Years of experience	Company size	Industry type
1	Chief technical officer	Masters	14	Large	Information and Communication Technology
2	Chief information officer	Masters	12	Large	Information and Communication Technology
3	UX lord	Bachelors	10	Small	Finance and insurance
4	Senior programmer	Bachelors	9	Large	Information and Communication Technology
5	Project manager	Bachelors	7	Medium	Health and Social work
6	Software developer	Masters	5	Small	Transportation and Storage
7	Software architect	Masters	5	Medium	Information and Communication Technology
8	Software analyst	Bachelors	4	Small	Information and Communication Technology
9	Programmer	Bachelors	3	Large	Information and Communication Technology
10	Junior engineer	Bachelors	3	Medium	Manufacturing
11	Junior developer	Bachelors	3	Micro	Information and Communication Technology
12	Web developer	Masters	2	Small	Real Estate
13	Full Stack developer	Bachelors	2	Small	Finance and insurance
14	DevOps developer	Masters	2	Medium	Information and Communication Technology
15	Junior programmer	Bachelors	2	Micro	Public administration
16	UX engineer	Masters	2	Small	Health and Social work

- **Which sustainability dimension/s are important to you for software sustainability and why?** This is to identify the most important sustainability dimensions to the workshop participants for software sustainability. This kind of data will be useful to align research on software sustainability to industry interests and priorities.

The data collected were coded and categorized into the Five sustainability dimension (economic, environmental, individual, social, technical) by the first two authors and the third and last authors cross validated the codes. Issues with code mismatched were documented and resolved by all the authors.

4 Results and Discussion

This section presents the results from the workshop and discussion based on the research questions and sub-research question.

1. Results Before Presenting Academic Definition of Software Sustainability: The first results from the workshop for software sustainability definition from practitioners in industry as shown in Table 3 and Fig. 1 indicates that 75% of software development practitioners in the workshop between entry level to junior level in industry has no clue as to the meaning of software sustainability. Only 25% of them provided some sort of definition. In contrast, 75% of mid-level to managerial level software development practitioners have a certain understanding of software sustainability definition.

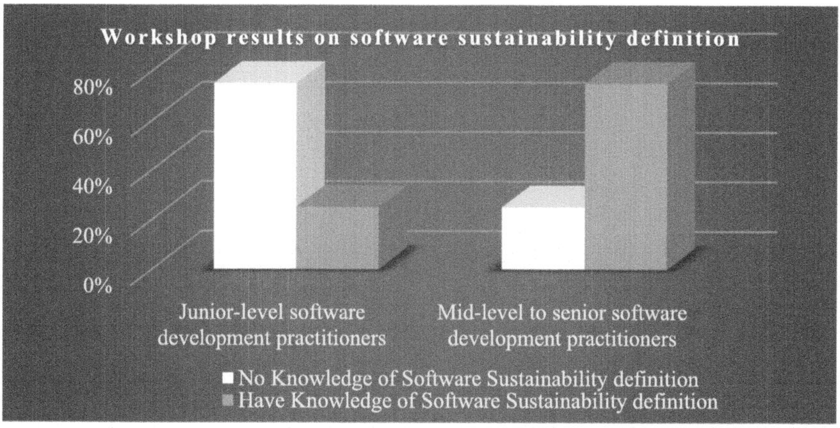

Fig. 1. First workshop results on software sustainability definition

Table 3. First workshop results of software sustainability definitions from software development practitioners in industry

Job title	What is Software sustainability
Chief technical officer	Software that meets the demands of our clients continuously, so they keep using our products for more revenue
Chief information officer	Software sustainability refers to a good piece of software that continue to evolve with business demands overtime. There is that sustainable pace of development to ensure business interest are met on time
UX lord	User friendly software that makes user satisfied while using the software. Software requirements will change from time to time because of the demands of younger generation but it must always meet their needs especially the user experience
Project manager	Software that is created in a sustainable way in which overtime it can continue to evolve to meet business demands
Software Developer	Software that you can manage
Software architect	Software with good technical structure that run efficiently using less computational resources
Junior engineer	Developing software in sustainable way, making it to meet the requirements
Junior developer	Green software, like software to help support Sustainable Development Goals

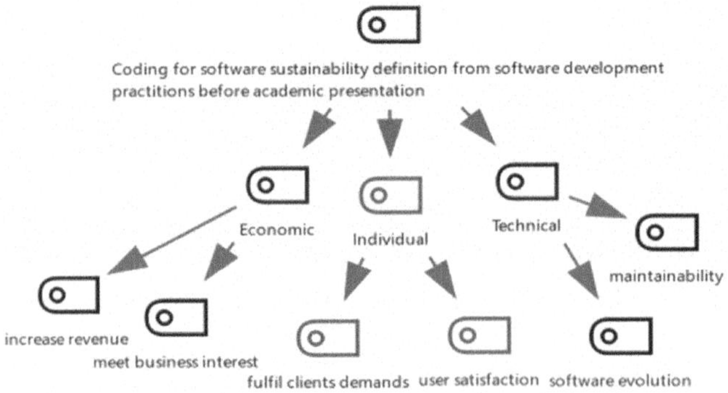

Fig. 2. Coding results of software sustainability definition from workshop participants before academic presentation of software sustainability definitions

Analysis of the coding results in Fig. 2 indicates that only economic, individual, and technical software sustainability dimensions are partially considered by software development practitioners. Responses from top management level (Chief Technical Officer and Chief Information Officer) as detailed in Table 3 shows that software sustainability is mainly linked to business demand (economic dimensions). Results from Table 3 supports research findings that software profession lacks a common ground that articulates its role in sustainability design [27] and also lack the knowledge, experience and methodological support that can enable discussion about sustainability effects in software design [9].

2. Results After Presenting Academic Definition of Software Sustainability and Software Sustainability Dimensions: All workshop participants were able to provide their perception of software sustainability after presenting academic definitions with the different software sustainability dimensions. However, all the definitions from the workshop participants as shown in Table 4 are strongly tied to their job role.

Table 4. Second workshop results of software sustainability from software development practitioners in industry

No	Job title	Software sustainability definition from software development practitioners in industry	Explanation by software development practitioners to clarify definitions of software sustainability with associated sustainability dimension
1	Chief technical officer	Software sustainability means a software that can grow efficiently and effectively with business and user demands without affecting the environment	**Economic, Technical and Environmental:** It is important for business to thrive, so software in this sense must be designed to continuously be profitable and at the same time ensure users are happy when using the software. It must also help reduce the impacts on environment through proper hosting in the cloud to reduce emissions that comes from using the software
2	Chief information officer	A good piece of software that meets business demands and ensure the health of the environment and people through proper software development	**Economic, Technical and Environmental:** Software that meets the demand of your business by using less human, hardware, financial, and even software resources. But there needs to be balanced to ensure the continuous usage of the software

(continued)

Table 4. (*continued*)

No	Job title	Software sustainability definition from software development practitioners in industry	Explanation by software development practitioners to clarify definitions of software sustainability with associated sustainability dimension
3	UX lord	Easy to use software developed using less hardware resources and operates in environmentally friendly manner	**Individual, Technical:** Software should have great user experience that supports user to achieve their task in quick and easy way, this will reduce the amount of time it takes to complete a particular task in the software which means less hardware and software resource usage
4	Senior programmer	Software sustainability is creating software with clean codes that are easily maintained and provide customers with their needs	**Economic, Technical:** Efficient coding that supports cost effective software development and ensure customer satisfaction
5	Project manager	Software that can continuously evolve overtime as business demands changes while ensuring value for business gain and user satisfaction	**Economic, Technical:** When a software is continuously useful to the business at different era, it is a sustainable software
6	Software developer	Software that continuously meet our customers demand	**Economic, Technical:** Meeting customers demand means user are satisfied and the software continuous to be useful
7	Software architect	Software that removes technical and social debt but still ensures business demands are met	**Technical, Economic:** when software demands changes in future, can the changes be easily integrated in the software based on the software architecture and how does it affect the development process
8	Software analyst	Software that uses less computational resources to achieve user task	**Economic, Technical:** Today we are in era of cloud and it is important to create software in a way that ensures less computational resources are used so the company can spend less for example in hosting services and also running the software
9	Programmer	Sustainable software that can easily be maintained without overspending compared to the cost of maintaining similar software	**Economic, Technical:** The software should be cost effective to meet the economic dimension and also easily maintained

(*continued*)

Table 4. (*continued*)

No	Job title	Software sustainability definition from software development practitioners in industry	Explanation by software development practitioners to clarify definitions of software sustainability with associated sustainability dimension
10	Junior engineer	Software that satisfies users and promotes better use of resources during development	**Technical:** It is essential to create software that user can use but also ensure that the software usage don't lead to poor use of hardware resources in the society
11	Junior developer	Software for positive climate change	**Environmental, Technical:** Software that help reduce pollution, protect the environment and help people make choices that wont affect the climate
12	Web developer	Software application that can be easily integrated with other application	**Economic, Technical:** Many software applications are part of other big software system. It is important for any software application to be easily integrated seamlessly for our users. This will make us continue to be in the business
13	Full stack developer	A software that ensures customers requirements are achieved and many users are happy to buy it for their home	**Economic, Technical:** User satisfaction is important in order to make profit from any software
14	DevOps developer	It is a software that is developed in a cost-effective manner that can adapt to changes in future	**Economic, Technical:** The economic gain from software of software sustainability can only be achieved through technical implementation
15	Junior programmer	Software which runs smoothly without downtime and process users request on time	**Technical:** Software sustainability require good coding implementation
16	UX Engineer	A Software design to guarantee continuous good user experience and support personalization for user	**Economic, Technical, Individual:** A good user experience will aid user to continue their subscription for any software

Results shows importance of economic dimension to top management for software sustainability. 95% of software development practitioners choose economic dimension of sustainability as a key factor for software sustainability. All the sixteen software development practitioners consider technical sustainability dimension as an important factor for software sustainability. Only three software development practitioners (Chief Technical Officer, Chief Information Officer and Junior Developer) considered the environmental dimension of sustainability in their definition. Interestingly, the results in Table 4 indicates that software development practitioners consider judicious and efficient usage of software and hardware resources as key elements for software sustainability but 90% of them did not select environmental sustainability as an important dimension for software sustainability. Also, the individual sustainability dimension was only selected by two software development practitioners (UX Lord and UX Engineer), this might have been influence by their job task of ensuring better user experience in software design and development.

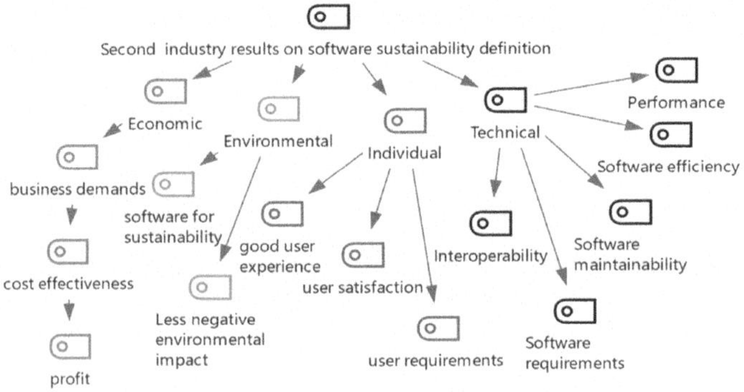

Fig. 3. Coding results of software sustainability perception from workshop participants after academic presentation of software sustainability definitions

From academia, different research [34–36] recognize social sustainability as an important element for achieving sustainability through software systems but social sustainability dimension was not considered by any of the software development practitioners as shown in Fig. 3 and Table 4. This shows there is need for more collaborative efforts between industry and academia for transfer of research to industry in a way that facilitate an efficient feedback loop between both parties. For example, research in academia indicates that sustainability perceptions by industry practitioners is centered around natural resources availability and waste reduction (environmental dimensions) [37]. However, the environmental dimension of sustainability was only considered important by 3 out of the 16 software development practitioners. This is a contrast between industry and academia because different research from academia have indicated the need to consider environmental, technical, social, economic and individual dimension for software sustainability [38, 39]. But the reality in industry (Table 4 and Fig. 3) shows economic and technical sustainability dimensions are the most important sustainability dimensions for software development practitioners. A report by IBM global chief executive office and Microsoft showed increase in business model redesign by organizations based on sustainability [40–42]. Such reports by IBM and Microsoft creates the expectation that industry practitioners are aware of sustainability. However, the results detailed in Table 3 and 4 shows only those from mid to top level management have that awareness about sustainability especially in software. Furthermore, research attention within software engineering has increased about sustainability [43]. Although, there is the challenge of consensus as to what sustainability means in software [44]. Cross disciplinary collaboration between academia and industry can help establish better understanding of software sustainability from theory (methodologies, processes, and tools) to practice in industry. New knowledge will be created through such collaboration which will foster better adoption of sustainability in software design and development overtime. One of such tool can be the sustainability awareness framework [9] for creating awareness about effects of software systems on sustainability and the Karlskrona Manifesto [27] to serve as guide for software sustainability design just like agile manifesto for software practitioners. The following outline key points from this study:

- There is need for consolidation of academic research towards a body of knowledge on software sustainability to help create a common consensus on software sustainability and standard curriculum for educating software development practitioners and students in universities.
- Cross disciplinary collaboration in academia and industry is required to exemplify each of the sustainability dimensions in software development project which can serve as practical guide to interested software development stakeholders in making informed design and engineering decisions on software sustainability.
- Academia perception of software sustainability differs from the current state in industry. Software development practitioners view sustainability from their job role and as such economic and technical dimension are the most relevant dimensions to them.
- The absence of social sustainability dimension from result in the workshop is possibly because software development practitioners currently see the direct effects of software sustainability (like in the case of individual dimension) and not the indirect effects which links to social sustainability dimension.

3. Threat to Validity

Construct Validity: Results from this research shows majority of software development practitioners have no idea what software sustainability means and there is contrast in perception of software sustainability between industry and theory in education (academia).

External Validity: The findings from this research were based on data in a workshop with software development practitioners from different background (company size, education, and specialization) to enable analytical generalization of data about the perception of software sustainability in industry.

Reliability: Triangulation was applied by the authors to ensure reliability of findings. The first two authors coded and analyzed data from this research with the other two authors reviewing and cross validating the codes. It is important to note that findings from this study involved only sixteen software development practitioners within Europe which might affect the result compared to a study with larger number of software development practitioners around the world.

5 Conclusion

Software plays a major role for achieving sustainability and it is important to ensure sustainability is core part of software design. As highlighted in this paper, the meanings and understanding of software sustainability differs between academia and software development practitioners in industry. Therefore, it is important to bridge that gap for better understanding of what sustainability means in software through proper collaboration between academia and industry on tools, processes and methodologies that can create consensus over time on software sustainability. This will aid more awareness and increase better avenues of engineering sustainability in software design and development.

We have identified through the workshop results that entry level to junior software development practitioners have no clue as to the meaning of software sustainability. This warrants more efforts towards sustainability in software design from academia to students who will later move to industry. Because graduates from universities and colleges are the future software development practitioners who will design and develop software applications for the future. Therefore, it is important to educate and equip them with all necessary knowledge of engineering sustainability into software. Furthermore, there is need for more studies between industry and academia involving large number of companies and organizations to gather enough information that can provide consensus understanding of what software sustainability means for practitioners in industry and enable researchers from academia identify avenues to consolidates existing research towards efficient engineering of sustainability in software.

References

1. Penzenstadler, B.: What does sustainability mean in and for software engineering ? In: 1st International Conference on ICT for Sustainability (ICT4S) (2013)
2. United Nations: Sustainable Development Goals, no. September 2000, pp. 8–23. https://www.un.org/sustainabledevelopment/sustainable-development-goals/. Accessed 28 July 2021
3. United Nations: World Economic and Social Survey 2013. Department for Economic and Social Affairs, New York (2013)
4. Mahaux, M., Heymans, P., Saval, G.: Discovering sustainability requirements: an experience report. In: Berry, D., Franch, X. (eds.) REFSQ 2011. LNCS, vol. 6606, pp. 19–33. Springer, Heidelberg (2011). https://doi.org/10.1007/978-3-642-19858-8_3
5. Bonini, S., Görner, S.: The Business of Sustainability: Putting it Into Practice, p. 6. Insights Publ. (2011)
6. Nielsen: Nielsen global online study. Web Report (2015). http://www.nielsen.com/eu/en/insights/news/2015/green-generation-millennials-say-sustainability-is-a-shopping-priority.html. Accessed 3 Aug 2021
7. Becker, C., et al.: Requirements: the key to sustainability. IEEE Softw. **33**(1), 56–65 (2016). https://doi.org/10.1109/MS.2015.158

8. Hankel, A.: Understanding higher order impacts of green ICT. In: 2nd International Conference on ICT Sustainability (ICT4S 2014), no. Ict4s, pp. 385–391 (2014). https://doi.org/10.2991/ict4s-14.2014.48
9. Duboc, L., et al.: Requirements engineering for sustainability: an awareness framework for designing software systems for a better tomorrow. Requirements Eng. **25**(4), 469–492 (2020). https://doi.org/10.1007/s00766-020-00336-y
10. Wiersum, K.F.: 200 years of sustainability in forestry: lessons from history. Environ. Manage. **19**(3), 321 (1995)
11. Heinberg, R.: What Is Sustainability? Watershed Media (2010). http://www.postcarbon.org/publications/what-is-sustainability/. Accessed 29 Apr 2019
12. Kuhlman, T., Farrington, J.: What is sustainability? Sustainability **2**(11), 3436–3448 (2010). https://doi.org/10.3390/su2113436
13. Cortese, A.D., Rowe, D.: Higher education and sustainability overview (2000). https://uwosh.edu/sirt/wp-content/uploads/sites/86/2017/08/Definitions-of-Sustainability.pdf. Accessed 03 Jan 2019
14. Clough, G.W., Jean-Lou, C., Carol, C.: Sustainability and the university, p. 2006 (2006)
15. Giovannoni, E., Fabietti, G.: What is sustainability? A review of the concept and its applications. In: Busco, C., Frigo, M., Riccaboni, A., Quattrone, P. (eds.) Integrated Reporting, pp. 21–40. Springer, Cham (2013). https://doi.org/10.1007/978-3-319-02168-3_2
16. Rondeau, E., Lepage, F., Georges, J.: Measurements and sustainability, green information technology. A sustainable approach, pp. 29–59. Elsevier (2015)
17. Oyedeji, S., Seffah, A., Penzenstadler, B.: Classifying the measures of software sustainability. In: Proceedings of 4th International Workshop on Measurement and Metrics for Green and Sustainable Software Systems co-located with 12th International Symposium on Empirical Software Engineering and Measurement (ESEM 2018) (2018)
18. Penzenstadler, B., Femmer, H.: A generic model for sustainability with process- and product-specific instances. In: Proceedings of the 2013 Workshop on Green in Software Engineering, Green by Software Engineering, pp. 3–7 (2013). https://doi.org/10.1145/2451605.2451609
19. Seacord, R., et al.: Measuring software sustainability. In: Proceedings International Conference on Software Maintenance ICSM 2003 (2013). https://doi.org/10.1017/CBO9781107415324.004.
20. Software sustainability institute. https://www.software.ac.uk/about
21. Koziolek, H.: Sustainability evaluation of software architectures: a systematic review. In: Proceedings of the joint {ACM} {SIGSOFT} conference–{QoSA} and {ACM} {SIGSOFT} symposium–{ISARCS} on {Quality} of software architectures–{QoSA} and architecting critical systems–{ISARCS}, pp. 3–12 (2011)
22. Venters, C.C., et al.: Software sustainability: the modern tower of babel. In: 3rd International Workshop on Requirements Engineering for sustainable Systems Workshop Proceedings, vol. 1216, pp. 7–12 (2014). http://ceur-ws.org/Vol-1216/
23. Naumann, S., Dick, M., Kern, E., Johann, T.: The GREENSOFT model: a reference model for green and sustainable software and its engineering. Sustain. Comput. Inform. Syst. **1**(4), 294–304 (2011). https://doi.org/10.1016/j.suscom.2011.06.004
24. Juha, T.: Good, bad, and beautiful software. In search of green software quality factors. CEPIS Upgrad. **XII**(4), 22–27 (2011)
25. Penzenstadler, B., Raturi, A., Richardson, D.: Systematic mapping study on software engineering for sustainability (se4s)—protocol and results. Technical report UCI-ISR-14-1 (2014)
26. Amsel, N., Ibrahim, Z., Malik, A., Tomlinson, B.: Toward sustainable software engineering (NIER track). In: 2011 33rd International Conference on Software Engineering, pp. 976–979 (2011). https://doi.org/10.1145/1985793.1985964

27. Becker, C., et al.: Sustainability design and software: the Karlskrona manifesto. In: Proceedings of 37th International Conference on Software Engineering, vol. 2, pp. 467–476 (2015). https://doi.org/10.1109/ICSE.2015.179
28. Chitchyan, R., Duboc, L., Becker, C., Betz, S., Penzenstadler, B., Venters, C.C.: Sustainability design in requirements engineering: state of practice, pp. 533–542 (2016)
29. Lammert, D., Betz, S., Porras, J.: Software engineers in transition: self-role attribution and awareness for sustainability. In: Hawaii International Conference on System Sciences (HICSS 2022) (2022)
30. Tainter, J.A.: Social complexity and sustainability. Ecol. Complex. **3**(2), 91–103 (2006). https://doi.org/10.1016/j.ecocom.2005.07.004
31. Glaser, B.G., Strauss, A.L.: The discovery of grounded theory strategies for qualitative research, vol. 66 (1967)
32. EU: European Comission Classification of Business Enterprise (2001). https://ec.europa.eu/growth/smes/sme-definition_en
33. EUROSTAT, Statistical classification of economic activities in the European Community (2008)
34. Condori-Fernandez, N., Lago, P.: Characterizing the contribution of quality requirements to software sustainability. J. Syst. Softw. **137**, 289–305 (2018). https://doi.org/10.1016/j.jss.2017.12.005
35. Al Hinai, M., Chitchyan, R.: Engineering requirements for social sustainability. In: Proceedings of ICT Sustainability 2016 (2016). https://doi.org/10.2991/ict4s-16.2016.10
36. Oyedeji, S., Adisa, M.O., Naqvi, B., Abdulkareem, M., Penzenstadler, B., Seffah, A.: The interplay between usability, sustainability and green aspects: a design case study from a developing country. In: Proceedings of 6th International Conference on ICT for Sustainability, (ICT4S), vol. 2382 (2019)
37. Chitchyan, R., et al.: Sustainability design in requirements engineering: state of practice. In: 38th International Conference on Software Engineering Companion (ICSE 2016), pp. 533–542 (2016)
38. Duboc, L., et al.: Do we really know what we are building? Raising awareness of potential sustainability effects of software systems in requirements engineering. In: Proc. IEEE International Conference on Requirements Engineering Conference, vol. 2019-Septe, pp. 6–16 (2019). https://doi.org/10.1109/RE.2019.00013
39. Kienzle, J., et al.: Towards model-driven sustainability evaluation to cite this version: HAL Id: hal-02146543 towards model-driven sustainability evaluation (2019)
40. IBM: Global CEO Study: The enterprise of the future, p. 76 (2010). https://www-935.ibm.com/services/uk/gbs/pdf/ibm_ceo_study_2008.pdf. Accessed 11 Aug 2021
41. Microsoft: Microsoft 2015 Citizenship Report (2015). http://download.microsoft.com/download/7/3/6/736CED21-9D8B-4CBB-98E8-DCBAE70262451/Microsoft%202015%20Citizenship%20Report.pdf . Accessed 11 Aug 2021
42. Nidumolu, R., Prahalad, C., Rangaswami, M.: Why sustainability is now the key driver of innovation. IEEE Eng. Manag. Rev. (2013). https://doi.org/10.1109/EMR.2013.6601104
43. Wolfram, N., Lago, P., Osborne, F.: Sustainability in software engineering. In: 2017 Sustainable Internet and ICT for Sustainability (2017). https://doi.org/10.1109/CSEET.2011.5876124
44. Venters, C.C., et al.: Software sustainability: beyond the tower of babel. In: 2021 IEEE/ACM International Workshop on Body of Knowledge for Software Sustainability (BoKSS), pp. 3–4 (2021). https://doi.org/10.1109/bokss52540.2021.00009

Engineering and Management

Tailored Design Thinking Approach - A Shortcut for Agile Teams

Dominic Lang[1], Selina Spies[2], Stefan Trieflinger[3](✉), and Jürgen Münch[3]

[1] ETAS GmbH, Borsigstraße 24, 70469 Stuttgart, Germany
Dominic.lang2@bosch.com

[2] Department of Cloud Services, Robert Bosch GmbH, 70442 Stuttgart, Germany
Selina.Spies@bosch.com

[3] Reutlingen University, Alteburgstraße 150, 72769 Reutlingen, Germany
{stefan.trieflinger,juergen.muench}@reutlingen-university.de

Abstract. Context: Agile practices as well as UX methods are nowadays well-known and often adopted to develop complex software and products more efficiently and effectively. However, in the so called VUCA environment, which many companies are confronted with, the sole use of UX research is not sufficient to find the best solutions for customers. The implementation of Design Thinking can support this process. But many companies and their product owners don't know how much resources they should spend for conducting Design Thinking. **Objective:** This paper aims at suggesting a supportive tool, the "Discovery Effort Worthiness (DEW) Index", for product owners and agile teams to determine a suitable amount of effort that should be spent for Design Thinking activities. **Method:** A case study was conducted for the development of the DEW index. Design Thinking was introduced into the regular development cycle of an industry Scrum team. With the support of UX and Design Thinking experts, a formula was developed to determine the appropriate effort for Design Thinking. **Results:** The developed "Discovery Effort Worthiness Index" provides an easy-to-use tool for companies and their product owners to determine how much effort they should spend on Design Thinking methods to discover and validate requirements. A company can map the corresponding Design Thinking methods to the results of the DEW Index calculation, and product owners can select the appropriate measures from this mapping. Therefore, they can optimize the effort spent for discovery and validation.

Keywords: Design thinking · Scrum · Discovery · Requirements management · UX strategy · Product management

1 Introduction

Agile practices as well as UX methods are nowadays well-known and often adopted to develop software and products more efficiently and effectively. One expected benefit is that software and products which are developed iteratively can better meet customer needs in the context of requirements management [1]. The tricky part when talking about

X. Wang et al. (Eds.): ICSOB 2021, LNBIP 434, pp. 37–49, 2021.
https://doi.org/10.1007/978-3-030-91983-2_4

requirements management is that, especially in software development, new requirements are continuously being submitted by the customer or through external influences. Often it is also not clear what is actually to be developed, and this must first be discovered. This significantly complicates the planning and management of requirements and, in practice, often leads to the need for continuous and comprehensive change management. This includes optimizing changes and developments to best match the users' needs. However, in a so called VUCA environment, which many companies are confronted with, the sole use of UX research is not sufficient to find the best solutions for customers. The acronym VUCA is described by Horney et al. [2] as a business environment that is characterized by 1) volatility (the nature, pace, volume magnitude and dynamic of change), 2) uncertainty (the lack of predictability of issues and events), 3) complexity (the mixing of issues and the mess that surround any organization) and 4) ambiguity (the fuzziness of reality and the mixed meanings of conditions). One reaction of affected companies to the increased need for research, analysis and discovery is the application of Design Thinking.

Design Thinking, which was named for the first time by the company Ideo in 1991 [3], can support this methodology for innovation and inventive thinking [4]. The implementation of Design Thinking can support the aforesaid process since it aims at understanding the user's problem first and provides an open space for discovering solutions [5, 6]. Many companies are already using Design Thinking. At Bosch Group, a large German company, for example, it can be observed that Design Thinking has become an important topic. A press release from January 2018 [7] on the opening of a new IoT campus in Berlin already mentions the "widespread innovation method" Design Thinking, which is used in particular in software development. In March 2019 [8], another area reports how they live innovation using Design Thinking and have made this methodology central to development. Furthermore, there are companies that have already integrated the Design Thinking approach. The company Brainbirds GmbH [9], for example, offers seminars on Design Thinking or agile methods. Besides Bosch, its close partnerships include Audi, BMW, Adidas, Allianz, Deutsche Post DHL, and McDonald's [9]. Applications of Design Thinking can also be found in the energy sector. The KIC InnoEnergy has founded a company "homeandsmart GmbH" [10] using Design Thinking and worked it out in detail. It offers solutions for a connected home like Bosch Smart Home [10]. A key insight that the company has gained through Design Thinking is, for example, that smart home systems are not bought to save energy. They are mainly bought for comfort or security [11]. In conclusion, there is a clear tendency to use Design Thinking in practice. But often when companies do adopt Design Thinking, they struggle to implement it into their agile processes and iterations. A major constraint is the high effort for conducting comprehensive Design Thinking methods to discover and validate features and requirements. On the one hand resources are limited and therefore not all features can be explored with methods of Design Thinking. On the other hand, it can easily happen that the effort spent on Design Thinking exceeds the actual value delivered by the respective feature. This leads to the issue that many companies and their product owners do not know how much resources they should spend for conducting Design Thinking methods for the discovery, evaluation, and validation of certain requirements. This paper is structured as follows: After the introduction, Sect. 2 gives an insight to related work and similar approaches. Section 3 describes the research approach, while Sect. 4 explains the results, which are interpreted in Sect. 5. Section 6 discusses validity, followed by a summary in Sect. 7.

2 Related Work

In the scientific literature, several authors have dealt with the topic of Design Thinking. Alhazmi et al. [12] describes an approach, which is an integrated framework with Design Thinking into Scrum in the context of requirements engineering management to increase productivity. They are writing about verifying development progress with making sure that the requirements and the needs of stakeholders are applied correctly. At this point the question about the how remains open, because it is missing from this work. In contrast to the previous work, the related work from Nudelman [13] considers a Lean UX approach, which provides the answer for how to implement it in practice. But it focuses more on a Design Framework for documentation and less on the amount of effort to be used for Design Thinking integrated in Scrum. In contrast the related work of Cheng [14] considers more the aspect of lean development and therefore the aspect of effort, which was missing in the previous work. The author employs a lean development cycle in the context of user acceptance testing, with the goal of not only creating a deliverable product as known from the Scrum process, but also validating the features that a customer is paying for. This means that the secondary objective is also to minimize the risk of undesirable developments, and this is similar to the DEW index. In addition to that, Cheng [14] considers a developed framework called MobileAppUsability Inspection (MAUi) that should be a reliable usability inspection method and can be used as a checklist for fine-tuning the readiness of any minimal viable product. This heuristics checklist based on a Likert scale is somehow like the DEW Index developed in this paper, because it is based on a scale approach where users order themselves. Nevertheless, the work focuses more on the aspect of usability and therefore it is only similar in a broader sense. Another related work that is considered is the work of Liikkanen et al. [15], which is in the context of user-centered agile development. It also deals with the problem of decision-making patterns but focuses more on their opportunities and challenges. It's also about implementation in practice, but more about implementing Lean UX and less about answering the question of how much effort should be put into it. Overall, most of these works do not provide an approach to how much effort should be spent on exploration in the context of requirements management, e.g., when using Design Thinking in Scrum. An exception is the approach of Gothelf and Seiden [16] in their book "Lean UX". Gothelf and Seiden describe a prioritization matrix for figuring out, based on assumptions, how much risk there really is and how much we know about a topic. The higher the risk is and the more unknown the topic is, the higher is the priority to validate these assumptions. That means, the prioritization matrix focuses on the question what is more important and therefore to be researched with UX and Design Thinking first. This is along the same lines as the Discovery Effort Worthiness (DEW) Index approach but focuses on a different aspect. The DEW Index focuses mainly on the level of effort and what that effort should look like, rather than on priority. Nonetheless, both approaches determine importance by evaluating unclarity and the risk-value relationship to reach conclusions. So, the related work from Gothelf and Seiden [16] uses a similar approach than the DEW

Index developed in this paper but aims at answering a different question. The company ETAS GmbH, for example, uses Lean UX and this prioritization matrix by Gothelf and Seiden [16] internally as part of "customer-centric risk management" [17] as an assumption-driven approach. It has the goal of reducing project risks and costs. The two dimensions that are used by ETAS GmbH are the business impact and the uncertainty to figure out which candidates should be validated first to reduce the uncertainty and risk [17]. In contrast to the presented DEW Index, it only considers the evaluation of priority but not the question of how much effort should be spent.

3 Research Approach

This paper aims at suggesting a supportive tool for product owners and their teams to determine a suitable amount of effort that should be spent for Design Thinking activities. For this purpose, following research question was defined:

- **RQ:** How can a product owner or agile team decide how much effort is needed and which methods are appropriate to apply Design Thinking to a particular backlog item?

Since the topic of developing the DEW Index is about complex content and different sources are used for data collection, the research method of a case study according to Yin [18] has been chosen. Yin describes a case study as an empirical investigation that examines contemporary phenomena in a real-world context. This method is particularly suitable when the boundaries between phenomenon and context are not clearly discernible. The investigation manages the technically distinct situation and draws on multiple sources of evidence [19]. According to Plag [20], the case study research method is suitable under the condition that the context of the complex phenomenon to be studied is of particular interest. Furthermore, a case study is suitable if current approaches and perspectives are to be broken open and new perspectives shall be defined. In addition, it is advantageous if the state of research tends to be in an early phase. With regards to the purpose of this paper, these conditions are met. This context is of particular interest for practice and for science. Current approaches and perspectives are examined, and new approaches are defined and optimized. Research in this context is still in an early phase.

In the case study, Design Thinking (according to the approach as proposed by IDEO [21]) was introduced into the regular process of fulfilling the definition of ready of a cross-functional Scrum team at Robert Bosch Smart Home GmbH. The Scrum team consists of one product owner, one Scrum master and a development team consisting of external and internal resources (IT architect, developers, marketing, logistics, sales). In the case study, user stories were evaluated with Design Thinking in order to mark them as ready and thus incorporate them into a sprint planning. To be able to develop a metric that allows the team to identify which effort should be invested into Design Thinking methods, first some kind of benchmark was needed. Therefore, the backlog items of the case study team were analyzed in workshops with the support of two UX and Design Thinking experts to assign corresponding Design Thinking methods that promise the best input-output-ratio (see Table 2). In surveys and workshops with the Scrum team, these assignments were reviewed and validated. While these assignments were set as the benchmark, the authors determined which dimensions were decisive to identify the right Design Thinking methods by asking the team and the UX and Design Thinking experts why they decided to pick a specific method and why they decided to spend the effort involved. These interviews with experts and team members revealed the major factors, called dimensions, that were used to come to the benchmark assignments. After identifying the decision driving dimensions, the next step was to select a set of user stories from the team's benchmark and rate them with regards to the identified dimensions following the Scrum poker principle of relative rating. That means one story for which the definition of the right Design Thinking method and therefore the appropriate effort was very clear, got rated and the following stories were rated in relation to it. The researchers decided to use a scale from 1–10 for the rating, where 10 means high and 1 means low. This was chosen because a scale of 10 offers enough variety but keeps the rating for the team simple, so adopting the approach is perceived easy in the team. The zero does not appear since ideas or user stories with a clarity of zero or a potential value of zero won't appear in practice and therefore won't be handled by a product owner.

When looking at the results of the dimension rating and the recommended effort by the UX and Design Thinking experts a correlation between the dimensions and the effort worth spending was observed. Based on these results, a formula was developed that enables the product owner to independently determine a score that allows agile teams to identify how much effort should be spend with Design Thinking without the need to continuously involve experts giving their recommendation. Depicting this on a more abstract level, the approach is as follows (see Table 1):

User Story A is rated on dimension 1 and dimension 2. User Story B is now rated on dimension 1 and 2 in comparison to User Story A. If User Story B seems too similar on dimension 1 but at least twice as relevant on dimension 2, a possible rating on a scale of 1–10 would be like:

Table 1. An example of the correlation between the dimensions.

	Dimension 1	Dimension 2
User Story A	5	3
User Story B	5	6

Since User Story A is well understood, there is a clear picture about which effort would be appropriate to be invested into Design Thinking for User Story A. User Story B can be rated in relation to User Story A but the rating itself will not reveal which research effort would be appropriate. Since this appropriate effort depends on dimension 1 and dimension 2, the relation between the dimensions and the effort must be determined to then derive the appropriate effort for User Story B.

Consequently, the research approach for this paper followed several phases: 1) create a benchmark by assigning research effort to a set of well-known user stories, 2) figure out the decisive dimensions that affected the effort assignment, 3) rate the user stories on the dimensions, 4) determine the relation between the dimensions, 5) calculate the

DEW Index, 6) create a mapping table with the relation between effort and DEW Index, and 7) select the appropriate effort for your team.

The relation between the dimensions that lead to the appropriate effort is the Discovery Effort Worthiness Index presented in this paper. To determine this relation, a set of more than 50 benchmark user stories, where the appropriate effort was known, was rated on the dimensions and a formula that connects the dimensions was derived.

While it has already been described how the dimensions and ratings were determined, the creation of the mapping table that is required to find the appropriate effort based on the DEW Index is not discussed yet. The creation of the mapping table can also be referred to as the 'calibration' step. Based on the benchmark set in step 1), the assigned Design Thinking methods (usually method bundles were assigned instead of single measures) were sorted according to their DEW Index. The scale of the DEW Index is based on a floating scale between one and ten and does not consider decimal places. The product owner can select methods from the ranges once, several times or not at all, depending on the user story and DEW Index. This abstraction and the relative scoring enable transferability of the approach to other teams and other discovery methods besides Design Thinking.

4 Results

Development of DEW Index. Looking at the backlog and discussing the selected Design Thinking methods that were assigned to the user stories by the team and the UX and Design Thinking experts, the interviews made clear that the DEW Index must be based on two dimensions that primarily affect the necessity for discovery and validation: 1) Clarity about the user's need – how well understood is the actual demand of the user? 2) Potential value – how much value does the feature deliver? It was observed that the need and willingness to invest time and resources is growing the higher the expected value and the lower the clarity about the customers' need is. Hereby, the authors determined that the impact of clarity is slightly higher than the expected value and therefore this dimension needs to be weighted higher. This was observed by looking at a set of more than 50 user stories that were rated on both dimensions and their assigned Design Thinking effort, as described in the research approach. To find the right weight for the dimensions, this set of more than 50 user stories was compared regarding their assigned Design Thinking effort. Knowing the relation of the selected efforts as well as the dimension ratings allowed the authors to determine the relation between the dimensions and therefore the weights that support the expert assignments. The suggested weighting is 3:2 for clarity and potential value. The weighting is done because a low level of ambiguity and thus a high level of certainty about a user story particularly increases the need for Design Thinking. Furthermore, it is expected that a high level of uncertainty directly leads to a higher inaccuracy in the estimation and rating of the potential value, what means that higher unclarity also might influence the rating of the second dimension and therefore has more impact on the necessity of discovery and validation.

Taking this weighting into account, the approach to calculate the DEW Index is to rate each feature request relative to each other against both dimensions on a scale from 1 to 10, where 10 represents high potential and high clarity respectively. The fact that the feature requests are rated relatively to each other allows easy adoption to various projects and environments. To be able to do the calculation of the DEW Index, the clarity rating must be inverted since the effort for discovery increases with high unclarity. Finally, due to the different weights (3 for unclarity and 2 for potential value), the score must be divided by 5 to get the index. Therefore, the formula to calculate the DEW Index looks like (Fig. 1):

$$\text{DEW Index} = \frac{3 * (10 - \text{clarity}) + 2 * (\text{potential value})}{5}$$

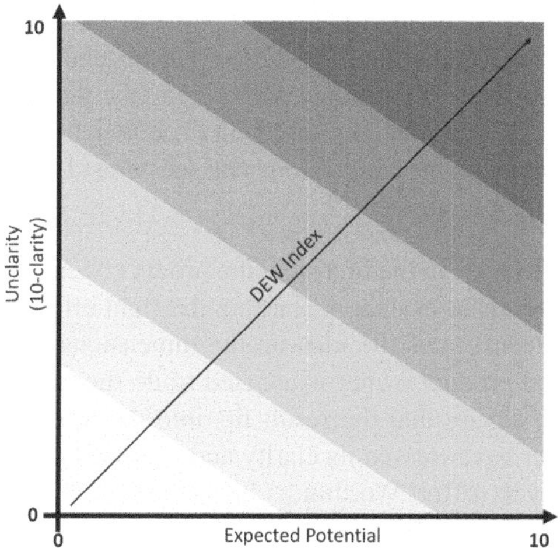

Fig. 1. Dimensions of the DEW index.

Calibration of DEW Index. The fact that the rating of the dimensions is done with a relative approach instead of absolute values leads to higher adoptability on the one hand but to the need for calibration on the other hand. To do the calibration, a company can proceed as follows: 1) assign corresponding Design Thinking methods to user stories from the backlog together with experts or based on experience, 2) rate this set of user stories from the backlog on the two dimensions, 3) calculate the DEW Index based on the rating, 4) map the corresponding Design Thinking methods to the results of the DEW Index calculation. That means that to enable product owners to easily select the appropriate measures from a mapping table and therefore optimize the effort spent for discovery and validation, a team must implement the DEW Index into their specific circumstances, since the relative dimension rating from 1 to 10 can vary between different teams. This calibration is suggested to be done with the same approach as chosen in this paper: 1) First, a set of user stories gets assigned to suitable Design Thinking methods with the support of UX and Design Thinking experts or based on the team's experience. 2) Then the stories are rated on the dimensions of clarity and potential value and 3) the DEW Index gets calculated. Having done this, the team can 4) create a mapping table that shows which DEW Index values are suggesting which methods and method bundles would be accurate. Here, the researchers observed that usually this mapping consists of method bundles instead of single methods. Executing just one single Design Thinking method is typically not sufficiently increasing clarity about the user demands or the expected value, so a bundle with a combination of methods can be more adequate. For example, such a bundle may consist of first conducting a brain dump, using the results for narrative interviews, and concluding the research with a Design Thinking workshop. The bundles that can be found in the mapping table are to be understood as a recommendation and orientation, not as a default. This is also why the methods and method bundles are not assigned to an exact DEW Index value and why the table should not show decimals. The DEW Index depicts the suitable effort for discovery and validation in a simplified way on a range from 1 to 10, taking the relation of the items into account. That means that also the methods and method bundles are sorted in relation to each other and to the DEW Index in this table. The product owner can take the calculated DEW Index of a user story, investigate the mapping table, and see which method range would be appropriate and then individually pick the ones he sees most feasible or promising. An example mapping can be seen in Table 2.

Application of DEW Index. In the first step, the product owner receives a new idea or a requirement that he needs to evaluate regarding the right effort for Design Thinking. Therefore, he (or the team) rates the idea on the dimensions of clarity and potential value. At this point, the product owner is advised to do the rating in comparison to a reference user story to ensure that the result fits into the team's calibrated mapping. Once the product owner has assessed its clarity and expected potential, the next step is to calculate the "Discovery Effort Worthiness Index" (or DEW Index) with the formula developed above. After the product owner has performed the calculation, he uses the calculated DEW Index to select one of the recommended Design Thinking methods or method bundles from the bundle mapping.

5 Interpretation of the Results

Through the DEW Index and Design Thinking, a continuous and user-centered way of working can be applied in everyday agile working life, ensuring that UX-optimized solutions are developed, customer requirements are correctly identified, and uncertainties are reduced through validation with the DEW Index. In addition to uncertainty, the Design Thinking approach also prevents undesirable developments and significantly reduces the risk of incorrect resource allocation. This becomes especially important when the effort for correction is taken into consideration. The difficulty of changing a wrongly delivered feature can vary significantly and the more difficult the correction is, the more important it is to have high clarity about the users' needs. In this initial version of the DEW Index, this dimension is not explicitly used since the authors decided to keep the simplicity and therefore usability high. The inclusion of the required change effort after implementation in the DEW Index could be subject of further research. Nevertheless, every validation through the DEW Index carried out provides the team with new insights and helps to learn from the findings for future implementations. In this way, the team can discuss

Table 2. Overview of an example of bundles.

1				6		DEW-	Index	7		9		10
Bundle 1	**Bundle 2**	**Bundle 3**	**Bundle 4**	**Bundle 5**	**Bundle 6**	**Bundle 7**	**Bundle 8**	**Bundle 9**	**Bundle 10**	**Bundle 11**	**Bundle 12**	**Bundle 13**
Stakeholder Map	Stakeholder Map	Stakeholder Map	Stakeholder Map	Stakeholder Map	Stakeholder Map	Stakeholder Map	Stakeholder Map	Stakeholder Map	Stakeholder Map	Stakeholder Map	Stakeholder Map	Stakeholder Map
Desk Research	Desk Research	Desk Research	Desk Research	Desk Research	Desk Research	Desk Research	Desk Research	Desk Research	Desk Research	Desk Research	Desk Research	Desk Research
Brain Dump	Brain Dump	Brain Dump	Brain Dump	Brain Dump	Brain Dump	Brain Dump	Brain Dump	Brain Dump	Brain Dump	Brain Dump	Brain Dump	Brain Dump
Online survey	Online survey	Online survey	Online survey	Online survey	Online survey	Online survey	Online survey	Online survey	Online survey	Online survey	Online survey	Online survey
	+	+	+	+	+	+	+	+	+	+	+	+
	Online survey	(Narrative) Interview 10<20	(Narrative) Interview >30	Online survey	Online survey	Online survey	(Narrative) Interview 10<20	(Narrative) Interview 10<20	(Narrative) Interview 10<20	(Narrative) Interview >30	(Narrative) Interview >30	(Narrative) Interview >30
	Semantic Analysis	Shadowing	DT-Workshop 4-8 pers.	Semantic Analysis	Semantic Analysis	Semantic Analysis	Shadowing	Shadowing	Shadowing	DT-Workshop 4-8 pers.	DT-Workshop 4-8 pers.	DT-Workshop 4-8 pers.
		Test of existing solutions					Test of existing solutions	Test of existing solutions	Test of existing solutions			
				+	+	+	+	+	+	+	+	+
				(Narrative) Interview 20<30	DT-Workshop 8-16 pers.	Prototype & Test <1 day	(Narrative) terview 20<30	DT-Workshop 8-16 pers.	Prototype & Test <1 day	(Narrative) Interview 20<30	DT-Workshop 8-16 pers.	Prototype & Test <1 day
				DT-Workshop 4-8 pers.	Role play	DT-Workshop >16 pers.	DT-Workshop 4-8 pers.	Role play	DT-Workshop >16 pers.	DT-Workshop 4-8 pers.	Role play	DT-Workshop >16 pers.

the learnings and necessary adjustments in retrospective and by doing so continuously improve its performance.

Furthermore, the acceptance of the employees for Design Thinking has been increased and ensured as a key to success, because through an iterative and closely coordinated development with many feedback rounds, the team was involved in the development at an early stage and the effort for discovery research was optimized. The advantages of the approach were thus clearly recognized and understood by the team and accepted and considered positive based on the user-centered working method through the team's own input. The possible skepticism of the team towards the presumed additional work through the implementation of an adapted Design Thinking approach with the DEW Index was not confirmed. Nevertheless, implementing the DEW Index in the everyday Scrum iterations requires some effort for calibration and the results vary based on the quality of this calibration. Having said this, the authors strongly recommend discussing the results of the DEW Index usage and the correctness of the calibration in the sprint retrospective to enable continuous improvement. The developed DEW Index is depicting the suitable effort for discovery and validation in a simplified way. It is not designed to master the high complexity of exactly determining the methods and amount of resources that should be spend for discovery and validation, but to simplify this process for product owners and their teams, by giving them orientation and avoiding wasting resources.

6 Threats to Validity

Like other research methods, the case study must also be critically examined. Here, requirements such as explanatory content, verifiability, lack of contradiction and proof are examined. There are different criteria for evaluating a case study. The following evaluation and examination of validity is carried out according to Yin's catalogue of criteria. It is based on classical evaluation criteria of empirical research. Accordingly, the following quality criteria are relevant [18].

The quality criterion of **construct validity** guarantees the most objective and thus verifiable case study results possible. However, it does not exclude subjective data collection and interpretation by the researcher. In this case, a comprehensible explanation must be recorded for third parties. To achieve a high construct validity, the collected data should be closely related to the research question. Furthermore, the analysis and interpretation of the results should be plausibly argued and a critical discussion of the results with experts can lead to a higher construct validity [22]. The case study is construct-valid, as data collection was carried out by means of interviews, surveys, and a workshop with several observers. Several stakeholders were involved in the preparation of the study. When formulating the questions for the interviews, surveys and workshops, care was taken to ensure objectivity and openness to avoid influencing the results.

Internal validity describes the extent to which the internal logic of the data analysis and the results is guaranteed. In this context, causal relationships are shown whether they were correctly derived, and all relevant explanatory approaches were considered. This is ensured, for example, by pattern matching, by writing explanatory approaches and critically questioning them, or by using logical models [22]. There is internal validity because the case study used both quantitative and qualitative methods. The results were verified using quantitative methods such as interviews and surveys and the qualitative method of the workshop, thus ensuring scalability.

External validity checks the results of the case study for their transferability to other cases [22]. The external validity of the case study is limited despite transferability being considered in the approach, as the results of the case study are only valid for the present framework conditions. Therefore, the results are not fully transferable to other research fields. It should be a team that already works successfully in an agile way and develops user-centered products. Furthermore, it must be noted that the distribution of the bundles on the scale was developed individually for a team in the calibration, that strongly depends on the experts and experience and thus only represents an internal validity. To apply the integration model in other teams, a new calibration is necessary.

Reliability is a quality criterion of the case study that describes the reliability, stability, and precision of the case study. It indicates the degree of reliability of a measurement. The measurement of reliability should lead to the same result when the case study is repeated [23, 24]. Reliability is present in this paper because the case study conducted did not collect measurement data, but qualitative criteria and their frequency. Therefore, unreliability or instability can only occur in the case of misunderstandings or misstatements.

Objectivity verifies the independence of subjective influencing factors. It considers the neutral attitude of the researcher regarding data collection, data analysis and data interpretation [23, 24]. The objectivity of the case study is not complete, as the researchers have their own opinion on the subject and may express it subconsciously. However, the case study tried to develop a neutral attitude towards data collection, data analysis and data interpretation.

7 Summary

The developed Discovery Effort Worthiness Index offers an easy-to-use tool for companies and their product owners to determine how much effort they should spend on Design Thinking methods to discover and validate features. It therefore simplifies the complex relations and dependencies and suggests a comfortable way to get orientation when trying to determine the suitable effort for discovery and validation based on the two dimensions with the most influence. A similar approach that uses the same dimensions is also applied by Gothelf and Seiden [16], with the difference that Gothelf and Seiden [16] focus on answering the question which features should be researched first, i.e. the priority of the backlog items. Gothelf and Seiden [16] make use of the research importance of a feature to prioritize, while the DEW Index uses the research importance to decide how much effort should be spent.

The approach of the DEW Index is that the effort worth spending for Design Thinking methods increases when high value can be expected but the clarity about the user's needs is low. The developed approach allows transferability to different teams and situations since it does not use absolute ratings, nevertheless it requires calibration when being used in a new environment. Besides that, the researchers recommend including a review of the application of the DEW Index in the Scrum retrospective to improve or even recalibrate, if necessary, e.g., after circumstances have changed. This especially becomes true when there are no experts or if there is only low experience with Design Thinking that could be used to create the benchmark that is needed for the calibration.

The mapping table can contain either single methods or method bundles that are sorted in accordance with the DEW Index and a product owner can use his calculated index value to identify and then pick the Design Thinking methods or method bundles in the respective range.

References

1. Lewin, D.: Change Management, vol. 1 (1980)
2. Horney, N., Pasmore, B., O'Shea, T.: Leadership agility: a business imperative for a VUCA world. People Strategy 33(4), pp-32–38. (2010). https://luxorgroup.fr/coaching/wp-content/uploads/Leadership-agility-model.pdf
3. Gerstbach, I.: Design Thinking im Unternehmen: Ein Workbook für die Einführung von Design Thinking. GABAL Verlag GmbH, Offenbach (2016)
4. Schallmo, D.R.A.: Design thinking erfolgreich anwenden. So entwickeln Sie in 7 Phasen kundenorientierte Produkte (2017)
5. Plattner, H., Meinel, C., Leifer, L.: Design Thinking: Understand - Improve - Apply. Springer, Heidelberg (2011). https://doi.org/10.1007/978-3-642-13757-0
6. Lahn, S.: Der businessplan in theorie und praxis (2015)
7. Robert Bosch GmbH: Bosch eröffnet IoT-Campus in Berlin (2018)
8. Becker, H.: Verwender im Fokus: Bosch Power Tools setzt auf Innovation und gestaltet die Entwicklung der Branche. https://www.bosch-presse.de/pressportal/de/de/verwender-im-fokus-bosch-power-tools-setzt-auf-innovation-und-gestaltet-die-entwicklung-der-branche-185293.html. Accessed 20 Aug 2021
9. Brain Birds GmbH: BrainBirds: Über uns. https://brainbirds.de/ueber-uns/. Accessed 20 Aug 2021
10. Homeandsmart GmbH: Home&Smart: Über uns. https://www.homeandsmart.de/ueber-uns. Accessed 20 Aug 2021
11. Majer, P.: Euroforum Deutschland: Hilfe, was will mein Kunde? Vom Design Thinking zum Smart Home Portal (2019). https://www.euroforum.de/stadtwerke/vom-design-thinking-zum-smart-home-portal/. Accessed 20 Aug 2021
12. Alhazmi, A., Huang, S.: Integrating design thinking into scrum framework in the context of requirement engineering management. In: Proceedings of 2020 3rd International Conference on Computer Science and Software Engineering (CSSE 2020), Bejing, China (2020). https://dl.acm.org/doi/pdf/10.1145/3403746.3403902
13. Nudelman, G.: Lean UX communication strategies for success in large organizations. Baker Hughes GE Digital (2018). https://dl.acm.org/doi/pdf/10.1145/3236683
14. Cheng, L.C.: The mobile app usability inspection (MAUi) framework as a guide for minimal viable product (MVP) testing in lean development cycle. In: CHIuXiD 2016, 13–15 April 2016, Jakarta, Indonesia (2016). https://dl.acm.org/doi/pdf/10.1145/2898459.2898460
15. Liikkanen, L.A., Kilpiö, H., Svan, L., Hiltunen, M.: Lean UX – the next generation of user-centered agile development? In: NordiCHI 2014, Helsinki, Finland (2014). https://dl.acm.org/doi/pdf/10.1145/2639189.2670285
16. Gothelf, J., Seiden, J.: Lean UX. O'Reilly Media, Inc., USA (2013)
17. ETAS GmbH: ETAS Lean UX – Customer centric Risk Management (internal document) (2019)
18. Yin, R.K.: Case Study Research - Design and Methods, Vol. 5. SAGE Publications, Inc. (2009)
19. Hoffmann, C.-A.: Methodik zur Steuerung modularer Produktbaukästen (2018)

20. Plag, M.: Veränderungsmanagement in Bundesministerien - Eine empirische Untersuchung auf Basis multipler Fallstudien, 1 edn. GWV Fachverlage GmbH Wiesbaden (2007).
21. IDEO: Design thinking. https://www.ideou.com/pages/design-thinking. Accessed 20 Aug 2021
22. Hansen, H.: Durchführung, Analyse und Bewertung der empirischen Erhebung, 1st edn. Gabler GWV Fachverlage GmbH, Wiesbaden (2009)
23. Matros, R.: Forschungsansatz. Gabler Verlag Springer Fachmedien, Wiesbaden (2012)
24. Preißner, A.: Marketing auf den Punkt gebracht. Oldenburg Wissenschaftsverlag GmbH, München (2008)

Deliberative Technical Debt Management: An Action Research Study

Nichlas Bødker Borup, Ann Louise Jul Christiansen, Sabine Hørdum Tovgaard, and John Stouby Persson(✉)

Department of Computer Science, Aalborg University, Selma Lagerlöfs Vej 300, 9220 Aalborg Øst, Denmark
{nichlasbb,annljc,sabineht,john}@cs.aau.dk

Abstract. Technical Debt (TD) has seen a growing interest from software companies and researchers since the term was first established almost 30 years ago. TD refers to concessions made for short-term advantages or conveniences, which may result in long-term difficulties. Numerous TD management strategies have been proposed to avoid the severe consequences of leaving TD unchecked. However, these strategies often suffer from being too abstract, making it difficult to initiate TD deliberations. To investigate how software development companies can initiate such deliberations, we conducted an Action Research study in collaboration with a Danish software development department, SoftShelf. Through two Action Research interventions at SoftShelf, we introduced strategies and tools for TD management and reified them to their situation in order to initiate deliberations on the matter. After reporting the interventions' practical consequences in SoftShelf, we discuss the usefulness of deliberation theory in TD management research and practice.

Keywords: Technical Debt · Deliberation theory · Action research

1 Introduction

The term Technical Debt (TD) generally reflects compromises made to gain short-term benefits that may incur long-term difficulties [17]. Although laying dormant for several years after its inception in 1992 [7], the term has recently become an increasingly popular field of study due to its economic implications, as well as the rise of agile software development, where the emphasis on rapid delivery makes the practice especially prone to TD [4,21]. Fowler's [12] TD Quadrant categorises TD based on the intention (deliberate or inadvertent) and awareness (reckless or prudent) of incurring the debt.

TD mainly affects the evolvability and maintainability of systems, making these costly and difficult, or downright impossible [17]. However, TD can also result in reduced productivity and system quality degradation, even requiring complete reworks of a system, as well as costing market value or business relationships in some cases [4]. Even so, not all TD is inherently bad. Intentionally

X. Wang et al. (Eds.): ICSOB 2021, LNBIP 434, pp. 50–65, 2021.
https://doi.org/10.1007/978-3-030-91983-2_5

incurring TD to achieve short-term benefits can be advantageous if the debt is managed properly [1,22]. Managing TD presents substantial challenges related to the abstract nature of the term, such as quantifying, visualising, and even agreeing on what TD is [36]. Still, little research has been done on how software developers view TD, even though this perspective is vital to enable developers to effectively manage TD [16,22]. Although the awareness of the term varies in practice, once familiar with the term, the consensus is that TD is a significant part of software development [9,16,22]. Nevertheless, it is difficult for software developers to initiate TD deliberations.

Deliberation covers "*mutual communication that involves weighing and reflecting on preferences, values, and interests regarding matters of common concern*" [23]. To get a team of developers, who are unfamiliar with TD, to become deliberate in managing it requires an initiating intervention. Action Research (AR) allows this, but very few studies have taken this interventionary approach [4]. One previous AR study [39] proposed processes for identification, documentation, and prioritisation of TD to increase its visibility and manageability, but without taking active decision-making on incurring new TD into consideration. Another AR study [28] implemented a TD management framework into two companies using Scrum to provide empirical evidence for its usefulness, but, as the other study, without an explicit focus on deliberation.

We report an AR study of introducing TD as a shared developer and management concern in an organisation. This AR study was conducted in collaboration with a Danish software development department – SoftShelf, a pseudonym, part of a large international intralogistics organisation. One of SoftShelf's main responsibilities is maintaining and evolving existing software solutions with customers in their region, making TD a central part of their practice, despite them not actively using the term. With this AR study, we pursue the dual purpose of helping SoftShelf manage their TD, as well as contributing to TD management research, through answering the research question: *How can we initiate Technical Debt deliberations at a software development company?*

Using the AR methodology [26], we demonstrate how to initiate TD deliberations at SoftShelf; supply further empirical evidence of the usefulness of Seaman and Guo's [33] TD management framework when used in conjunction with Rubin's [30] TD visualisation approaches in a Scrum process, and; nuance Fowler's [12] TD Quadrant using deliberation theory.

2 Background

2.1 Technical Debt Management

Technical Debt (TD) was first coined in 1992 as a way of expressing the act of writing immature code under deadline pressure by Cunningham [7]. Since then, a wide range of definitions has been suggested by several authors, often expanding the definition to a more widespread and general perspective on software development costs, including architectural, testing, or documentation related TD. As a consequence of the absence of a singular definition, researchers have argued that the metaphor may be losing some of its strength [18], as it exacerbates the challenge of identifying and managing the debt adequately [36]. However, the consensus on the term is that it describes trade-offs between some expedient short-term decisions and the resulting long-term costs [21,22].

TD can be categorised into types based on the cause of the debt [18,22], which may pertain to requirements, architecture, design, code, test, build, documentation, infrastructure, and versioning [21]. Notably, McConnell [25] categorises TD into two basic types based on intention: intentional and unintentional. Fowler [12] nuanced this categorisation by adding the consideration of awareness (prudent or reckless) when incurring debt; introducing his TD Quadrant (Fig. 1). We use Fowler's [12] quadrant, but with McConnell's [25] intention categorisation (intentional or unintentional) instead of Fowler's [12] (deliberate or inadvertent) to avoid confusion between this categorisation and deliberation theory.

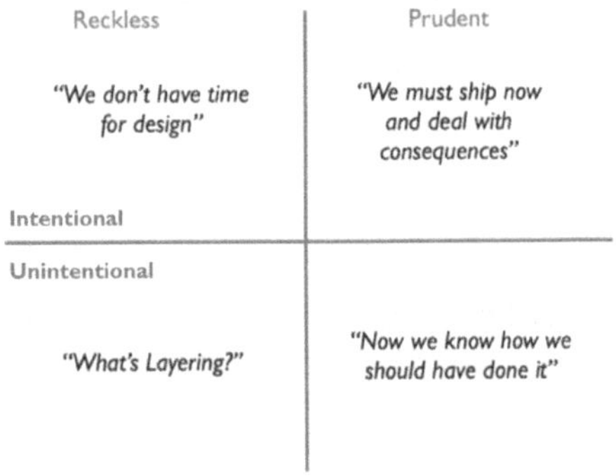

Fig. 1. Adapted Fowler's [12] TD Quadrant

TD is considered intentional and prudent if the debt is incurred proactively through a well-thought-through decision, e.g. a team choosing to forgo proper documentation and testing to be able to ship quickly. In such a situation, TD is not inherently negative. Inherent to this terminology is that prudent debt is preferable to reckless debt, since unintentional TD is difficult to handle [16]. Taking on debt is inevitable, and the focus is therefore not on eliminating it, but managing it [1]. However, managing TD can be strenuous, as measuring the debt and assigning business value to it proves challenging in practice [19,21]. Furthermore, many different stakeholders may induce TD beyond the control of the development team [21]. When managing TD, there are different elements which must be considered; these are TD items, principal, interest, interest probability, impact, automated means, expert opinion, scenario analysis, time-to-market, when to implement decisions, evolution, and visualisation [10].

TD management involves eight key activities; repayment, identification, measuring, monitoring, prioritisation, communication, prevention, and representation/documentation [21]. However, most literature is focused on repayment, identification, and measurement. There exist a plethora of tools for managing TD, however, the majority of these tools pertain to only code debt with the fewest tools pertaining to requirement and documentation debt [21,31]. Furthermore, few TD management strategies have been validated through empirical evidence, and as such, the field calls for further research refining TD management strategies to ensure their real-world practicality [21].

TD management itself must not exceed the cost of simply leaving TD unattended and should therefore be integrated into the existing project management process [13]. Following this notion, [28] implemented Seaman and Guo's [33] TD management framework in two software projects using Scrum. This framework includes listing TD as items using the template seen in Table 1.

Table 1. Seaman and Guo's [33] TD items template

ID	TD identification number
Date	TD identification date
Responsible	Person who identified TD
Type	TD type
Location	Description of where TD is
Description	Justification of why item needs to be considered
Estimated Principal	Work required to pay off item
Estimated Interest Amount	Extra effort needed in the future if item not paid off
Estimated Interest Probability	Probability of extra work needed if item not paid off

The *Estimated Principal, Estimated Interest Amount* and *Estimated Interest Probability* in Table 1 may be simple approximate ratings of high, medium or low. The framework proposes using the items to perform a Cost-Benefit analysis to assess whether, how much, and which TD to pay off. This use can be supported by Rubin's [30] visualisation approaches: (1) Logging TD like defects into an existing defect-tracking system, (2) Creating product backlog items that represent TD, and (3) Creating a special TD backlog. Nevertheless, while such visualisation can help a software development organisation learn about its debt, it does not in itself ensure deliberative TD management.

2.2 Deliberation

Deliberation is defined as "*mutual communication that involves weighing and reflecting on preferences, values and interests regarding matters of common concern*" [23]. Essential to this definition are three main principles of deliberation. Firstly, deliberation is mutual communication – it requires communication between two or more people. Secondly, deliberation is weighing and reflecting, which captures the thoughtful consideration ordinarily associated with the term deliberation. Finally, deliberation is regarding matters of common concern and does not include matters only relevant to the individual. This definition is relatively neutral and does not consider the concepts of good and bad deliberations. As such, standards for good deliberation must be defined separately.

Research in the field of deliberations has yielded a broad array of standards for good deliberations. At the forefront of these standards are building a strong information base, considering a range of solutions and evaluating all of these equally, mutual respect, and adequate opportunities to speak so that a diversity of views may be heard [6]. Additional standards for good deliberation include absence of power, rational and emotional considerations, aim at consensus and clarifying interests, orientation to the common good, equal opportunity of access to influence, the inclusion of all affected individuals, accountability to constituents, publicity/transparency, sincerity, epistemic value, and substantive balance [23]. However, many of these standards are contestable and may conflict with one another, and should therefore be interpreted as regulative ideals.

There are four essential prerequisites for deliberation [6]. Firstly, deliberation must be perceived to be an appropriate mode of discourse by participants. Secondly, participants must also perceive a potential for reaching a common ground, as deliberation may seem futile otherwise. Thirdly, deliberation requires some analytical and communicative competencies from its participants to thoughtfully consider the wide range of perspectives of the deliberative process. Fourthly, participants must be motivated to deliberate instead of simply forgoing the process.

Intuitively, improving deliberation would entail ensuring a selection of the standards of good deliberation. However, improved deliberation can also be achieved through good facilitation, with vital aspects of this being maintaining a positive atmosphere and making progress [24]. From these definitions, it can be proposed that what would be categorised as prudent and intentional TD is incurred through what would be considered good deliberations.

3 Methodology

To understand how we can initiate TD deliberations, we performed an Action Research (AR) study [26], which juxtaposes action and research to create new knowledge, through seeking solutions to real-world practical problems [27]. In this study, we follow an iterative process [26] for industry-research collaboration [37] as exemplified in [2] with SoftShelf, a Danish software development department, over the course of 10 months. SoftShelf was contacted as one of several candidates for the collaboration of this study. Our primary contact from SoftShelf, the UX and QA Manager, has previously worked as a researcher in the fourth author's research group.

3.1 The Company – SoftShelf

SoftShelf is a software development department of a large international organisation making intralogistics solutions and products, whose main office is located in Germany. While the organisation was founded in the 1930s, SoftShelf was not created until 2008 and was not the first software development department of the organisation. This means that SoftShelf's responsibilities include working with legacy systems from other departments. SoftShelf operates from two different locations, and the department is divided into two teams: Project and IT service. However, employees are not necessarily strictly assigned to a single team and thus sometimes work across both. The Project team develops new software according to specifications from the organisation's sales department, while the IT service team is responsible for software maintenance, communicating directly with the customers. As such, TD was a central part of SoftShelf's practice, but was not a term they used in their process.

SoftShelf had seen significant growth in recent years, with the number of employees increasing from seven in 2017 to 25 at the time of our study, and still increasing. Due to increased demand, the department had to work extremely fast even with additionally hired consultants. As speed had taken precedence, the development process and structure had fallen by the wayside. The department decided that this situation was no longer sustainable and had begun restructuring its development processes. To facilitate this restructuring, a task-force of four employees with relevant expertise had been set: the UX and QA Manager, a Developer, a Solution Architect, and a Project Manager. The task-force had defined new feature driven development processes that fitted into SoftShelf's overall process. A feature is a reportable and testable ability of the system that has value to the customer. While working on these features, the teams used Scrum to iterate through the design and build phases. As SoftShelf were undergoing this restructuring, they were highly interested in introducing TD management into their process to optimise their restructuring even further. We approached the problem situation first at the department level involving both the IT Service and Project teams and next on a specific Project team. As a pilot project, we aided a team's TD management. This team included a projects manager, lead logistics consultant, quality controller, product owner, external consultant, lead developer, Scrum master, and three developers. As the team roles covered a wide range of responsibilities, we were able to initiate deliberations on TD across different stakeholder levels.

3.2 Research Activities

Our analytical approach to the problem situation at SoftShelf was abductively driven by questions and breakdowns [5]. Unlike the data-driven analysis of induction and the theory-driven analysis of deduction, abduction is breakdown-driven analysis – when something breaks with the normal understanding of a situation. Abduction is used for understanding and explaining, e.g., when exploring Fowler's [12] Quadrant, we wondered what it meant to be prudently intentional (deliberate) in one's TD decisions, which lead us to the vast field of deliberation theory as a way of framing TD management.

We performed research activities over 10 months (Fig. 2). To investigate **the problem situation**, we initially observed a virtual meeting concerning the department's restructuring and internal processes. Next, we conducted seven semi-structured interviews. These interviews followed the practical guidelines in [29] to ensure quality and an interview guide with open-ended questions designed to elicit the interviewees' experiences with and opinions of TD. These questions were based on research topics from our study of relevant TD literature, and included TD types, TD assessments, actors and stakeholders, and valuation of TD. The full table of research topics and the interview guide can be requested from the authors.

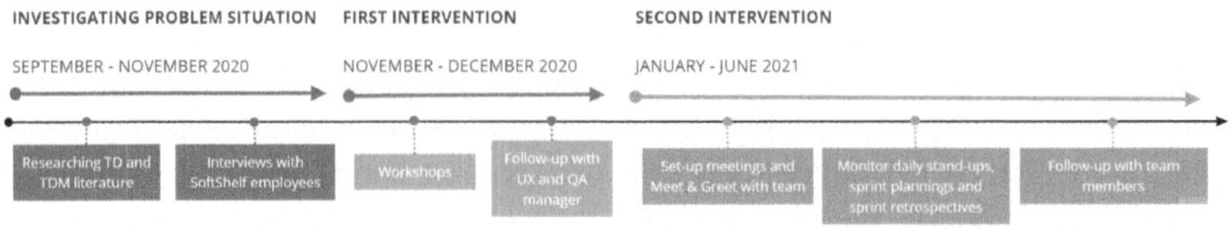

Fig. 2. Action Research study timeline

These interviews were spread out between SoftShelf's two teams, with two developers from the IT service team and its team lead being interviewed, as well as two developers and a solution architect from the Project team. We selectively transcribed interviewee statements relevant to our research, discussing and noting any breakdowns. In a follow-up interview with the UX and QA Manager, she helped deepen our understanding of the software department's roles, structure, and daily work routines. After these seven interviews, the answers were evaluated and used to guide further research of relevant literature as we aim to conceptualise and reify TD in the context of SoftShelf. This juxtaposition of relevant literature and the in-depth inquiries into the problem area [27] links our problem-solving activities to our research activities, with each activity helping the other.

Our **first intervention** into the problem situation at SoftShelf was to organise a workshop with the restructuring task-force and relevant managers. The findings from the interviews were presented and backed by relevant literature on TD to conceptualise their current situation as a starting point for deliberation. We then presented several methods and tools for managing the specific TD problems identified in SoftShelf for them to conceptualise the future, and to improve deliberation. Throughout the workshop, the participants were asked to reflect on the findings presented. All reflections were noted to monitor and evaluate the effect of the interventions on both solving the problem and answering our research question. Finally, we interviewed the UX and QA Manager again to evaluate the effects of the workshop sessions on SoftShelf's TD deliberations after a longer incubation period. While the UX and QA Manager was pleased with our intervention, they requested further practical support of initiating TD deliberation on the project level, which led to our second intervention.

Our **second intervention** focused on implementing TD management strategies [30,33] identified during our first intervention with a specific Project team in SoftShelf. We first conducted a meeting with the UX and QA Manager and the Lead Developer of the pilot project team to understand the team's specific process and how our research could be carried out with the best possible outcome for both parties. After this meeting, we organised a workshop with the team, to present the framework and tools we thought could aid them in their TD deliberations. To best facilitate the implementation of the framework and tools, we were present for all significant meetings, where there was a possibility that TD deliberations could unfold. This summed up to 25 daily stand-up meetings, two bi-weekly sprint plannings, and two sprint retrospectives. At these meetings we were present to help facilitate TD deliberations if necessary and aided them in conceptualising their debt, e.g., providing them with a list of TD types. We also presented the concept of deliberation to improve their communication and juxtapose our research with their problem solving in our collaboration. Finally, to conclude this intervention, we conducted follow-up interviews and a group session with the entire team to evaluate the intervention.

4 Findings

In this section, we present the problem situation at SoftShelf, as well as our two interventions to improve their TD deliberation.

4.1 Problem Situation at SoftShelf – Lack of Deliberation

In SoftShelf there was no consensus on the concept of TD – some employees coined TD as "*duplicate code*", others as "*missing documentation*", and some were not familiar with the term at all. However, the legacy aspect of projects in both the IT service and Project teams was a clear source of frustrations pertaining to "*much of the code is pre-made*" leading to "*a lot of time spent changing old code*". Several developers expounded the issue of addressing TD when reworking older systems. As the maintainability decreases with every new line of code, the customer seemed to play a significant role in decisions regarding whether or not to pay off debt. It was evidently "*hard to communicate debt to the customer, as it was something they cannot see*". Moreover, "*the customer does not pay for our documentation*" seems to lay the grounds for no actual deliberation on whether or not to address the issue. The customers and the sales department inducing TD is broadly agreed upon between developers. However, when asked if they ever discussed these issues amongst each other, no deliberation on managing it was apparent.

TD was occasionally mentioned as an annoyance within teams but most often dealt with on an individual rather than an organisational level. There was little communication about what to do when TD was discovered or when the possibility of incurring TD occurred. They had no standard procedure for, or communication about, how to handle, for instance, loosely defined specifications. Decisions like these, where a developer attempts to solve loosely defined specifications in isolation, are intentional [12], as the developer was unsure of how the specifications should be carried out and therefore purposely risked incurring debt. Nevertheless, it is also reckless behaviour [12], since communicating with the right stakeholders could have clarified the specifications and averted the possibility of incurring debt altogether. However, some of our interviewees felt that TD was indeed communicated within the organisation. A solution architect stated that decisions concerning TD were communicated across different levels of the organisation, and the leader of the IT service team mentioned that obstacles, such as poorly written code, were discussed regularly:

> "*We talk about it – also poorly written code and how we can solve it. It should not be taboo. It is not difficult, and people are nice about it.*"
> (IT service Team Lead)

We found this difference in perception of the level of TD communication at SoftShelf interesting. Most TD decisions were made individually and in the moment, with a few exceptions briefly being discussed with the closest colleagues. Furthermore, our interviewees expressed that these decisions were mostly made recklessly [12], since the repercussions were rarely considered. Deliberation is based on mutual communication and cannot be done in isolation by the individual [23]. In our first intervention to improve deliberation at SoftShelf, we introduce the TD term and reify it to their specific present situation.

4.2 First Intervention – Organisational Deliberation

Our first intervention at SoftShelf consisted of a workshop with the relevant managers and the restructuring task-force. All of our previous interviewees, not already included, were also welcomed to join if they could find the time.

We initiated the workshop by briefly introducing the concept of TD to supply them with a vocabulary for discussing their own issues regarding TD. Once we had established this knowledge base, we presented the current issues related to TD in SoftShelf based on our interviews. We took care to relate these issues to relevant literature, reifying the term in their specific context. This included how their current TD considerations placed in Fowler's [12] TD Quadrant, where we categorised most of their statements as reckless and intentional – e.g. "*deadlines gave us no time to review*" and "*it is "fire and forget", not something we talk about again*" leaving little room for any thoughts on action. We also presented how several types of debt were present in SoftShelf, including code debt, documentation debt, and design debt. The UX and QA Manager commented that she was not surprised by the amount of TD we had identified within the company, but she did not realise how many aspects TD covered outside of coding.

Next, we outlined different TD management strategies to provide a context from which their own TD management could be understood. Here, we presented three focus areas specific to the TD at SoftShelf: communicating about TD, estimation of TD, and handling TD in legacy systems. An overview of these strategies and tools and the specific challenges they target is presented in Table 2.

Table 2. Strategies presented at workshop

Focus Area	Strategy	Tool
Communication	Internal	Discuss TD – e.g. put it on the agenda [36,39]
		Document TD – e.g. create a TD list [35,39]
		Agree on TD [39]
	External	Visualisation of TD [15]
		Estimate TD – e.g. Cost-Benefit Analysis, Portfolio Management [34]
Value Estimation	Decisions	Cost-Benefit Analysis, Portfolio Management [34]
	Code	Software analysis tool – SQALE [20]
Legacy Systems	Decisions	Decisional Framework for Legacy System Management [8]
	Code	Eclipse plugin for Java – JDeodorant [11]
General	Agility	Extended Definition of Done [4]
	Maturity	CMMI with TD focus [38]

When asked to reflect upon the presented strategies, they were predominantly positive. One developer was particularly interested in the software tool SQALE, calling it a "*really good idea*", while others expressed interest in using an extended Definition of Done to include requirements to minimise the risk of incurring TD. A solution architect stated that he could see the tools possibly having a direct effect on SoftShelf's collaborations with customers:

> "*As we are implementing new standard solutions and trying to sell these to the customers, we might be able to use these tools as an argument in convincing customers to choose a more standardised solution.*"
> (Solution Architect)

We were pleased to hear that the employees could envision some of the tools and strategies being used in their daily work to improve their processes. Their willingness to change their methods showed that they want more deliberation within the department. In a much later follow up meeting with the UX and QA Manager, evaluating the intervention's effect on the problem situation at SoftShelf and their overall TD deliberation, we were also pleased to hear they had begun talking about TD in their day-to-day work:

> "*It is something we think about now, something that we are aware of. It has become easier for us to talk about it. We have to be aware of the meaning of technical debt, and we have become better at articulating it.*"
> (UX and QA Manager)

Having gained a conceptualisation of TD, the employees at SoftShelf were now able to discuss issues constructively through a new common vocabulary. According to the UX and QA Manager, SoftShelf's older projects accumulated the most

TD and for this reason, they had now decided to focus on setting time aside to "*patch things together properly*" on these projects.

Overall, SoftShelf had begun analysing their current situation and deliberating on the occurrence and management of TD. When starting up new projects, a common Definition of Done is now created for the project, including measures to manage TD. Nevertheless, SoftShelf also wanted us to aid them in initiating TD deliberation on a pilot project using some of our suggested frameworks and tools. SoftShelf still needed further assistance reifying TD to their specific situation. The department-wide awareness and information base from our first intervention was not adequate to initiate SoftShelf's TD deliberations on its own. Thus, we turned our focus from the organisational perspective of our first intervention to a project-centred perspective for our second intervention.

4.3 Second Intervention – Project Deliberation

For our second intervention at SoftShelf, we collaborated closely with a specific Project team over a couple of months, helping them initiate TD deliberations. To accomplish this, we introduced Seaman and Guo's [33] TD management framework (cf. Sect. 2.1) into their Scrum process, as it is flexible [13] and has empirical evidence of its usefulness [28]. It fit well with the incremental nature of Scrum, where their bi-weekly sprint planning would frequently allow the team to repay urgent TD items. The daily stand-up events would allow them to discuss any new-found TD items with the rest of the team within 24 h.

We presented the framework at our Meet & Greet with the team. Here, we also detailed how to fill out the framework's TD items and that these were then to be used for a Cost-Benefit analysis at their upcoming sprint planning sessions, as to prioritise what TD to pay off. The team was positively disposed towards the framework. It seemed simple for them to implement and matched well with their existing process. We also presented Rubin's [30] three visualisation approaches (cf. Sect. 2.1) and asked the team to choose the one they found best suited their process, which they decided would be the third approach.

When attending our first sprint planning session, we began by contextualising the meeting with what is considered good deliberation, such as mutual respect and adequate opportunities to speak (cf. Sect. 2.2). To aid the team in prioritising their debt, we proposed evaluating all identified items against the elements of TD decisions [10], while also taking Seaman and Guo's [33] framework's Cost-Benefit prioritisation into account. Next, the team presented and evaluated all of their identified TD items, filled into Seaman and Guo's [33] template. As a testament to their positive disposition, the team had been very thorough in the identification work, both documenting issues as they arose day-to-day and reviewing older components. The team identified more than 20 TD items; one such item can be seen in Table 3. Based on the ensuing discussions, each item was evaluated and prioritised, with some being incorporated into the following sprint. The team's determining factors in these evaluations included the feasibility of resolving the TD item, the benefit to be gained from resolving it, and if there was adequate time left over in the sprint to resolve it.

Table 3. Example of SoftShelf TD item

ID	G3
Date	2021-04-16
Responsible	`<developer>`
Type	Design/Documentation
Location	build.gradle, build-core.gradle, build-deploy.gradle
Description	The gradle tasks build all aspects of the project, including the parts which are not in use. [...]
Estimated Principal	1 week
Estimated Interest Amount	1–2 days per new developer
Estimated Interest Probability	Medium

Following the execution of the second sprint, for the sprint retrospective session, the Lead Developer put forth that "*getting technical debt prioritised alongside regular tasks*" had helped, but there were no other direct mentions of TD. However, there was another point that we found interesting. A developer wrote up "*previous sprint planning circus / long discussions during meetings*" as an anchor holding them back. For this point, he elaborated that their discussions, in general, would become excessively long-winded, as some members of the team would dwell on discussing specific topics, which were not of immediate priority to the rest of the team. We were excited to see this point brought up, as it displays them trying to be deliberate in their communication.

For the final sprint planning session in our study, the team appreciated that the list of new TD items was much shorter, as prioritising them became more manageable. For the upcoming sprint, the team agreed to prioritise items with a high *Estimated Interest Probability* and a low *Estimated Principal* as resolving these items would yield the highest reward with the lowest effort. At our final sprint retrospective session, there were only fleeting off-hand mentions of TD, similar to the daily stand-up meetings we attended throughout the intervention.

To conclude and evaluate this second intervention, we conducted follow-up interviews, both individually and as a group, to assess the effect using the TD framework had on the team's TD deliberations. From these we found that everyone agreed that it had indeed had a positive effect, with a developer stating:

> "*It has been really really good – we're lifting [TD] from being a secondary task to being on equal footing with other tasks. It gives us an opportunity to communicate about [TD]. [The TD] is not magically solved for that reason, but it gives us a common language.*"
>
> (Developer)

Another developer elaborated further on these positive effects, stating:

> *"It has taken this big 'black box' of unorganised annoyance and broken it down into simple and manageable little pieces, where we can actually do something about some of it."*
>
> (Developer)

The remainder of the team agreed with this notion, saying that the framework had actually empowered them to be able to handle and manage their TD. While, they found the framework to be rudimentary, the team agreed that using the framework had helped them resolve some identified TD. Although the developers did not see any effect on SoftShelf's organisational TD deliberations, the Scrum Master and the Lead Developer stated it has helped them communicate the team's struggles upwards in SoftShelf's hierarchy. The Lead Developer also stated that the SoftShelf's restructuring task-force would be bringing the framework and other results from the intervention with them to future talks with upper management. This statement was also echoed by the UX and QA Manager, the team's quality controller, and the Product Owner, who were both also part of the restructuring task-force. The three also stated that they would definitely be incorporating TD awareness into their process restructuring, as they had witnessed its usefulness first-hand through the pilot project.

5 Discussion

Understanding and managing Technical Debt (TD) has been a research interest for the past three decades [7], with multiple studies explaining the TD metaphor [12,17,18,36] and discussing the use of different TD management strategies [1,4,38]. However, few studies have been conducted using the Action Research (AR) approach [28,39], and none have to our knowledge taken the approach of incorporating deliberation theory. On this basis, we expound that the notion of communication within TD management can be extended using deliberation theory [6,23,24]. Against this backdrop, this paper investigated: *How can we initiate TD deliberations at a software development company?*

To do this, we collaborated with SoftShelf on initiating their TD management, as it was something they struggled with daily but were not deliberate in managing. We first had to ensure that the four prerequisites of appropriateness, potentiality, competencies and motivation for deliberations were present [6]. All SoftShelf's participants were highly educated and all already had the common ground of wanting the best for their company. Therefore, we only had to create the motivation for, and perceived appropriateness of, deliberation. We did this by building their TD information base, both about their present problem situation and relevant TD literature through two AR interventions.

An important contribution of our AR study is a nuancing of Fowler's [12] TD Quadrant, using the theory of deliberation to evaluate whether an intentional debt is reckless or prudent. The theory of deliberation (cf. Sect. 2.2) offers standards of what is considered good deliberation. TD incurred through poor deliberation, as was the case at SoftShelf, is decidedly reckless, while debt incurred based on good deliberation is distinctly prudent. Improving one's deliberation standards is a TD management strategy that depends on practical tools for weighing and reflecting about TD, for which Seaman and Guo's [33] Cost-Benefit framework of identified TD items was found to be useful at SoftShelf. Parts of such a framework have been implemented in prior research [28], but we propose to use it as part of the deliberation strategy. By facilitating good deliberation with this framework, it is ensured that the debt is properly reflected upon before any action is taken. Specifically, the TD items were useful in SoftShelf by first demanding a proper information base about TD and next for serving as a common ground for deliberation about the specific item itself. Our study also corroborates the prior research on implementing the Cost-Benefit framework in Scrum projects [28], in that Scrum suits the deliberation-focused TD management strategy well, since both emphasise open communication and the absence of a structural hierarchy [23,32].

The benefits of reducing debt are largely invisible, sometimes intangible, and usually long term, while the costs of actually handling the debt are significant and immediate [10]. The Cost-Benefit analysis [30,33] with its estimates of interest, interest probability, and refactoring costs improved the stakeholder's understanding of TD and their communication about it between levels of the company hierarchy. SoftShelf's management were interested in costs, and the developers were now able to provide actual costs related to TD. Therefore, initiating deliberation on a project level also sparked further communication about TD on an organisational level. As such, by giving SoftShelf a common vocabulary, we have enabled the project team to communicate their TD with stakeholders at higher levels of the department.

A limitation of our study concerns our methodology, AR, which has been criticised for being little more than consultancy [3]. We were attentive to biases and did not consider the AR interventions and their presence as contamination but as an inevitable part of the social construction of scientific knowledge [2,14]. Our AR approach's dual imperative of a problem solving interest cycle and a research interest cycle [26] ensured simultaneous contributions to SoftShelf's problem solving and the research on TD management. While our study revolves around a specific company with a specific problem, SoftShelf's TD issues are not unique. We see our practice of first using a theoretical foundation to identify specific issues in a company, and then using deliberations as a TD management strategy, as transferable to other contexts. In this study, the simple tactics used to create deliberations clearly helped SoftShelf's TD management. This simplicity makes it achievable to recreate in other organisations and projects. However, further research is needed to investigate this transferability on a larger scale.

References

1. Allman, E.: Managing technical debt. Commun. ACM **55**(5), 50–55 (2012)
2. Ananjeva, A., Persson, J.S., Bruun, A.: Integrating UX work with agile development through user stories: an action research study in a small software company. J. Syst. Softw. **170**, 110785 (2020)

3. Avison, D.E., Davison, R.M., Malaurent, J.: Information systems action research: debunking myths and overcoming barriers. Inf. Manag. **55**(2), 177–187 (2018)
4. Behutiye, W.N., Rodríguez, P., Oivo, M., Tosun, A.: Analyzing the concept of technical debt in the context of agile software development: a systematic literature review. Inf. Softw. Technol. **82**, 139–158 (2017)
5. Brinkmann, S.: Doing without data. Qual. Inq. **20**(6), 720–725 (2014)
6. Burkhalter, S., Gastil, J., Kelshaw, T.: A conceptual definition and theoretical model of public deliberation in small face–to–face groups. Commun. Theory **12**(4), 398–422 (2002)
7. Cunningham, W.: The WyCash portfolio management system. ACM SIGPLAN OOPS Messenger **4**(2), 29–30 (1992)
8. De Lucia, A., Fasolino, A.R., Pompelle, E.: A decisional framework for legacy system management. In: International Conference on Software Maintenance (2001)
9. Ernst, N.A., Bellomo, S., Ozkaya, I., Nord, R.L., Gorton, I.: Measure it? Manage it? Ignore it? software practitioners and technical debt. In: 10th Joint Meeting on Foundations of Software Engineering, pp. 50–60 (2015)
10. Fernández-Sánchez, C., Garbajosa, J., Yagüe, A., Perez, J.: Identification and analysis of the elements required to manage technical debt by means of a systematic mapping study. J. Syst. Softw. **124**, 22–38 (2017)
11. Fokaefs, M., Tsantalis, N., Chatzigeorgiou, A.: JDeodorant: identification and removal of feature envy bad smells. In: International Conference on Software Maintenance, pp. 519–520. IEEE (2007)
12. Fowler, M.: Technical debt quadrant, October 2009. https://martinfowler.com/bliki/TechnicalDebtQuadrant.html. Accessed 09 Nov 2020
13. Guo, Y., Seaman, C., da Silva, F.Q.: Costs and obstacles encountered in technical debt management-a case study. J. Syst. Softw. **120**, 156–169 (2016)
14. Hayes, G.R.: The relationship of action research to human-computer interaction. ACM Trans. Comput.-Human Interact. **18**(3), 1–20 (2011)
15. Klimczyk, P., Madeyski, L.: Technical debt aware estimations in software engineering: a systematic mapping study. e-Informatica Softw. Eng. J. **14**(1), 61–76 (2020)
16. Klinger, T., Tarr, P., Wagstrom, P., Williams, C.: An enterprise perspective on technical debt. In: 2nd Workshop on Managing Technical Debt, pp. 35–38 (2011)
17. Kruchten, P.: Refining the definition of technical debt, April 2016. https://philippe.kruchten.com/2016/04/22/refining-the-definition-of-technical-debt/
18. Kruchten, P., Nord, R.L., Ozkaya, I.: Technical debt: from metaphor to theory and practice. IEEE Softw. **29**(6), 18–21 (2012)
19. Lenarduzzi, V., Besker, T., Taibi, D., Martini, A., Fontana, F.A.: A systematic literature review on technical debt prioritization: strategies, processes, factors, and tools. J. Syst. Softw. **171**, 110827 (2021)
20. Letouzey, J.L.: The SQALE method for evaluating technical debt. In: 3rd International Workshop on Managing Technical Debt, pp. 31–36. IEEE (2012)
21. Li, Z., Avgeriou, P., Liang, P.: A systematic mapping study on technical debt and its management. J. Syst. Softw. **101**, 193–220 (2015)
22. Lim, E., Taksande, N., Seaman, C.: A balancing act: what software practitioners have to say about technical debt. IEEE Softw. **29**(6), 22–27 (2012)
23. Mansbridge, J.: A minimalist definition of deliberation. In: Heller, P., Rao, V. (eds.) Deliberation and Development - Rethinking the Role of Voice and Collective Action in Unequal Societies, chap. 2, pp. 27–50. World Bank Publications (2015)
24. Mansbridge, J., Hartz-Karp, J., Amengual, M., Gastil, J.: Norms of deliberation: an inductive study. J. Public Deliberation **2**(1) (2006)

25. McConnell, S.: Managing technical debt. Best practices white paper, Construx Software, June 2008. https://www.construx.com/resources/whitepaper-managing-technical-debt/
26. McKay, J., Marshall, P.: The dual imperatives of action research. Inf. Technol. People **14**(1), 46–59 (2001)
27. Nielsen, P.A., Persson, J.S.: Engaged problem formulation in is research. Commun. AIS **38**, 720–737 (2016)
28. Oliveira, F., Goldman, A., Santos, V.: Managing technical debt in software projects using scrum: an action research. In: Agile Conference (2015)
29. Patton, M.Q.: Qualitative Research & Evaluation Methods: Integrating Theory and Practice. Sage publications (2015). chap. 7 Qualitative Interviewing
30. Rubin, K.S.: Essential Scrum: A Practical Guide to the Most Popular Agile Process. Addison-Wesley, Boston (2012)
31. Saraiva, D., Neto, J.G., Kulesza, U., Freitas, G., Reboucas, R., Coelho, R.: Technical debt tools: a systematic mapping study. In: Proceedings of the 23rd International Conference on Enterprise Information Systems, pp. 88–98 (2021)
32. Schwaber, K., Sutherland, J.: The scrum guide. Scrum Alliance **21**, 1 (2011)
33. Seaman, C., Guo, Y.: Measuring and monitoring technical debt. In: Advances in Computers, vol. 82, pp. 25–46. Elsevier (2011)
34. Seaman, C., et al.: Using technical debt data in decision making: potential decision approaches. In: 3rd International Workshop on Managing Technical Debt (2012)
35. Spínola, R.O., Zazworka, N., Vetro, A., Shull, F., Seaman, C.: Understanding automated and human-based technical debt identification approaches-a two-phase study. J. Braz. Comput. Soc. **25**(1), 1–21 (2019). https://doi.org/10.1186/s13173-019-0087-5
36. Tom, E., Aurum, A., Vidgen, R.: An exploration of technical debt. J. Syst. Softw. **86**(6), 1498–1516 (2013)
37. Wohlin, C., Runeson, P.: Guiding the selection of research methodology in industry-academia collaboration in software engineering. Inf. Softw. Technol. **140**, 106678 (2021)
38. Yli-Huumo, J., Maglyas, A., Smolander, K.: How do software development teams manage technical debt?-An empirical study. J. Syst. Softw. **120**, 195–218 (2016)
39. Yli-Huumo, J., Maglyas, A., Smolander, K., Haller, J., Törnroos, H.: Developing processes to increase technical debt visibility and manageability – an action research study in industry. In: Abrahamsson, P., Jedlitschka, A., Nguyen Duc, A., Felderer, M., Amasaki, S., Mikkonen, T. (eds.) PROFES 2016. LNCS, vol. 10027, pp. 368–378. Springer, Cham (2016). https://doi.org/10.1007/978-3-319-49094-6_24

Blockchain Governance: A Dynamic View

Gabriella Laatikainen(✉), Mengcheng Li, and Pekka Abrahamsson

Faculty of Information Technology, University of Jyväskylä, Jyväskylä, Finland
{gabriella.laatikainen,mengcheng.m.li,pekka.abrahamsson}@jyu.fi

Abstract. The governance of blockchain systems is unique due to its decentralized nature and automatically enforced rules and mechanisms. Moreover, blockchain governance is crucial in achieving success and sustainability. With this study, we aim to advance the theory of blockchain governance and support practitioners by defining blockchain governance from a holistic viewpoint and identifying its building blocks. As a result of a systematic literature review of 75 recent articles focusing on blockchain governance, we propose a dynamic model that deepens the researchers' and practitioners' understanding of blockchain governance. The conceptual model can serve as a reference framework and structured foundation for analyzing, discussing, and developing the governance of blockchain systems.

Keywords: Blockchain governance · Dynamic view · Systematic literature review

1 Introduction

Blockchain and distributed ledger technologies may disrupt industries by providing means for decentralization, enabling automation, reengineering business processes, and improving the management of information systems [1–3]. Blockchain relies on cryptography consisting of an interconnected and unmodifiable list of digital records shared within a peer-to-peer network [4]. One of its advantages is its ability to enforce automatic rules without intermediaries [5]. Smart contracts (i.e., code representing a self-executing digital contract) and consensus mechanisms (i.e., fault-tolerant methods of authenticating and validating a value or transaction on a distributed ledger) enable agreement assurance within the nodes of a network. These technological advances infer a deeper investigation of blockchain governance [1].

Indeed, a key factor in developing sustainable blockchain systems is related to their governance. Governance refers to the regulation of decision-making processes among actors towards shared objectives that lead to the development, reinforcement, or reproduction of social norms and institutions [6, 7]. The governance of blockchain systems differs from existing governance structures, such as markets, hierarchies, platforms, or organizations [8, 9]. First, due to its decentralized nature, blockchain governance needs to balance integrity and autonomy without a central authority [1]. Second, blockchain enables embedding governance mechanisms into blockchain transactions,

X. Wang et al. (Eds.): ICSOB 2021, LNBIP 434, pp. 66–80, 2021.
https://doi.org/10.1007/978-3-030-91983-2_6

and this automating self-governing characteristic of the technology opens new opportunities and challenges that need further investigation [10]. Thus, while effective governance is crucial in developing and operating blockchain systems, its differences to already investigated governance structures claim further research [11].

Blockchain governance has been studied through the lens of several theories including IT governance theory (e.g., [1, 9, 11]), platform governance (e.g., [12–14]), the organizational and corporate governance literature (e.g., [15–17]), agency theory (e.g., [9]), internet governance (e.g., [17]), and open-source software governance (e.g., [11]). While there is no consensus on one specific definition of blockchain governance, several terms share a common understanding among researchers. First, blockchain governance can be understood as both governance of the infrastructure (i.e., means and processes of directing, controlling, and coordinating actors within a blockchain system) and governance by the infrastructure (i.e., using blockchain to govern actions and behavior) [18]. Second, there is a distinction between on-chain governance (i.e., direct encoding of rules and decision-making processes into the blockchain infrastructure) and off-chain governance (i.e., non-technical rules and decision-making processes affecting the development and operation of blockchain systems) [19]. Third, technology governance refers to governing the technical development of the blockchain system, while network governance implies governance of the associated blockchain networks [20]. Fourth, studies drawing on organizational and corporate governance literature distinguish between external and internal governance [15, 16]. External governance refers to decisions made outside the blockchain system (e.g., the media, general public) but impacting managerial decision-making within the system [15]. Internal governance, in contrast, describes governance practices inside the system [15]. While distinguishing between these aspects is necessary and useful, there is also a need for a general definition that provides a shared common language for researchers and practitioners to understand and communicate this concept similarly and avoid confusion.

Current literature has identified different components of blockchain governance. For example, studies building on IT governance theory identify the dimensions of decision rights, accountability, and incentives [9]. Researchers inspired by organizational and corporate governance literature describe decision-making related to (i) owner control on the blockchain level, (ii) formal voting on the protocol level, and (iii) centralized funding at the organizational level [16]. Further, governance has been found to be concerned with decisions related to (i) demand management, (ii) data authenticity, (iii) system architecture development, (iv) membership, (v) ownership disputes, and (vi) transaction reversal [8]. Moreover, studies based on the theory of platform governance identify the following three key components of blockchain governance: (i) access, (ii) control, and (iii) incentives (e.g., [12]).

Besides these essential works that focus on some aspects of blockchain governance, there is a need to define blockchain governance from a holistic viewpoint and identify its key components. There are several reasons for this. First, blockchain governance models based on a single theory focus on particular aspects while neglecting many others. For instance, on-chain governance rules are more efficient and predictable than the off-chain counterpart. At the same time, on-chain governance is less adjustable to the unknown or changing environment [44]. On the contrary, off-chain governance is ambiguous, but it can respond to unusual cases more humanly and flexibly to the changing circumstances [44]. Therefore, it is crucial to have an integrative view of blockchain governance to balance the pros and cons of a single model. Second, analyzing blockchain systems from a holistic viewpoint and identifying the decision-making needs is essential, especially in distributed settings. In these decentralized systems, there are contradictory forces of autonomous actors with different incentives and goals, while there is a need for collaboration to achieve the shared objectives. Thus, governance decisions cannot be made to one aspect of the system without considering its possible consequences to other parts. Third, in some of the distributed systems (e.g., self-sovereign identity ecosystems), the governance framework (i.e., consisting of business, legal, and technical rules and policies of a system) is an essential building block beside the technological architecture [21, 22]. The development and management of a governance framework require similar development work as building the technical architecture. Thus, it requires a holistic understanding of different, interrelated parts of blockchain governance [21, 22]. Therefore, it is essential to identify the building blocks of blockchain governance and their interrelations, and propose a systematic way to determine the decision needs and understand, analyze, and communicate blockchain governance decisions throughout the whole lifecycle of a blockchain system.

Despite the growing body of literature, existing research falls short in providing a holistic understanding of the components of blockchain governance and their possible interrelations. The only work providing an integrative blockchain governance framework has been developed and proposed by van Pelt et al. [11]. The authors build on the definition of open-source software (OSS) governance and define blockchain governance as "The means of achieving the direction, control and coordination of stakeholders within the context of a given blockchain project to which they jointly contribute" [11, p. 7]. In this work, blockchain governance is a combination of six dimensions (formation and context, roles, incentives, membership, communication, and decision making) and three layers (off-chain community, off-chain development, and off-chain protocol). While this work provides an excellent framework for studying blockchain governance, it does not emphasize the dynamic, evolving nature of blockchain systems, it does not incorporate the legal and regulatory aspects, and also, the business aspects get less attention. However, governance decisions cannot ignore the legal and business context that both sets the constraints and provides opportunities for alternative governance structures. Furthermore, governance decisions need to consider the lifecycle stage of the blockchain system. For example, governance is typically more centralized in the formation phase, with more ad-hoc decisions made via traditional, social decision-making means. Still, it is continuously evolving towards decentralized governance structures and more routinized and automatized decisions in the operating phase.

Thus, while understanding blockchain governance from a holistic viewpoint is essential, there is a clear research gap in the literature in providing an integrative framework and a definition of blockchain governance that integrates insights from various theories. In our study, we aim to answer the research question "what is blockchain governance, and what are its building blocks?" by carrying out a systematic literature review and integrating the existing viewpoints to define blockchain governance holistically and identify its components.

The paper has several contributions to both theory and practice by proposing a dynamic model of blockchain governance that offers a holistic viewpoint and a more comprehensive understanding of blockchain systems and their governance. Researchers and practitioners (e.g., users, organizations, regulators) can use the proposed model as a reference framework in further studies and as a tool to systematically design, analyze and communicate the different aspects of the governance of blockchain systems throughout the various lifecycle stages.

2 Research Methodology

A systematic literature review is an appropriate approach to synthesizing the existing studies to facilitate theory development and support policymakers and entrepreneurs for better decisions [23]. This methodology has high reproducibility and objectivity due to its transparency in data collection and synthesis [23]. Following the five-stage grounded theory method of Wolfswinkel et al. [24] for conducting a systematic literature review, we applied a review by defining, searching, selecting, analyzing, and presenting, which we will describe in the following subsections.

2.1 Defining

A well-written and detailed protocol document is essential for ensuring consistency throughout the whole review process by defining the criteria for inclusion, the fields of research, the appropriate sources, and specific search terms. For our study, all articles focusing on or partially mentioning blockchain governance can provide valuable insights into blockchain governance's definition and components. Therefore, we defined the inclusion criteria as follows: articles focused on studying blockchain governance or presenting the occurrences of blockchain governance. Since research on blockchain governance has just emerged in recent years, any relevant article might provide interesting views for our research in different fields. Therefore, we did not limit the fields of research, which may result in a multidisciplinary or holistic perspective for the studies on blockchain governance.

In this study, we used three multidisciplinary, electronic databases for keyword searching: the Web of Science, Proquest, and ScienceDirect. Those databases were considered appropriate sources since they cover a wide range of literature and are frequently used by previous scholars (e.g., [25, 26]).

Blockchain governance can be mentioned and discussed using different terms. Thus, we decided on the following string for searching in the three databases:

(blockchain OR ((distributed OR decentralized)
AND (ledger OR platform OR "autonomous organization")))
AND (governance OR management OR ecosystem)

2.2 Searching and Selecting

In Fig. 1, the searching and selecting stages are presented. In the Searching phase, we applied the defined search terms on the three online databases. We got the following results: 142 articles from the Web of Science, 323 articles from Proquest, and 473 articles from ScienceDirect.

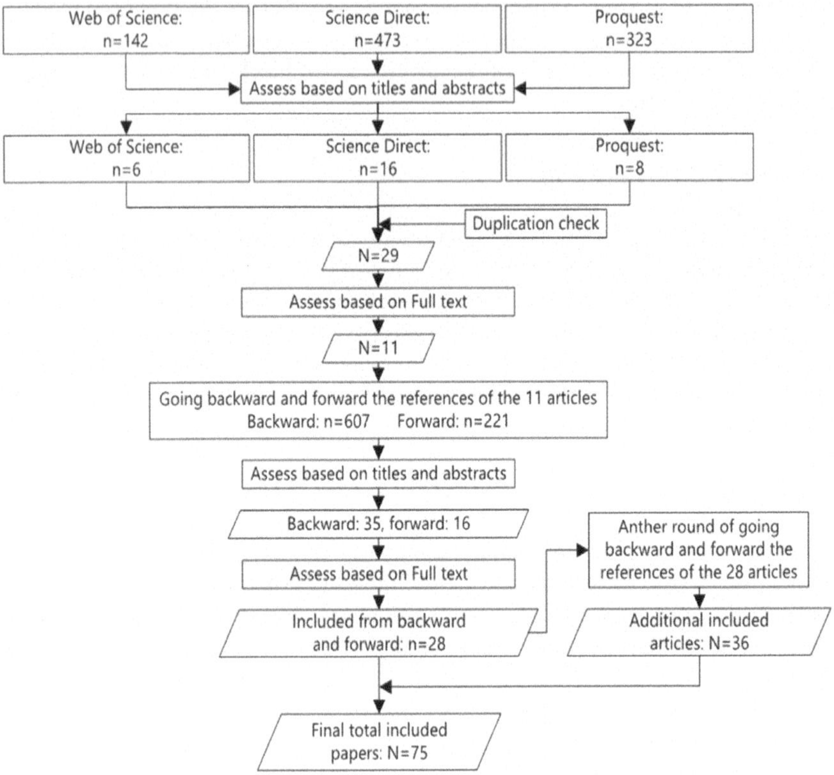

Fig. 1. Searching and selecting stages of the systematic literature review process

In the selecting phase, we filtered the articles based on their titles and abstracts using the defined inclusion criteria. This phase resulted in six relevant articles from the Web of Science, eight relevant articles from Proquest, and 16 relevant articles from ScienceDirect. In this step, we eliminated duplicates and identified 29 primary articles based on title and abstract. Next, we filtered the articles based on their content against the same inclusion criteria and received 11 articles. Later, we went backward and forward in the references of the 11 articles to find additional relevant articles with the same inclusion criteria. We found 607 articles by going backward through the references, and 35 articles were relevant based on the titles and abstracts. Within forward references (i.e., from the papers citing the referred articles), 16 out of 221 articles were found relevant based on the titles and abstracts. Then, we went through the 51 articles and filtered them based on their content against the same inclusion criteria and got 26 articles. Next, we did another round of backward and forward reference searches at the 26 included articles and found an additional 36 relevant articles. Therefore, the total number of final included articles was 75. During this stage, we made descriptive notes about each included article to offer a general overview.

2.3 Analyzing

We performed the data analysis of the final articles in three phases, each phase in an iterative manner. We used ATLAS.ti qualitative data analysis software [27] for open coding and axial coding. First, we did open coding using the constant comparative method [28] to identify the main characteristics of blockchain governance and gather descriptive statistics of the articles (e.g., objective, theories, and the research method). In this phase, we also used the code in vivo and automatic coding functionality of the software. As a result, the coding was detailed, and in many cases, followed the wording of the original articles [29, 30]. Example codes of this phase include "exit strategy", "benevolent dictator", "platform developers", and "economic rewards".

In the axial coding phase, we reorganized these codes into larger, overlapping categories using the code group functionality of the Atlas.ti software. These categories represented the different aspects of blockchain governance, such as "business aspects" and "actors and roles". Then, we reduced the number of codes by renaming and merging the codes that referred to similar issues. This task resulted in a hierarchical code structure with a maximum of three levels (for example, "actor: developer", "incentive: nonpecuniary: networking" and "descriptive: method: design science"). This code structure represented the building blocks of blockchain governance and provided the base for our conceptual framework.

In the theoretical coding phase, our objective was to formulate a definition and a dynamic model of blockchain governance from a holistic perspective. To achieve this, we integrated the theoretical insights from the articles and the building blocks of blockchain governance resulting from the axial coding phase. Both the definition and the model have been informed by the various definitions and components of blockchain governance and related concepts, such as, for example, governance, open-source software governance, platform governance, corporate governance, internal governance, endogenous governance, collaborative governance, distributed governance, and IT governance.

All phases of the data analysis have been carried out as an ongoing, iterative, co-creative process. First, the authors discussed the code structure several times and modified it according to the agreements. The code structure was considered final when all the codes belonged to a category, and there were no more questions from any of the authors. Second, several blockchain practitioners discussed the conceptual model during several meetings. After the first meeting, the model was refined based on the feedback. Later on, the attendees found the model easy to understand, and they used it as a tool to discuss issues related to the governance of their blockchain system. As a final step, we reviewed the quotations behind the codes and summarized the findings in this article.

3 Findings

3.1 Descriptive Statistics

In Fig. 2, the number of different article types are presented each year. As visible from the figure, blockchain governance has gained increasing attention since 2018. More than half of the total included articles were published between 2018–2020. The included articles are journal articles (36%), conference articles (23%), and others (such as book chapters, theses, and university publications; 41%).

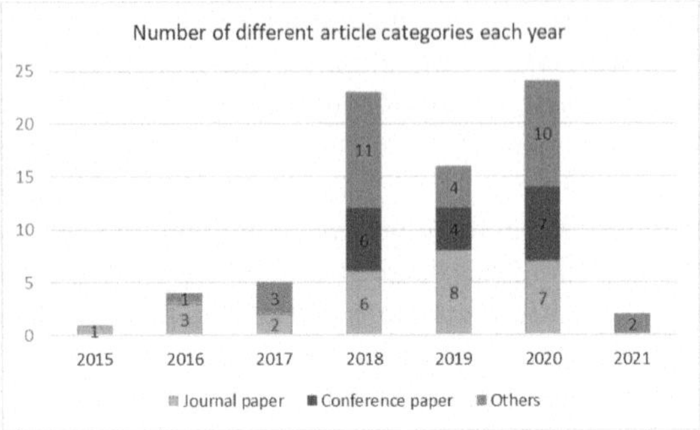

Fig. 2. Number of different article categories each year

Various research methods have been applied in the included papers. Case study was the most frequently used approach, accounting for more than 50% of the included papers. Most of these case studies offered discussions related to Bitcoin and/or Ethereum, while some other studies analyzed EOS.IO [11], the Swarm City [9], Cardossier [8, 43], and Tezos [17]. In addition to case studies, other research methods included design science research approach [11, 31] and action research [20].

3.2 A Dynamic Model of Blockchain Governance

The diversity of theoretical lenses and viewpoints and the various dimensions of blockchain governance mentioned in the included articles lead us to investigate blockchain governance from a holistic perspective. Thus, as a result of our systematic literature review, we define blockchain governance as follows:

Blockchain governance encompasses technical and social means to make decisions on the different levels (e.g., individual, community, organizational, national, international) related to actors, roles, rights, incentives, responsibilities, rules, and the business, technological, legal, and regulatory aspects of a blockchain system during its whole lifecycle.

Furthermore, we propose a dynamic model of blockchain governance that can be seen in Fig. 3. In line with the definition, the model captures the dynamic nature of blockchain governance where technology-based and social means impact the various facets of blockchain governance. In the following subsections, we describe the different aspects of the model of blockchain governance.

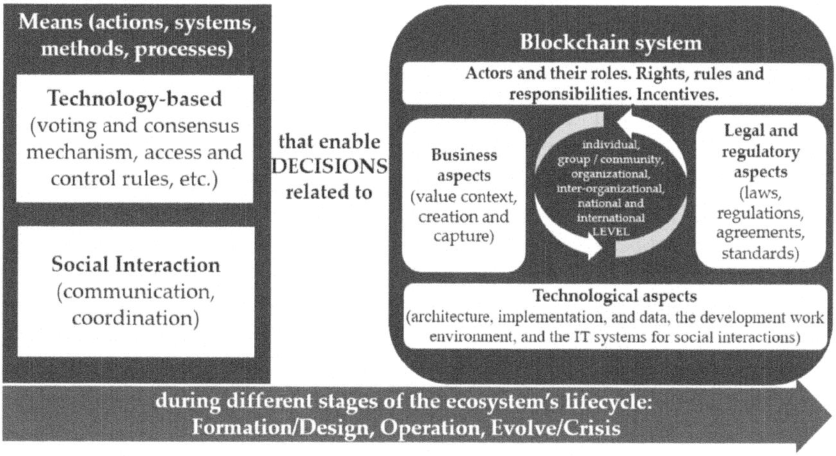

Fig. 3. A dynamic model of blockchain governance

Technical and Social Means for Governance

This building block of our model encompasses both governance *of* and governance *by* the infrastructure. Governance means refer to actions, systems, methods, and processes designed for decision making. Blockchain technology allows *on-chain governance* (referred to also as automated self-governance); that is, automatizing governance decisions by technical means, in the form of voting mechanisms, smart contracts, DApp frameworks, and blockchain network protocols (e.g., [10, 44]). Embedding governance into technology refers to managing and maintaining systems of legal agreements, voting and property rights, and validating, maintaining, and enforcing social and functional properties or contracts in the system [32]. Technical means enable the standardization of interactions, embedding quality standards into the technical architecture, and providing incentives [12]. Automatizing governance decisions entails embedding social trust and determining the bargaining power of the actors [17, 18].

However, the technology cannot solely be held accountable for governance decisions. Besides these technical means, there is a need for *off-chain governance* enabled by traditional, social means for governance, such as communication, collaboration, and coordination among actors [11]. Social interactions among the actors are needed in different forms and channels [9, 11, 12, 18, 45]. Social governance means refers to formal and informal communication and collaboration among the actors, such as discussions via coordination systems, tracking systems, meetings, and working groups [11].

A key challenge in blockchain governance is to find the right balance between the technical and social means of governance (i.e., what, how, and when to automatize). A decision on embedding governance into technology should also be made based on other aspects of the system (for example, the lifecycle stage [8]). In blockchain systems, on-chain technical governance interacts with traditional governance mechanisms in both substitutionary and complementary ways [33].

Blockchain System

Actors and Their Roles

Governing a system requires identifying the actors (i.e., stakeholders, agents) that are influenced by, or can affect the system [17]. Blockchain systems have a boundary problem: defining the actors of the system is challenging [17]. Some actors are not even aware that they contribute to governance decisions [11]. Furthermore, some actors are affected by the decisions, but they do not interact [17]. Moreover, a group of actors with the same role may not be homogenous in their incentives and actions (e.g., token holders [17]). Another problem comes from the different preferences of different actors towards the chosen governance models [34].

Actors can be individually governed as a community or according to other affiliations (cf. the subsection Governance levels). Actors can be categorized into *passive* (i.e., users of blockchain, for example, to transfer money) or *active* users (i.e., users who contribute and support the operations of the network) [18]. Actors might be *public* or *private* [43]. Finally, they can be considered *internal* (i.e., users) or *external* (i.e., regulators or standard-setting bodies) [8].

Based on our review, actors can be grouped based on their roles in the infrastructure development processes or their roles in the ecosystem. Roles can be defined as a characteristic set of behaviors or activities undertaken by the actors [11]. Roles related to *infrastructure development* are nodes, miners or validators, users, developers, architects, and so forth (e.g., [11, 18, 42]). Roles related to a *system* can be owners, founders, leaders, providers, investors, contractors, complementors, standard-setting bodies, regulators, observers, operators, suppliers, and so on (e.g., [1, 12, 34, 46]). In some cases, there is a hierarchy between the roles, and specifying this hierarchy plays an important role in governance decisions [11].

Rights, Rules, and Responsibilities

One of the key factors for successful governance is the rights and responsibilities of the roles/actors and the rules in the system [10]. Rights and rules have been mentioned in various forms in the literature. First, access rights and rules have been referred to as rights/rules for entry, membership, input control, and participation (e.g., [8, 11, 15]). Second, decision rights and rules "concern the rights governing control over certain assets" [9] (p. 1022). Third, rights and rules should be developed related to development, software updates, data policies, and hard forks [15, 34, 35]. Fourth, rules and rights are needed for voting, validation/verification, overrides, and ownership (intellectual property) [8, 16, 17, 32, 34]. Rights and rules could be endogenous (i.e., developed by the community for the community, as a form of self-governance) or exogenous (i.e., rules established by external actors that have the power of influence) [44].

Governing a blockchain system implies designing the responsibilities and the accountabilities assigned to the roles [9, 11, 34, 45]. The importance of responsibility management has been emphasized in both the open-source software governance and the corporate governance literature [16, 36]. Accountability captures the level on which actors are and can be held accountable for their actions and behavior [11]. Accountability represents one of the key concepts in the theory of IT governance, platform governance, digital infrastructure governance, corporate and organizational governance [1, 7, 9, 10, 37].

Incentives
Incentives refer to actors' motivations for participation and actions [11]. Incentives play a key role in governance decisions because they encourage desirable behavior in the system [9]. Aligned incentives allow actors to choose their own behavior and actions that coincide with the shared objectives of the system [9]. Incentives can be pecuniary (monetary) or nonpecuniary (non-monetary) (e.g., [11]). Besides financial benefits, blockchain systems offer a wide range of value, such as privileges, reputation, and visibility [9, 42]. Some actors contribute to the system to gain experience, do research, carry out technical and market testing, simulate business processes, collaborate or build new strategic alliances [20].

Technological Aspects
Blockchain systems cannot be governed without decisions related to technology. In particular, these decisions are related to (i) the architecture, implementation, and data, (ii) the development work environment, and (iii) the IT systems for social interactions, knowledge, and memory management (e.g., [8, 9, 11, 34]). First, related to the architecture, implementation, and data, decisions are to be made related to the technical details of consensus mechanisms and voting mechanism, technical choices for the software stack, third-party software, technical requirements on connectivity and firewalls, the monitoring and maintenance of key performance parameters, the sharing of node-IPs, online or offline funding storage, transaction enforcement, validation and conflict resolution mechanisms, data authenticity, activity tracking, identity management and interoperability (e.g., [18, 20]). Second, decisions are needed related to software repository management, versioning, testing, and monitoring. Third, decisions related to coordination systems are important for enabling traditional governance using social interactions.

Business Aspects
In blockchain systems, the actors co-create value together, and a key question is how to ensure a fair share of value among them. A successful business model is beneficial for all actors [38], and it is essential for a sustainable blockchain system. In this view, a fit between value capture, value creation, and value context is key to achieve dynamic stability [39]. According to this view, we grouped the governance decisions related to the business aspects into three groups: decisions related to value context, value creation, and value capture.

The decisions related to *value context* encompass identifying the purpose and context, the business requirements, and the strategies and mission of the system (e.g., [8, 11, 45]). For this task, there is a need to understand where the value resides in the system, considering all other aspects, such as the actors, their roles, their (possible) incentives, the opportunities enabled by the technology and its limitations, and the legal and regulatory context.

The decisions related to *value creation* are primarily related to cost factors and funding sources (e.g., [12, 20, 42]). Furthermore, decisions are needed related to core activities and how to split the funding fairly among the actors to establish incentives and facilitate innovative outputs.

Value capture entails not only the provision and negotiation but also the realization of value [12]. The decisions related to *value capture* typically deal with revenue streams and pricing models (e.g., [11, 12]). In blockchain systems, different actors might have different revenue models that need to be considered in decision-making processes.

Legal and Regulatory Aspects
While there are considerable advances related to the legal and regulatory environment of blockchain systems in different countries, uncertainty still exists related to the legal and regulatory aspects of the technology and the ecosystems built around it [40]. Blockchain governance encompasses decisions related to laws, regulations and industry policies, standards, and agreements (e.g., [10, 35, 40]).

In an uncertain *legal and regulatory* environment, decisions are needed on the specific regulations to comply with or in regard to lobbying for changes in the existing regulations [40]. In particular industries (e.g., financial or data services), the choice of jurisdiction or accountability over multiple jurisdictions is crucial [10].

Viable blockchain solutions need to have a *standard* industry policy strategy or an alternative strategy when standards are not yet fully established. Choices could be, for example, (i) creating a proprietary blockchain protocol, (ii) working with existing standards groups to adopt standards for blockchains, or (iii) joining an industry blockchain consortium [40].

Besides the decisions related to laws, regulations, and standards, one of the key tasks in developing blockchain systems is to create *agreements* among the actors that set out the rules and policies of the system. Agreements can exist in different forms, such as legal documents, shared understanding, or code (e.g., [8, 32, 45]).

Lifecycle Stages
Blockchain governance evolves over time [8, 10, 34]. Blockchain systems are orchestrated in the formation/design phase (also called exploration/ bootstrapping), where the key question is "How should the system work?" In the operation phase, the key governance decisions have been made already, and the main question is "How should the system operate?" In some cases, the system can enter into the crisis phase, when the key question is "How should the system handle the conflicts?" Crisis situations can lead systems to death or to forming a new blockchain system via hard forks, or the system can go back to the operation phase via the self-renewal/soft fork.

While blockchain governance is typically considered decentralized, an evolution pattern can be observed that a central authority makes the first design decisions, and the system becomes more decentralized when maturing [34]. Furthermore, the level of automatizing governance also evolves over time: while ad-hoc decisions cannot be automatized, the planned decisions can be implemented later using technical means [8]. Thus, blockchain governance needs a dynamic, evolutionary viewpoint.

Governance Levels
Understanding the scope of the decisions (i.e., the targets that the decisions have an impact on) is crucial in governance because it helps to understand the possible consequences of the decisions. We argue that decisions can be related to individuals or a group/ community [11]. Furthermore, some decisions (such as business, legal or regulatory ones) are made at the organizational, inter-organizational, national, or international levels [40].

4 Conclusions

Governance decisions in decentralized systems cannot be made solely by focusing on the key components from one specific theory (e.g., decision rights, accountability, and incentives from IT governance theory). Instead, making governance decisions needs a comprehensive analysis of the system. In this work, we synthesize findings from a systematic literature review of 75 articles related to blockchain governance. By integrating insights from recent work, we define blockchain governance from a holistic perspective. That is, blockchain governance encompasses technical and social means to make decisions on the individual, community, organizational, inter-organizational, national, international levels related to actors, roles, rights, incentives, responsibilities, rules, and the business, technological, legal, and regulatory aspects of a blockchain system during its whole lifecycle. This definition is novel due to its comprehensive characteristic. It provides a systematic viewpoint on the governance decisions that need to be made during designing, operating, and managing blockchain systems during crises.

Blockchain governance is multifaceted and complex [34], and decisions related to one aspect of the system affect other parts. In our model, we incorporated on-chain and off-chain governance, governance *of* the infrastructure, and governance *by* the infrastructure in one model, facilitating the investigation of how the technical and social governance means substitute for and complement each other [33]. This model emphasizes the dynamic, evolving nature of blockchain governance [34]: decisions should consider the lifecycle stage of the system. For example, governance might be more centralized in the formation phase but evolving towards decentralized governance structures. Furthermore, the complexity and ad-hoc nature of governance decisions also differ in different lifecycle stages. Our model also emphasizes the context-dependent nature of blockchain governance: for example, decisions should consider the legal and regulatory context and the value context of the system. While all components of blockchain governance have been mentioned in recent literature, our model is the first one that incorporates all.

This research has several theoretical and empirical contributions. First, the work contributes to IS research by providing a unique, holistic view of blockchain governance and its multifaceted, complex, and dynamic nature. In particular, the holistic definition of blockchain governance advances theory by integrating the different theoretical viewpoints and can serve as a reference definition for further studies. Furthermore, researchers can use the model as a reference framework in future work, such as empirical, comparative case studies. This integrative framework is significant since it balances the benefits and drawbacks of a single blockchain governance model and intends to cover all relevant components. Second, for practitioners, such as the actors of blockchain systems, the definition, and the model provide a structured foundation and a shared language to understand, analyze and communicate blockchain governance decisions. In particular, similarly to Business Model Canvas [41] that has been commonly used in business model development, this model can serve as a tool for identifying the gaps and questions, and provides a systematic way of documenting governance decisions throughout the whole lifecycle of the system, such as formation/design, operations, and crisis.

The study has limitations that we aim to address in our future work. First, we will describe our conceptual model more extensively and include some more insights from the articles on which our conceptual model is based. Second, we will describe future research avenues that we identified using our conceptual model. However, we believe that the comprehensiveness of our proposed model advances theory and practice also in this short form.

Acknowledgment. This research has been conducted in the Security And Software Engineering Research Center (S^2 ERC, 2020–21) in the COOL-Appia and StrokeData projects funded by Business Finland.

References

1. Zachariadis, M., Hileman, G., Scott, S.: Governance and control in distributed ledgers: understanding the challenges facing blockchain technology in financial services. Inf. Organ. **29**(2), 105–117 (2019). https://doi.org/10.1016/j.infoandorg.2019.03.001
2. Chang, V., Baudier, P., Zhang, H., Qianwen, X., Zhang, J., Arami, M.: How blockchain can impact financial services – the overview, challenges and recommendations from expert interviewees. Technol. Forecast. Soc. Change **158**, 120166 (2020). https://doi.org/10.1016/j.techfore.2020.120166
3. Panin, A., Kemell, K.-K., Hara, V.: Initial coin offering (ICO) as a fundraising strategy: a multiple case study on success factors. In: Hyrynsalmi, S., Suoranta, M., Nguyen-Duc, A., Tyrväinen, P., Abrahamsson, P. (eds.) ICSOB 2019. LNBIP, vol. 370, pp. 237–251. Springer, Cham (2019). https://doi.org/10.1007/978-3-030-33742-1_19
4. Trump, B., Marie-Valentine Florin, H., Matthews, S., Sicker, D., Linkov, I.: Governing the use of blockchain and distributed ledger technologies: not one-size-fits-all. IEEE Eng. Manag. Rev. **46**(3), 56–62 (2018). https://doi.org/10.1109/EMR.2018.2868305
5. Wang, Y., Singgih, M., Wang, J., Rit, M.: Making sense of blockchain technology: how will it transform supply chains? Int. J. Prod. Econ. **211**, 221–236 (2019). https://doi.org/10.1016/j.ijpe.2019.02.002
6. Kolehmainen, T., Laatikainen, G., Kultanen, J., Kazan, E., Abrahamsson, P.: Using blockchain in digitalizing enterprise legacy systems: an experience report. In: Klotins, Eriks, Wnuk, Krzysztof (eds.) ICSOB 2020. LNBIP, vol. 407, pp. 70–85. Springer, Cham (2021). https://doi.org/10.1007/978-3-030-67292-8_6
7. Shermin, V.: Disrupting governance with blockchains and smart contracts. In: Strategic Change, pp. 499–509. Wiley, Hoboken (2017)
8. Ziolkowski, R., Parangi, G., Miscione, G., Schwabe, G.: Examining gentle rivalry: decision-making in blockchain systems. In: Hawaii International Conference on System Sciences (2019). https://doi.org/10.24251/HICSS.2019.550

9. Beck, R., Müller-Bloch, C., King, J.: Governance in the blockchain economy: a framework and research agenda. J. Assoc. Inf. Syst. **19**, 1020–1034 (2018). https://doi.org/10.17705/1jais.00518
10. Rikken, O., Janssen, M., Kwee, Z.: Governance challenges of blockchain and decentralized autonomous organizations. Inf. Polity **24**, 397–417 (2019). https://doi.org/10.3233/IP-190154
11. van Pelt, R., Jansen, S., Baars, D., Overbeek, S.: Defining blockchain governance: a framework for analysis and comparison. Inf. Syst. Manag. **38**(1), 21–41 (2020). https://doi.org/10.1080/10580530.2020.1720046
12. Schmeiss, J., Hoelzle, K., Tech, R.P.G.: Designing governance mechanisms in platform ecosystems: addressing the paradox of openness through blockchain technology. California Manag. Rev. **62**(1), 121–143 (2019). https://doi.org/10.1177/0008125619883618
13. Mattila, J., Seppälä, T.: Distributed governance in multi-sided platforms: a conceptual framework from case: bitcoin. In: Smedlund, Anssi, Lindblom, Arto, Mitronen, Lasse (eds.) Collaborative Value Co-creation in the Platform Economy. TSS, vol. 11, pp. 183–205. Springer, Singapore (2018). https://doi.org/10.1007/978-981-10-8956-5_10
14. Chen, Y., Pereira, I., Patel, P.C.: Decentralized governance of digital platforms. J. Manag. 0149206320916755 (2020). https://doi.org/10.1177/0149206320916755
15. Hacker, P.: Corporate governance for complex cryptocurrencies? A framework for stability and decision making in blockchain-based organizations. In: Regulating Blockchain. Techno-Social and Legal Challenges, pp. 140–166. Oxford University Press, Oxford (2019)
16. Hsieh, Y.Y., Vergne, J.P.J., Wang, S.: The internal and external governance of blockchain-based organizations: evidence from cryptocurrencies. In: Bitcoin and Beyond (Open Access), pp. 48–68. Routledge, Oxfordshire (2017)
17. Allen, D.W., Berg, C.: Blockchain governance: what we can learn from the economics of corporate governance. Presented at the Blockchain International Scientific Conference, March 11, 2020, Edinburgh Napier University, Scotland, UK. (Forthcoming in the Journal of the British Blockchain Association) (2020)
18. De Filippi, P., Loveluck, B.: The invisible politics of bitcoin: governance crisis of a decentralised infrastructure. Internet Policy Rev. (2016). https://hal.archives-ouvertes.fr/hal-01382007
19. Reijers, W., et al.: Now the code runs itself: on-chain and off-chain governance of blockchain technologies. Topoi **40**(4), 821–831 (2018). https://doi.org/10.1007/s11245-018-9626-5
20. van Deventer, O., et al.: Techruption consortium blockchain–what it takes to run a blockchain together. In: Proceedings of 1st ERCIM Blockchain Workshop 2018. European Society for Socially Embedded Technologies (EUSSET) (2018)
21. Laatikainen, G., Kolehmainen, T., Li, M., Hautala, M., Kettunen, A., Abrahamsson, P.: Towards a trustful digital world: exploring self-sovereign identity ecosystems. In: 2021 PACIS 2021 Proceedings, p. 19 (2021). https://aisel.aisnet.org/pacis2021/19
22. Laatikainen, G., Kolehmainen, T., Abrahamsson, P.: Self-sovereign identity ecosystems: benefits and challenges. In: 12th Scandinavian Conference on Information Systems, p. 10 (2021). https://aisel.aisnet.org/scis2021/10
23. Kraus, S., Breier, M., Dasí-Rodríguez, S.: The art of crafting a systematic literature review in entrepreneurship research. Int. Entrep. Manag. J. **16**(3), 1023–1042 (2020). https://doi.org/10.1007/s11365-020-00635-4
24. Wolfswinkel, J.F., Furtmueller, E., Wilderom, C.P.: Using grounded theory as a method for rigorously reviewing literature. Eur. J. Inf. Syst. **22**, 45–55 (2013)
25. Bakkalbasi, N., Bauer, K., Glover, J., Wang, L.: Three options for citation tracking: google scholar, scopus and web of science. Biomed. Digit. Libr. **3**, 1–8 (2006). https://doi.org/10.1186/1742-5581-3-7
26. Mckeown, K.R.: Challenges and solutions for libraries in serving entrepreneurship needs: findings from ProQuest research. J. Bus. Finan. Librariansh. **15**, 253–260 (2010)

27. ATLAS.ti 8 Windows. (n.d.). ATLAS.ti. https://atlasti.com/product/v8-windows/. Accessed 1 Sept 2021
28. Locke, K.: The grounded theory approach to qualitative research. In: Measuring and Analyzing Behavior in Organizations. Advances in Measurement and Data Analysis, Jossey-Bass, Hoboken pp. 17–43 (2002)
29. Gioia, D., Corley, K., Hamilton, A.: Seeking qualitative rigor in inductive research: notes on the gioia methodology. Org. Res. Methods **16**(1), 15–31 (2013). https://doi.org/10.1177/1094428112452151
30. Strauss, A., Corbin, J.: Grounded theory methodology: an overview. In: Handbook of Qualitative Research, pp. 273–285. Sage Publications, Thousand Oaks (1994)
31. McCurdy, D.: The role of collaborative governance in blockchain-enabled supply chains: a proposed framework. Business Administration Dissertations, Georgia State University, Atlanta, GA (2020). https://scholarworks.gsu.edu/bus_admin_diss/131
32. Reijers, W., O'Brolcháin, F., Haynes, P.: Governance in blockchain technologies & social contract theories. Ledger **1**, 134–151 (2016). https://doi.org/10.5195/ledger.2016.62
33. Lumineau, F., Wang, W., Schilke, O.: Blockchain Governance – a new way of organizing collaborations? Organ. Sci. **32**, 1–22 (2020)
34. Lacity, M., Steelman, Z., Cronan, P.: Blockchain governance models: insights for enterprises. University of Arkansas (2019)
35. Tasca, P., Tessone, C.J.: Taxonomy of blockchain technologies. Principles of Identification and Classification arXiv:1708.04872 [Cs] (2018)
36. Midha, V., Bhattacherjee, A.: Governance practices and software maintenance: a study of open source projects. Decis. Support Syst. **54**(1), 23–32 (2012). https://doi.org/10.1016/j.dss.2012.03.002
37. Reyes, C.L., Packin, N.G.: Distributed governance. SSRN J. (2016). https://doi.org/10.2139/ssrn.2884978
38. Wells, P.: Economies of scale versus small is beautiful: a business model approach based on architecture, principles and components in the beer industry. Organ. Environ. **29**, 36–52 (2016)
39. Demil, B., Lecocq, X.: Business model evolution. in search of dynamic consistency. Long Range Plan. **43**, 227–246 (2010)
40. Lacity, M.: Addressing key challenges to making enterprise blockchain applications a reality. MIS Q. Exec. (2018). https://aisel.aisnet.org/misqe/vol17/iss3/3
41. Osterwalder, A., Pigneur, Y., Tucci, C.L.: Clarifying business models: origins, present, and future of the concept. Commun. Assoc. Inf. Syst. **16**(1), 1 (2005)
42. Pereira, J., Tavalaei, M.M., Ozalp, H.: Blockchain-based platforms: decentralized infrastructures and its boundary conditions. Technol. Forecast. Soc. Change **146**, 94–102 (2019). https://doi.org/10.1016/j.techfore.2019.04.030
43. Schwabe, G.: The role of public agencies in blockchain consortia: learning from the cardossier. Inf. Polity **24**, 1–15 (2019)
44. De Filippi, P., Mcmullen, G.: Governance of blockchain systems: governance of and by distributed infrastructure. Research Report, Blockchain Research Institute and COALA, Toronto (2018). https://hal.archives-ouvertes.fr/hal-02046787
45. Gasser, U., Budish, R., West, S.M.: Multistakeholder as governance groups: observations from case studies. SSRN Electron. J. (2015). https://doi.org/10.2139/ssrn.2549270
46. Arruñada, B., Garicano, L.: Blockchain: the birth of decentralized governance (SSRN Scholarly Paper ID 3160070). Soc. Sci. Res. Netw. (2018). https://doi.org/10.2139/ssrn.3160070

Framework for Creating Relevant, Accessible, and Adoptable KPI Models in an Industrial Setting

Arttu Leppäkoski(✉), Outi Sievi-Korte, and Timo D. Hämäläinen

Tampere University, Tampere, Finland

{arttu.leppakoski,outi.sievi-korte,timo.hamalainen}@tuni.fi

Abstract. The development of software for modern products with lots of interfaces, layers and stakeholders has become very complex, increasing the risk of inefficiency. Key Performance Indicators (KPIs) can be used to identify bottlenecks and problems, but the challenge is how to create KPI models, processes and dashboards that help improving the development processes and can be adopted by all the stakeholders. We introduce the RelAA Framework - a bottom-up approach for monitoring product-focused software development. The RelAA (Relevant, Accessible and Adoptable) Framework is created in an industrial setup that currently includes around 350 persons in different phases of the software life cycle. The RelAA Framework is formed by analyzing existing KPIs and tools, gathering feedback from development teams, management, business representatives, and other stakeholders, and creating intuitive ways to share information related to KPIs. The RelAA Framework itself does not define exact KPIs for the organization to adopt, but it provides a process and model how to create, document and utilize KPIs. The RelAA Framework ensures relevance, accessibility, and adoption of KPIs across stakeholders and organization.

Keywords: KPI · KPI model · KPI framework · Metrics · Software life cycle · Dashboard · Visualization · Agile

1 Introduction

Large organizations have increasingly adopted performance measurement programs to aid decision-making and control quality. Key Performance Indicators (KPIs) are often at the center of these programs, as they are the concrete measures used to quantitatively assess performance of critical factors [1]. However, companies may struggle with creating pro-active measures and selecting the right set of KPIs for long-term analyses, among other issues [2]. Increasing software complexity and development team sizes set further limitations and new prerequisites for the KPIs. In most cases, both the KPIs and goals have been defined and given "as is" by the management. This can lead to some of the KPIs not having clear linkage to the daily work of the development teams and can even be considered confusing or disturbing. In the worst case, the KPIs that are designed to be used by only certain types of teams are used by other teams as well. This

X. Wang et al. (Eds.): ICSOB 2021, LNBIP 434, pp. 81–97, 2021.
https://doi.org/10.1007/978-3-030-91983-2_7

increases the risk of teams not committing or taking actions to improve their work, and thus, KPIs not being optimally exploited in optimizing the overall operations. We thus set the following research questions:

RQ1: Relevance - *How to ensure that the used set of KPIs is relevant, up-to-date and focuses on the right context to the stakeholders and teams?*
RQ2: Accessibility and adoption - *How to ensure KPIs are seamlessly accessible and a natural part of the daily work?*

Via an action research process to answer these questions, we propose the RelAA (Relevant, Accessible and Adoptable) Framework which consists of RelAA Process, RelAA Model and RelAA Dashboard. We suggest a process where the KPI model is developed bottom-up and provide facilitation for the creation and management of the model with web-based tooling. Instead of defining and offering a fixed KPI model, we introduce a process to engage stakeholders to contribute to the model, which is also expected to evolve according to the needs, relevance, and usefulness to each stakeholder group. In addition, the framework provides methods to ensure that company business model and targets are aligned with KPIs. Piloting the framework in our case company has shown promising results on rising commitment to KPIs.

The rest of the paper is organized as following. Section 2 discusses the background for this research. We first go through the related work on KPI models and processes, and then introduce the industrial background. Section 3 describes the utilized action research process, resulting in an introduction of the RelAA Framework within the case study company. Section 4 introduces the RelAA Framework. Section 5 evaluates the completeness of the RelAA Framework. Section 6 includes lessons learnt and lists possible threats and weaknesses. Section 7 concludes the paper and introduces ideas for the future work.

2 Related Work and Background

2.1 Related Work

Performance measurement is a widely studied phenomenon in a variety of business domains (see, e.g., [3–6]). Utilizing KPIs is an inherent part of performance measurement. In this study, our scope is on KPIs targeted particularly for software development, which is distinctly different from, e.g., manufacturing or construction. There is scarce research on the processes for creating KPI models, utilizing KPIs and on the actual KPI models targeted specifically for SW engineering processes. While SW *metrics* and measures are widely used and discussed, an *indicator* is more complex, being comprised of several measures [7]. For example, Briand et al. [8] propose the GQM/MEDEA method - a general process that can be used as a guideline to design sound measures particularly in the field of SW engineering. However, more steps would be needed to further refine such measures into KPIs.

There are some studies suggesting the processes to define KPI models in the context of software development. Tsunoda et al. [9] present a general model for discussing SW projects and their success with a variety of stakeholders, and KPIs or Key Goal Indicators

(KGIs) are an essential part of that model. In their paper, a mock example of a KPI/KGI model is presented, based mainly on counting defects and program size. Their main contribution is a set of requirements that need to be met when designing a model to enable communication between stakeholders.

Staron et al. [10], in turn, present a KPI Quality model, defining 59 quality attributes that a well-defined KPI needs to meet. The attributes are based on three key drivers: Transparency, Actionability, and Traceability. Additionally, Staron and Meding [11] present the MeSRAM method for assessing robustness of measurement programs particularly in SW development. While MeSRAM considers measurement programs at large, KPIs are an essential part of it.

There are some studies giving examples of KPI models in software engineering. Antolic [12] presents a KPI model for SW development. While the KPIs are based on data and experiences from Ericsson Software Development, the process of how the KPI model was established and how it has evolved has not been enclosed.

Kazi et al. [13], in turn, use a balanced scorecard approach for monitoring performance in SW projects, where KPIs make the scorecard. While the KPIs are based on data stores used in the business process model, and the KPI model is carefully mapped to serve existing process models, there is no report on how the KPI model would evolve, and what kind of practical experiences there are in using the model.

Finally, a review shows [14] that there is little research on visualizations related to SW processes, including visualizing KPIs alongside other process information, as most SW visualization studies focus on visualizing programs.

According to our study, we find the gaps in existing research as listed in Table 1. We will contribute to filling in these gaps. Proposed solutions are linked to the gaps in the later parts of this paper.

Table 1. Gaps in the existing studies

ID	Description	Research question
GAP1	How are teams included in the process of defining KPIs?	RQ1
GAP2	How to create a set of KPIs that are applicable for monitoring a larger entity than just one SW project?	RQ1
GAP3	How to create a set of KPIs that are targeted for different stakeholders?	RQ1, RQ2
GAP4	How to support evolution in KPIs?	RQ1

2.2 Case Company Background

The research in this paper sparked from acute needs in a large multi-national company, providing industrial products in all continents. The products include mechanics, electronics and both embedded and cloud scale software. Software is involved in controlling mechanical devices, connecting millions of devices to cloud, executing cloud analytics and delivery of user interfaces for different stakeholders.

The number of persons working in the SW department from 2013 to 2021 has increased from 75 to more than 300 and the development sites (USA, India, and Finland) are now more geographically distributed than before. The growth requires both new organizational structures and development processes.

The SW department includes three different programs which include tens of Scrum teams. Scrum teams have two-week sprints starting with sprint planning, having daily standups, and ending to sprint demo session. Programs and Scrum teams plan their backlogs for the next three months in quarterly planning sessions together with the business and other stakeholders such as maintenance. Quarterly planning is used to align the backlogs and schedules according to the given business priorities and make sure that possible dependencies to the HW development is aligned.

In the case company, the main purpose of KPIs is to ensure that all activities and initiatives are providing additional customer value and that operations are carried out effectively. KPIs can be either strategic or operational and both short-term and long-term targets can be set. KPIs are used in different levels of the organization and for different target audience and roles.

3 Research Process

Our research process follows the action research [15] method which includes four phases: plan, act, observe, and reflect. The design and development of the RelAA Framework has been carried out in phases as depicted in Fig. 1.

Phase	Action research	2018	2019	2020
SW development life cycle assessment	Plan			
Planning phase	Plan			
Development program	Not applicable			
Identification of the existing KPIs and tools	Plan			
Definition of the RelAA Framework and new KPIs	Act			
Feedback gathering (workshops & discussions)	Observe, reflect			
Development of the Minimum Viable Product (MVP)	Act			
RelAA Framework launch	Act			
Feedback gathering (RelAA Dashboard & discussions)	Observe, reflect			
Continous development	Observe, reflect			

Fig. 1. The action research phases and timeline in the RelAA Framework development

3.1 Planning Phase and Initial Observations

The planning phase included schedule setting, stakeholder identification, analysis of the existing KPIs and processes, and goal setting. All the major stakeholders have been involved in the process: SW teams, HW teams, management, business, quality managers, SW testing department, steering group, and Human Resources (HR). The planning phase included an analysis of the characteristics of the existing KPIs, tools and processes, as well as several workshops and face-to-face discussions to gather feedback. The following questions were applied in the workshops and discussions:

- Do you understand why we have KPIs?
- Are you able to find required documentation for each KPI?
- Have you been able to use the existing KPI tool?
- Which KPIs and metrics have been useful?
- What kind of things would you like to measure in your team?
- What would help your team to get more committed on KPIs?

Workshops, discussions, and interviews included persons from different parts of the organization and different roles such as program managers, developers, test specialists, product owners, agile coaches, quality managers, and test managers. Table 2 includes a summary of the feedback gathered from the workshops and interviews grouped into strengths, weaknesses, opportunities, and threats. For example, the interviews revealed that only 10 out of the 20 persons interviewed considered the existing KPIs useful and that KPIs had been guiding teams into better performance. Thus, there was a clear need to improve the existing model and its adoption. The first draft of the framework was offered for stakeholders' evaluation and further evolution based on their contributions.

Table 2. SWOT analysis

Strengths
• Lots of existing KPIs for teams and programs
• Automatic system to gather data from existing systems (e.g. backlog management)
• Story point burnup charts are widely used by development teams and visible in info screens
• Lots of different kind of visualizations and chart types available in the existing tool
• KPIs are used for measuring the performance of development teams instead of individuals
Weaknesses
• Lack of documentation, only small set of KPIs have documentation available
• Ambiguity and obscurity of KPIs
• Disorganized and unintuitive user interface and no means to enter data points manually
• Missing linkage between the KPIs and objectives defined by the management
• Missing linkage between the KPIs and company processes
• No KPIs for measuring customer value and other levels than team and program
• Lack of SW testing related KPIs
• Goals are not understandable and justifiable by the development teams
• Only part of the KPIs have goals in place
Opportunities
• New KPIs for other levels than team and program
• Definition of KPIs and goals for each role (Product Owner, Scrum master etc.) separately

(continued)

Table 2. (*continued*)

• Soft KPIs to measure motivation and feelings of the organization
• Appropriate balance between agility and stability to increase commitment
• Automatization of measurement of new KPIs
Threats
• Insufficient quality of data
• Incorrect and misleading goals and results
• Team adjusts daily routines to meet the goals without understanding the reasons
• Lack of common goals due to the diversity of teams
• Usage of KPIs as incentives arouses controversy in the organization
• Negative attitude towards KPIs
• Excessive amount of KPIs
• Excessive and complex documentation

3.2 Acting Phase

Acting phases include defining the process for continuous KPI development, setting guidelines for the documentation of the KPIs and implementation of the facilitation tool. Development of these entities is tied to a larger company-wide program, dedicated for improving the SW life cycle processes in an industrial setting. The outcome of the acting phase, RelAA Framework, is described in Sect. 4. One of the authors is working in the program within the company. The program started in 2018 and completed at the end of 2020. A dedicated info session for the teams involved in the SW development life cycle was arranged in June 2019 to launch the RelAA Framework. The implementations of an automatic data gathering system, a simple KPI tool and a set of KPIs for automated testing and continuous SW integration was started by Oinonen [16].

3.3 Observe and Reflect

Development of the RelAA Framework was followed in a weekly program status meeting in which the program core team provided their observations and guidance. Development of the RelAA Framework was coordinated, and observations were discussed in regular sessions with the RelAA development team. Additions to the RelAA Framework were reviewed and discussed in dedicated sessions with the program core team and selected stakeholders. For example, new RelAA Dashboard views, changes to the RelAA Process, and additions to the RelAA Model were demonstrated to the program core team and stakeholders to collect feedback. In addition, feedback was gathered from the RelAA Dashboard users by providing a built-in feedback form and having informal discussions with many people. With methods above we gathered observations continuously throughout the iterative development of the RelAA Framework. Observations were reflected to adjust and improve the RelAA Framework iteratively.

4 RelAA Framework

RelAA Framework consists of RelAA Process, RelAA Model and RelAA Dashboard which are tightly integrated with each other to provide seamless user experience. Figure 2 describes the characteristics of these components. *RelAA Dashboard* is a facilitation tool that supports the creation, usage and analysis of the RelAA Model and RelAA Process. *RelAA Model* defines guidelines and templates for documenting the KPIs for better visibility and transparency. *RelAA Process* defines processes and methods to enable the continuous development of the KPIs.

4.1 RelAA Process

KPIs require continuous development due to the changing development processes, organizational structures, and evolving architectures. Thus, it is important to have proper methods in place to ensure that the KPI model remains in good shape. In this section we introduce the RelAA Process, providing steps for 1) managing the KPI life cycle, 2) setting clear roles and responsibilities, 3) enabling the incremental development, 4) validating the defined KPIs and 5) providing training for the end users.

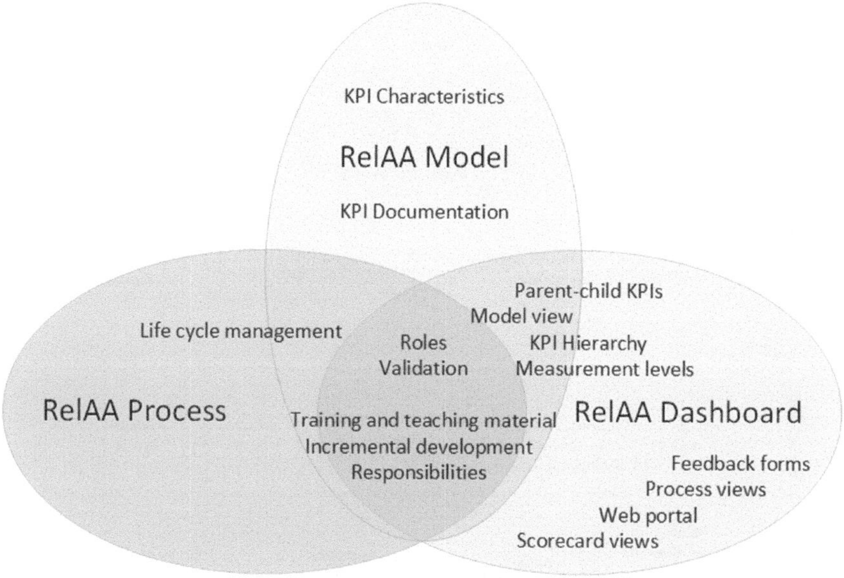

Fig. 2. RelAA Framework

Life Cycle Management. The purpose of the RelAA Process is to allow teams and stakeholders to be involved in the KPI specification from the beginning and thus increase the adoptability and transparency of KPIs, as well as and commitment to them. Additionally, there was a need to identify KPIs that are not seen valuable by the users. This approach requires that each KPI has a predefined status as listed in Table 3. Each status phase includes various tasks that need to be carried out before the next phase can be reached. The KPI life cycle and roles and responsibilities are illustrated in Fig. 3.

Table 3. Status values

Status	Description
Define	Definition of KPI and its characteristics (like measurement criteria) is in progress. Changes may occur during this phase
Baseline	KPI and its characteristics have been defined. Data is being collected to set the baseline and targets. Measurement results and measurement criteria are being validated by relevant stakeholders, teams, and persons
Measure	KPI and its characteristics have been defined and baseline and targets have been set. KPI is being followed by the responsible person or team

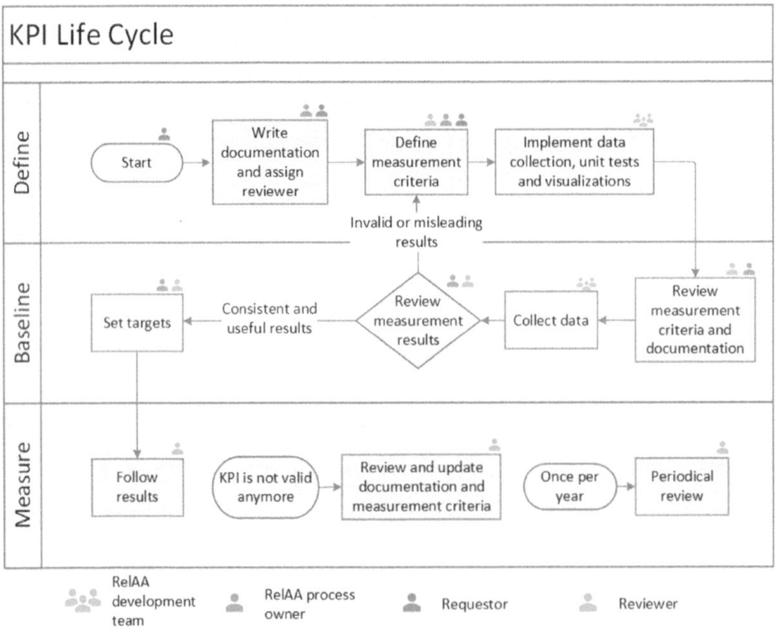

Fig. 3. KPI life cycle

Roles and Responsibilities. One of the key targets was to set clear roles, responsibilities, and accountabilities to ensure that KPIs are being developed and followed continuously. We have defined following roles and responsibilities.

- *RelAA Development team* is responsible for implementing data collection, dashboards, and visualizations. Team consists of developers that implements and maintains the system that is gathering data from different sources and components required in the RelAA Dashboard. Development team owns the RelAA Dashboard.
- *RelAA Process owner* is responsible for creating roadmaps and schedules for implementation of new KPIs, collecting ideas and feedback, and participating to KPI documentation reviews. Process owner interacts with the RelAA development team actively. Process owner owns the RelAA Process and RelAA Model.
- *Requestor* is a person or team that proposes a new KPI to be taken into use or existing KPI to be modified.
- *Reviewer* is a person that is responsible for following the measurement results, setting targets, and checking that the measurement criteria and documentation is up to date. Reviewer is assigned for each KPI separately.
- *End user* is a person or team that uses the RelAA Framework to follow the KPIs.

Incremental Development. Sometimes it is required to modify existing KPIs, introduce a new KPI or completely stop using some KPI. To enable the required incremental development process, we decided to include version numbers and histories to both the KPI model and RelAA Dashboard. This should allow comparison of different versions and provide visibility on how KPI model and RelAA Dashboard change and evolve.

Several reasons (triggers) can cause a new version of the KPI model to be released. Table 4 includes triggers that we have identified to result in releasing a new version. For each trigger, we have defined a set of actions to be executed. Predefined actions are targeted to help ensuring that KPI model remains up to date in all circumstances. In addition, we have defined an update interval for the KPI model. The purpose of the update interval is to provide information and visibility about the pace and scope of changes in relation to the nature of changes. The KPI model can be updated weekly, monthly, or yearly (Table 5).

Table 4. Triggers for new version of KPI model

Trigger	Description	Actions
Process change	Many KPIs are usually related to process milestones or phases	Review process views
		Review documentation
Organizational change	Changes in the organization may cause changes in responsibilities and teams	Assign reviewers
		Review measurement levels

(*continued*)

Table 4. (*continued*)

Trigger	Description	Actions
Architectural change	KPIs may become obsolete or invalid due to architectural changes	Review measurement criteria
		Assign reviewers
Invalid goals	Goals are not realistic or have been achieved	Review Target and Stretch goals
Invalid or insufficient results	Poor quality of the measurement results. KPI does not provide any additional value in finding problems or bottlenecks	Review measurement criteria
		Review data quality
Development tool set change	New tool or new version of existing tool is taken into use	Review data sources
		Review measurement criteria
KPI missing	New KPI has been identified	Add KPI into the KPI model

Table 5. KPI model update interval

Interval	Description of changes	Examples
Weekly	Minor changes that do not have long-term impact or do not require any actions from teams or stakeholders	Documentation improvements
		Bug fixes
Monthly	Medium changes that may require some minor actions from teams or stakeholders	Changes to measurement criteria
		Changes in reviewers
		Adding of new KPIs
Yearly	Major changes that must be communicated to whole organization	Setting of goals used for incentives
		Process view updates

Validation Measures. To ensure the validity of the KPIs through the whole KPI life cycle, we have defined the following validation measures.

Validity of New KPI. RelAA Development team together with the reviewer and relevant stakeholders validates the measurement results and reviews the documentation of the new KPI during the Baseline phase.

Validity of Existing KPIs. Each KPI is being reviewed (documentation and measurement results) periodically at least once per year to ensure that the underlying data is in good shape and reliable and documentation corresponds with the actual ways of working. Reviewer is responsible to execute the periodical review.

Validity of Data and Visualizations. RelAA Development team creates the necessary unit tests and other tests to ensure that the measurement results are being calculated and visualized correctly. Tests are executed automatically always when changes occur.

Training Sessions and Teaching Material. During the development of the RelAA Framework we discovered that even if the tools and processes would be intuitive and documentation is available, separate training sessions and teaching material need to be arranged. Developing the RelAA Framework we defined training sessions for different target audiences and added a description of the RelAA Process and a dedicated help view to the RelAA Dashboard.

Training sessions are tailored for each role (such as Product Owner), but each training session has a common frame including two parts (2 h). The first part focuses on basics and theory and includes description of the RelAA Framework. Second part is a hands-on session in which participants are getting familiar with the RelAA Framework by trying it by themselves.

4.2 RelAA Model

In the RelAA Model, KPIs are organized hierarchically (parent-child) to increase the accessibility and adoptability and to illustrate relationships. The value of the parent KPI is calculated using the values of the child KPIs using pre-defined measurement criterium. Figure 4 includes a small exemplary set of KPIs and their hierarchical relationships.

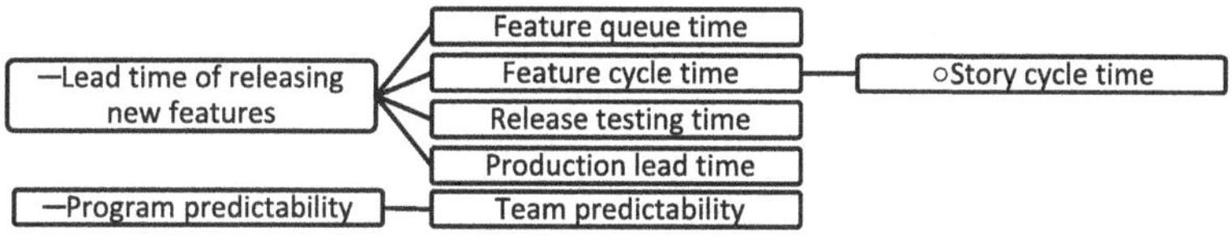

Fig. 4. Hierarchically organized KPIs

The RelAA Model includes eight documentation fields (free-form text) that are used for documenting each KPI as listed in Table 6. The purpose of these is to elaborate the background, provide practical examples and to increase the acceptance and commitment in teams.

KPIs are divided into measurement levels based on the level in which a KPI is used. Each KPI is mapped to one or more measurement levels. The measurement levels are listed in Table 7.

Each KPI is mapped to one category and one or more SW life cycle phase based on the characteristics. The categories are Speed, Efficiency, Customer centricity, and Motivated & capable team. SW life cycle phases are Planning, Requirements, Development, Testing, Maintenance. In addition, Each KPI is also tagged either Lagging or Leading. Lagging KPI is for measuring and analyzing past performance and Leading KPI is for measuring and predicting future performance.

Table 6. Documentation fields

Documentation	Description
Why is this needed?	Description about the background and purpose of the KPI
	Example: *Cycle time indicates how fast team delivers new features. Fast and consistent delivery of stories is an indicator of high productivity*
Measurement criteria	Equation or other description on how KPI value is being measured
	Example: *Story cycle time is the time (days) each story spent in 'In Progress' state before it is moved to 'Done' or 'Accepted' states*
Target goal	Target goal is defined only for KPIs that can have some meaningful target. Goal is set only after baselining period is completed. Target goal is set so that it is easier to achieve than stretch goal
	Example: *Story cycle time < 10 days*
Stretch goal	Stretch goal is defined only for KPIs that can have some meaningful target. Goal is set only after baselining period is completed
	Example: *Story cycle time < 5 days*
Reviewer	Person in charge of reviewing the results. Ideally, only one person should be nominated to avoid shared responsibilities
	Examples: *Product Owner, Program Manager, Quality Manager*
Data source	List of tools, applications and systems from which data is retrieved
	Examples: *Version control system, issue and task tracking system*
Measurement frequency	How often KPI is being measured
	Examples: *daily, weekly, monthly*
Reporting frequency	How often KPI is being reported
	Examples: *daily, weekly, monthly*
Unit of measurement	Unit of the KPI value
	Examples: *days, story points, number of defects*

Table 7. Measurement levels

Measurement level	Description
North Star	Overall status in company and product level
R&D	Overall status in R&D level
Solution	KPIs for getting more detailed information about specific solutions
Release	Detailed status and progress of each SW release
Program	KPIs for each SW development program
Team	Detailed status of the performance of each team
Component	Detailed status of the development of each component

4.3 RelAA Dashboard

The development of the RelAA Model was tightly coupled to the RelAA Dashboard which is a web portal user interface to the KPIs. We decided to build documentation into the Dashboard as there must be a way to intuitively explore the concrete KPI model (built according to the RelAA Model).

The RelAA Dashboard includes a dedicated *Model view*, which contains a built-in tree-view to visualize the hierarchies, and a possibility to see all the documentation related to the KPI by selecting any KPI.

Process view is used to map each KPI to the development process and the RelAA Dashboard includes several process views. Available process views are North Star, Release, Program, and Team, which have been defined as measurement levels. Colors (green, yellow, red) indicate the status of the KPI in each process view. Status is defined according to the Target and Stretch goals. The Trend is shown using arrows (up, right, left). Process views are kept rather simple to easy understanding.

Scorecard view includes documentation (items listed in Sect. 4.2), charts, and values related to the selected KPI. All this information is shown in a single view to increase the accessibility of the documentation and adoption of KPIs. In addition, the Scorecard view includes dedicated discussion panel that is intended for discussing about KPI results, anomalies identified in the KPIs etc.

Feedback view includes a built-in form to give feedback about the KPI model and RelAA Framework. Feedback is made visible for all allowing users to browse given feedbacks and check which feedback has been already processed and in which version it has been taken into consideration.

5 Results

5.1 Observed Effect

As part of the action research process, the RelAA framework was actively piloted in the case company while it was being created. Based on the feedback gathered during this research and development of the framework, most of the team members feel positive about the RelAA Framework and KPIs after they have been involved. They understand the background, measurement criteria and linkage to the daily work. The RelAA Framework has increased the accessibility and adoptability of the KPIs by providing intuitive, approachable, and understandable means to explore the model itself and analyze the performance of the organization.

Since the framework was completed, many of the KPIs introduced using the RelAA Framework have proven to be very useful. For example, *Engagement & Satisfaction* KPI provides detailed insights about the motivation of the development teams, *Team Predictability* KPI indicates whether it is realistic to expect the business commitments to be fulfilled and *Story Definition of Ready* KPI depicts if teams are having enough information available before starting stories. All the KPIs together help to ensure that the teams are proceeding according to the business targets.

5.2 Fulfilling Requirements

Tsunoda et al. [9] have defined a set of requirements that need to be met when designing a model to enable communication between stakeholders. These requirements are in line with our research questions and objectives, and thus, provide a useful method to validate the completeness of the current RelAA Framework. The requirements and comparison to the RelAA Framework are listed in Table 8. Requirements and models introduced in other studies were not seen comparable due to the differences in the applicability of the models. Other models are more narrowly scoped for smaller SW projects whereas the RelAA Framework is applicable for a larger entity.

Table 8. Evaluation of requirements set by Tsunoda et al. [9]

Requirement by Tsunoda et al. [9]	RelAA Framework
(R1) Goals of each stakeholder separately, and a metric which directly indicates whether the goal is achieved or not	Yes
(R2) Distinction between a metric indicating goal achievement and metrics indicating progress toward the goal	Yes
(R3) How to collect metrics	Yes
(R4) How to analyze metrics	Yes
(R5) Timing of analyzing metrics with stakeholders	Yes
(R6) Countermeasures to correct abnormal process or products identified on check phase	Yes

5.3 Fulfilling Gaps

In Table 1 we introduced gaps that were found in the existing studies and in Sect. 4 we have introduced solutions to fulfill these gaps. Table 9 includes summary about gaps and our solutions.

Table 9. Evaluation of gaps

ID	Description	Proposed solution
GAP1	How are teams included in the process of defining KPIs?	RelAA Process: KPI Life cycle
		RelAA Process: Incremental development
		RelAA Process: Training sessions
		RelAA Dashboard: Feedback database
GAP2	How to create a set of KPIs that are applicable for monitoring a larger entity than just one SW project?	RelAA Model: Measurement levels
		RelAA Dashboard: Process view
GAP3	How to create a set of KPIs that are targeted for different stakeholders?	RelAA Model: Measurement levels
		RelAA Dashboard: Process view
GAP4	How to support evolution in KPIs?	RelAA Process: KPI Life cycle
		RelAA Process: Incremental development
		RelAA Dashboard: Feedback
		RelAA Dashboard: Discussion section

6 Discussion

6.1 Lessons Learnt

Developing the RelAA Framework gave an intense insight into how KPIs are utilized within a large, multi-national company. Getting different stakeholders committed to KPIs required continuous discussions, active inclusion, and many training sessions. When taking the RelAA Framework to use, we particularly advice to take note of reserving a great deal of time and resources to involve all the necessary stakeholders to have all the aspects covered in the defined KPI model. It is also important to notice that something that fits one team, might not be suitable for some other team. For this reason, it is not reasonable to expect every team to follow the exact same set of KPIs and targets. Finally, we will revisit the research questions.

RQ1: Relevance - How to ensure that the used set of KPIs is relevant, up-to-date and focuses on the right context to the stakeholders and teams?

First, one should **engage** different stakeholders from the beginning of the KPI process. There should be **life cycle management** of the KPIs with distinct **roles** and **responsibilities**, and the organization should further allow **incremental development** of KPIs. The KPIs should also be **validated**, and **training material** provided for different users. The proposed RelAA process captures these elements to ensure that KPIs are up-to-date and that they are both designed to be relevant and understood as such by different stakeholders. Relevance is further improved by **comprehensive documentation**, describing the context and purpose of KPIs (as proposed by the RelAA Model).

RQ2: Accessibility and adoption - How to ensure KPIs are seamlessly accessible and a natural part of the daily work?

A key part in having accessible KPIs is to provide **relevant information** for **a variety of stakeholder** with **technical solutions** that are easy to adopt. Our solution for this is the constructed RelAA Dashboard. With the Dashboard different stakeholders can **view** KPIs, **suggest** new ones, **give feedback**, and **monitor** KPI values. Particularly, by providing **a number of visualizations** for different purposes and stakeholders, we have found that KPIs are more easily taken aboard in the organization. However, in order to have the Dashboard taken in as part of daily work, **a working process** for introducing it on an organizational level is required. The RelAA Process defines that stakeholders must be engaged from early on in defining the KPIs.

6.2 Threats to Validity

Using the classification presented by Wohlin et al. [17] we identified the following threats to validity.

Construct Validity and Internal Validity. We recognize that our view on how KPIs are being interpreted and understood is dependent on successfully selecting a varied set of interviewees and accurately constructing the interview questions. To minimize this risk, we have had discussions with several different types of teams to identify the distinction between common issues and team specific issues. In addition, the RelAA Framework has been reviewed with selected stakeholders during the development phase. The complexity of the development process increases the risk of not finding the causal relationships that are required to ensure the quality of KPIs. This risk has been minimized by defining several measurement levels and mapping the KPIs to process views.

External Validity. The RelAA Framework has been used only in one organization so far, and thus, we do not have evidence of the RelAA Framework's suitability in other organizations. However, we consider this as a low risk since the organization is rather large and includes a large variety of products, teams, and stakeholders. Therefore, the RelAA Framework by nature supports diverse products and processes.

Conclusion Validity. Risk of low conclusion validity exists due to the lack of numerical and statistical evaluation. This risk has been minimized by evaluating the requirements set by Tsunoda et al. [9] and reviewing the results and conclusions with the stakeholders.

7 Conclusions

We set out to create a methodology for flexibly defining KPIs for monitoring product-focused software development. Our aim was to ensure relevance (RQ1) and accessibility and adoption (RQ2) of KPIs across stakeholders and organization.

Following an action research-based process, we introduced the RelAA Framework defined for monitoring SW life cycle in an industrial setup. The RelAA Framework has been taken into use in a large company including 350 persons in SW development and in total of 56 KPIs have been documented and categorized using the methods introduced in the RelAA Framework. The defined KPI model is being updated constantly using the methods described in this paper. The RelAA Process, Model and Dashboard have been designed to fulfill the gaps (GAP1-GAP4) described in Sect. 2.

We will 1) continue arranging surveys about the experiences, 2) raise the level of commitment to SW process metrics by using regular workshops, info letters, and allowing teams more control over KPIs, and 3) validate of the KPIs used in the presented industrial setup using the KPI Quality Model [10] and MesRAM method [11].

References

1. Sinclair, D., Zairi, M.: Effective process management through performance measurement: part III-an integrated model of total quality-based performance measurement. Bus. Process Re-eng. Manag. J. **1**(3), 50–65 (1995)
2. Staron, M.: Critical role of measures in decision processes: managerial and technical measures in the context of large software development organizations. IST **54**, 887–889 (2012)
3. Neely, A., Gregory, M., Platts, K.: Performance measurement system design: a literature review and research agenda. Int. J. Oper. Prod. Man. **15**(4), 80–116 (1995)
4. Gosselin, M.: An empirical study of performance measurement in manufacturing firms. Int. J. Product. Perform. Man. **54**(5/6), 419–437 (2005)
5. Sanchez, H., Robert, B.: Measuring portfolio strategic performance using key performance indicators. Proj. Manag. J. **41**(5), 64–73 (2010)
6. Ishaq Bhatti, M., Awan, H.M., Razaq, Z.: The key performance indicators (KPIs) and their impact on overall organizational performance. Qual. Quant. **48**(6), 3127–3143 (2013). https://doi.org/10.1007/s11135-013-9945-y
7. Garcia, F., et al.: Towards a consistent terminology for software measurement. IST **48**, 631–644 (2006)
8. Briand, L.C., Morasca, S., Basili, V.R.: An operational process for goal-driven definition of measures. TSE **28**(12), 1106–1125 (2002)
9. Tsunoda, M., Matsumura, T., Matsumoto, K.: Modeling software project monitoring with stakeholders. In: Proceedings of the ICCIS 2010, pp. 723–728 (2010)
10. Staron, M., Meding, W., Niesel, K., Abran, A.: A key performance indicator quality model and its industrial evaluation. In: Proceedings of the IWSM-Mensura, 2016, pp. 170–179 (2016)
11. Staron, M., Meding, W.: MeSRAM – a method for assessing robustness of measurement programs in large software development organizations and its industrial evaluation. JSS **113**, 76–100 (2016)
12. Antolic, Z.: An example of Using Key Performance Indicators for Software Development Process Efficiency Evaluation, Ericsson Nikola Tesla R&D Center, p. 6 (2008)
13. Kazi, L., Radulovic, B., Kazi, Z.: Performance indicators in software project monitoring: balanced scorecard approach. In: Proceedings of the SISY, 2012, pp. 19–24 (2012)
14. Mattila, A.-L., Ihantola, P., Kilamo, T., Luoto, A., Nurminen, M., Väätäjä, H.: Software visualization today – systematic literature review. In: Proceedings of the 20th International Academic Mindtrek Conference. 2016, ACM, pp. 262–271 (2016)
15. Dickens, L., Watkins, K.: Action research: rethinking lewin. Manag. Learn. **30**(2), 127–140 (1999)
16. Oinonen, T.: Key Performance Indicators for Automated Testing and Continuous Software Integration. Master's thesis, Aalto University, p. 70 (2018)
17. Wohlin, C., Runeson, P., Höst, M., Ohlsson, M.C., Regnell, B., Wesslén, A.: Experimentation in Software Engineering, p. 236 (2012)

Risk Exposure and Management in Software Development – A Survey of Multiple Software Startups

Gholamhossein Kazemi[1(✉)], Orges Cico[2(✉)], Quang-Trung Nguyen[3(✉)], and Anh Nguyen-Quang[4(✉)]

[1] University of South Eastern Norway, Ringerike, Norway
238834@usn.no
[2] Norwegian University of Science and Technology, Trondheim, Norway
orges.cico@ntnu.no
[3] Thuongmai University, Hanoi, Vietnam
trungnq@tmu.edu.vn
[4] University of Transport and Communications, Hanoi, Vietnam
anhnq@utc.edu.vn

Abstract. Context: Software startups perform many high-risk activities regarding both business and product development. Being aware of important risks and effectively managing them is important for startups, particularly in an era of a global pandemic such as this. Even though there are many studies about the failure and success factors of software companies, not much is understood about risk management for startups. **Aim:** Our aim is to characterize how startups identify, manage, and control different kinds of risks during their software product development. We also intend to investigate whether there is a mismatch between startups' risk exposure and their risk management approaches. **Method:** We designed an online questionnaire with 72 questions and collected opinions from 89 software startups in different stages. **Results:** we preliminarily revealed the relevant team composition, methodology, and product risks in each stage of a startup. Our findings suggest that perceived risk exposures are reduced as startups progress from early to later stages. There was no observable difference in the ways risks are managed among startups in different stages. Startups rely on team-based, informal, and unstructured methods to identify, analyze, and control their risks. **Contribution:** Our results have direct implications for startup founders and project managers to become effective in managing software startup risks.

Keywords: Software startups · Project management · Risk management

1 Introduction

Turning ideas into a profitable business is a long and risky endeavor. 75% of startups fail within three years of their operations for various reasons. We refer to startups as companies with innovation focus, lack of resources, uncertain and time-pressured working conditions, high reactivity, and rapid evolution [1]. Startups are heavily dependent on

X. Wang et al. (Eds.): ICSOB 2021, LNBIP 434, pp. 98–104, 2021.
https://doi.org/10.1007/978-3-030-91983-2_8

the concepts of minimum viable product and technical debt in their business models [2]. Previous research has shown that technical risks, including uncertainties associated with products, engineering processes, and practices, are all threats to the startups' businesses [3]. For instance, technical debt, a common phenomenon in startups, can also be considered a software project risk with observable future consequences [4]. For software startups, risk management might be unconventional, because startups might get involved in more complex domains with more uncertainties than traditional businesses.

While methodological approaches dealing with technical debts [3] can be used to deal with different kinds of risks during startups' product development, we have limited knowledge about how other types of technical risks are managed in startup contexts. Besides, startups are sensitive to non-technical factors, like change funding situations or new market demands. Particularly, they are more vulnerable than established software companies to disruptive changes in the company's environment, such as those imposed by the coronavirus disease 2019 (COVID-19) pandemic. According to *Startup Genome*, more than 70% of startups have been seriously impacted since the start of the pandemic [5]. Similar to research about software engineering activities in software startups [6], our knowledge about risk management, as a sub-area of project management, should be revisited to contribute to research-driven processes and practices specifically applied to the startup context.

Our aim is to characterize how startups identify, manage, and control different kinds of risks during their software product development. We propose two research questions (RQs) that guide the exploration of startup practices in two parts: (1) risk and (2) risk management.

- **RQ1:** What is the relevance of the exposure of a team, methodology, and product to risks across different stages of a software startup?
- **RQ2:** How do startups perform risk management activities across different stages of a software startup?

To answer our RQs, we used Barki et al.'s theoretical framework [7] and the risk management practices described by Schwalbe [8]. In particular, Barki et al. [7] proposed a contingency model of software risk management, arguing that successful organizations establish a fit between risk and risk management practices. We conducted an extensive survey with 72 questions answered by 89 startups. This paper presents a preliminary result from this survey research.

The paper is organized as follows: section one outlines the introduction, section two presents related work, and section three is the research methodology. Section four presents our results and main observations while section five contains the discussion and conclusion.

2 Related Work

Barki et al. [7] proposed a contingency model of software risk management, proposing that successful organizations establish a fit between the risk exposure and risk management activities conducted. "Risk exposure" is defined as this probability multiplied by the loss potential of the unsatisfactory outcome. "Risk management practices" can be decomposed and assessed by the types and extents of performed risk identification, analysis, and control activities. According to the author, too much emphasis on the use of formal risk management is thought to be inappropriate for high-risk exposure projects, while employing formal approaches is seen as useful in low-risk exposure projects.For startups in high-tech domains, known risk factors have been discussed, for example staffing risk, technical risk, and market risk [9, 10]. Risk factors of startups are associated with the complexity of the work environment and competence in dealing with uncertainty. Todeschini et al. found that startups have different ways of understanding the concept of risk management and suffer from a lack of familiarity with the concept of risk management [9]. Previous research suggests that start-ups should minimize the risk of failure by minimizing the expenses of learning [10].

3 Research Methodology

The survey design is based on Barki's theoretical framework [7] and risk management practices described by Schwalbe [8]. The survey questions were tested in the first round with three researchers and in the second round with three project managers and two startup founders. The "final" version of the survey consists of 72 questions in nine sections: (1) welcome message, (2) meta-information, (3) market risk, (4) finance risk, (5) team risk, (6) business risk, (7) methodology risk, (8) product risk, and (9) evaluation. We mostly used either closed questions with a five-point Likert scale or questions with multiple-choice pre-given answer options. For each type of risk, we made queries regarding used risk identification methods, relevant product-related risks, risk occurrence frequency, risk affection, used risk identification analysis methods, frequency of rick management activities, and used risk control methods.

The target population of this survey is startup companies that develop software-intensive products or services. The survey aims at collecting opinions from startup key personnel (CEOs, CTOs, etc.) about their experience with risk exposure and risk management practices. Data collection was done in two rounds, lasting more than one year. In the first round, the invitation was sent to potential participants in our network. In the second round, we also shared the survey invitation to a crowd-sourced platform, which gave us more responses than any other single channel. Participants were asked to complete the survey online (using a Google form) and participation was voluntary and anonymous. Respondents could withdraw their results from the survey at any time. Researchers agreed to publish only a summary and aggregate information from the survey.

Our unit of analysis is the company, and all our observations were made at the company level. Data were preprocessed by removing invalid responses. We recoded the raw data into a common quantitative coding scheme. We also recoded the risk frequency and risk severity. For most of the survey questions, descriptive statistics, such as minimum, maximum, median, and mean values were calculated.

4 Results

Our sample included many startup companies from Europe, specifically in Norway. There were also participants from America (USA, Canada, Mexico, etc.) and Asia (Japan, India, Nepal, etc.). We did not have any startups from Australia and Africa.

Regarding company size, 34% (the majority) of the sample had less than 10 employees (as shown in Fig. 1). 8% of the sample were companies with more than 500 employees. We had 32 companies (36%) that did not provide this information. This categorization helps to have a better view of the size of the participant companies.

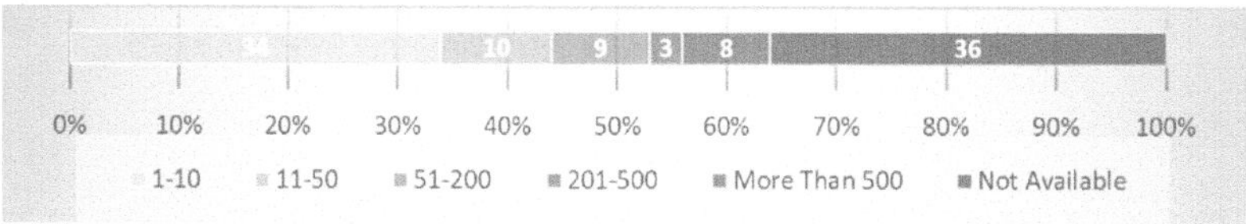

Fig. 1. Distribution of companies by number of employees

Regarding the company stage, we had 29% of the sample at the early stage (26 companies), 47% at the startup stage (42 companies), and 24% at the later stage (21 companies). We used this category to compare the risk management practices between startup companies and companies at the other stages.

4.1 RQ1: What is the Relevance of the Exposure of a Team, Methodology, and Product to Risks Across Different Stages of a Software Startup?

In this section, we focus on answering RQ1. Overall, our sample does not find the common risk factors much relevant to their context. Interestingly, neither team nor methodology was relevant. Product is the area where most of the risks were relevant. Products were concerned at the early-stage and startup-stage. The legal issue is the only product risk item with a value larger than three in later-stage companies. In comparing the early-stage and later stages, the perceived risk relevance tends to be higher at the startup stage. There are also five risk items relevant at the startup stage: (1) lack of project management methodology, (2) bad scheduling, (3) product user experience, (4) product quality, and (5) product functionalities.

Risk exposure is calculated with the formula in Sect. 3.3, representing the perceived risk level for the survey participants. Figure 2 presents nine boxplots for team risk, methodology risk, and product risk of companies at the early-stage, startup stage, and later stages.

Regarding risk types, the median values of risk exposures are the same for team, methodology, and product risk (value of four). In general, product risks are of greater exposure in comparison to team risk and methodology risk. On average, the risk exposure level is highest at an early-stage startup, followed by startups and then later-stage companies.

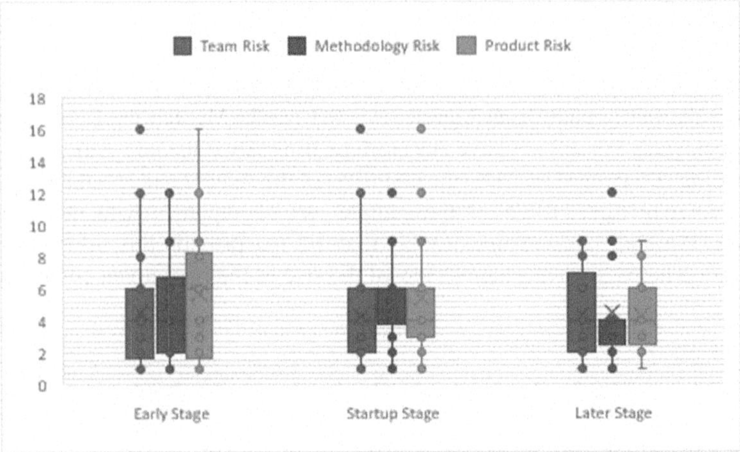

Fig. 2. Risk exposure of team, methodology, and product risks across different companies' stages

4.2 RQ2: How Do Startups Perform Risk Management Activities Across Different Stages?

In this section, we focus on answering our RQ2. Figure 3, Fig. 4, and Fig. 5 Present the frequency of risk management activities regarding team risk, methodology risk, and product risk respectively. Overall, startups perform little risk management activities (more than 50% of responses choose either "never" or "minor" responses). Our samples show more risk management activities regarding product risks than they do regarding team and methodology risks (which aligns with observations in Sect. 4.1).

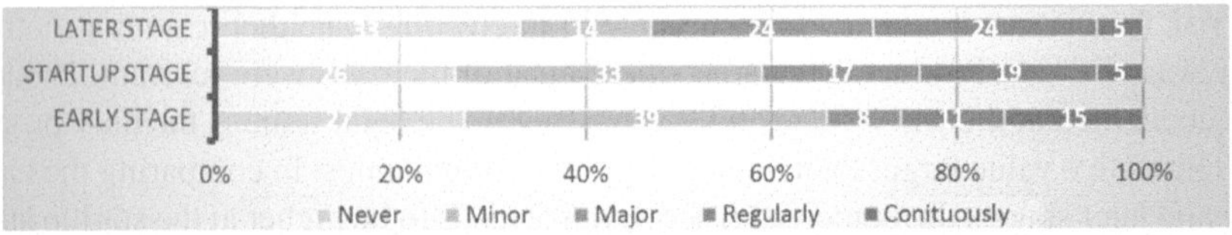

Fig. 3. Frequency of team risk management activities

Regarding team risk, the number of companies regularly or continuously performing risk management activities is larger at the later stage than at the startup or early stages. Regarding methodology risk and product risk, the number of companies regularly or continuously performing risk management activities is larger at the startup stage than at the other two stages.

Common Risk Identification Approaches. Team brainstorming is the most common risk identification method used across risk types (57% for team risk, 55% for methodology risk, and 47% for product risk), followed by interviews/ talks with the experts (35% for team risk, 36% for methodology risk, and 38% for product risk). Formal forms of risk identification, for instance, root-cause analysis and Delphi technique, seem to be used little regarding team risk identification methods. Our sample is also not data-driven regarding risk identification.

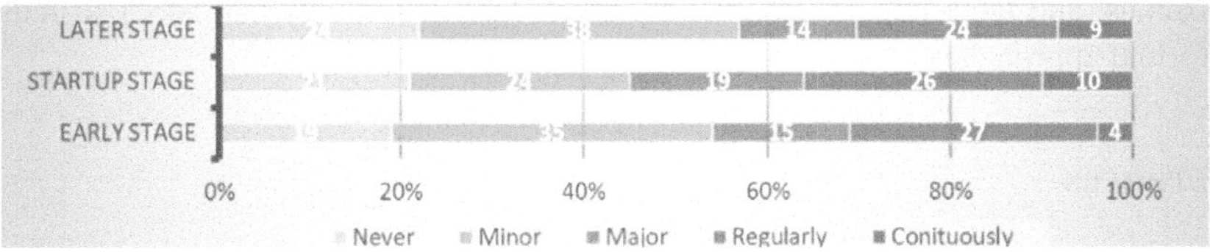

Fig. 4. Frequency of methodology risk management activities

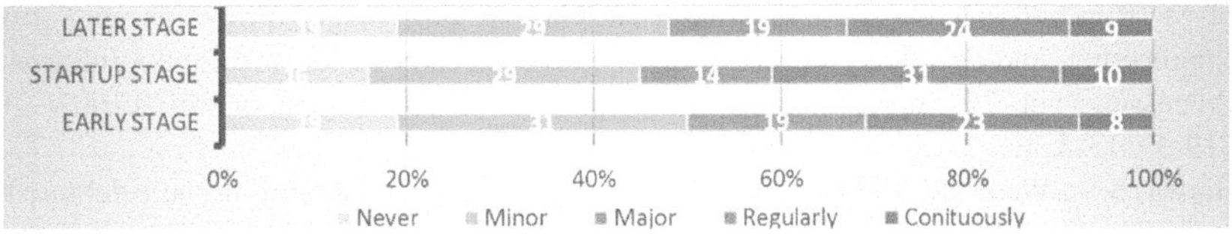

Fig. 5. Frequency of product risk management activities

5 Discussion and Conclusions

In this study, we reported the results of our observations from one year of research about risk management in software startups. We collected responses to 72 questions from 89 startup companies, many of which were from Norway and Europe. Our observation is that product risks are relatively more concerning to startup project managers than team and methodology risks. Software products, including functional and quality features, are directly connected with startup outcomes and play a critical role in the access to funding and success of a software startup. This is not a surprise, as literature in software project management has acknowledged the relative importance of requirement risks in comparison to user risks or organization risks [11]. Our observations also support the argument that startups in earlier stages are exposed to more risks. At the early stages, startups would probably face more uncertainty and consequently, more unforeseeable risks, which could lead to secondary unforeseeable risks. The amount of uncertainty can be reduced over time, or the experience of the startup project manager increases over time, leading to the reduction of perceived risks in later stages.

There are many startups that do not perform risk management. It might be argued that startups are risk-oriented activities by nature and staying with the risks might be a natural thing to do for startup project managers. However, most of the survey participants think that risk management is useful to them. We also observed that risk management activities are positively correlated with product satisfaction. This might be the gap for risk management research to address.

Our observations recommend that project managers should gain information regarding the risks from their team members to conduct risk management, including risk identification, risk analysis, and risk control in an effective way and in the right context. This highly mitigates chance of failure. It can also be useful to explicitly consider the stage of the startups to select the most suitable risk management approaches. According to the contingency approach [7], startups that have more uncertainty can adopt more flexible approaches, and later-stage companies that have less uncertainty can adopt structured and formal approaches.

References

1. Nguyen-Duc, A., Münch, J., Prikladnicki, R., Wang, X., Abrahamsson, P.: Fundamentals of Software Startups. Springer, Heidelberg (2020). https://doi.org/10.1007/978-3-030-35983-6
2. Duc, A.N., Abrahamsson, P.: Minimum viable product or multiple facet product? The role of MVP in software startups. In: Sharp, H., Hall, T. (eds.) Agile Processes, in Software Engineering, and Extreme Programming. XP 2016. Lecture Notes in Business Information Processing, vol. 251, pp. 118–130. Springer, Cham (2016). https://doi.org/10.1007/978-3-319-33515-5_10
3. Bajwa, S.S., Wang, X., Nguyen Duc, A., Abrahamsson, P.: "Failures" to be celebrated: an analysis of major pivots of software startups. Empir. Softw. Eng. **22**(5), 2373–2408 (2016). https://doi.org/10.1007/s10664-016-9458-0
4. Guo, Y., Spínola, R.O., Seaman, C.: Exploring the costs of technical debt management – a case study. Empir. Softw. Eng. **21**(1), 159–182 (2014). https://doi.org/10.1007/s10664-014-9351-7
5. The Impact of COVID-19 on Global Startup Ecosystems. https://startupgenome.com/covid19
6. Klotins, E., et al.: A progression model of software engineering goals, challenges, and practices in start-ups. IEEE Trans. Softw. Eng. **47**(3), 498–521 (2019)
7. Barki, H., Rivard, S., Talbot, J.: An integrative contingency model of software project risk management. J. Manag. Inf. Syst. **17**(4), 37–69 (2001)
8. Schwalbe, K.: Information Technology Project Management. Cengage Learning (2015)
9. Todeschini, B., Boelter, A., Souza, J., Cortimiglia, M.: Risk management from the perspective of startups. Eur. J. Appl. Bus. Manag. EJABM **3**(3), 40–54 (2017)
10. Razdan, R., Kambalimath, S.: Super lean software startup engineering management. In: 2019 IEEE Technology & Engineering Management Conference (TEMSCON), pp. 1–6. IEEE (2009)
11. Wallace, L., Keil, M., Rai, A.: Understanding software project risk: a cluster analysis. Inf. Manag. **42**(1), 115–125 (2004)

Software Startups

Supporting Entrepreneurship with Hackathons - A Study on Startup Founders Attending Hackathons

Maria Angelica Medina Angarita[1(✉)] and Alexander Nolte[1,2]

[1] University of Tartu, Ülikooli 18, 50090 Tartu, Estonia
{maria.medina,alexander.nolte}@ut.ee
[2] Carnegie Mellon University, 5000 Forbes Avenue, Pittsburgh, PA 15213, USA

Abstract. Entrepreneurial hackathons are generally perceived to foster the creation of new startups, support networking, and acquire entrepreneurial skills. Current research work about entrepreneurial hackathons focuses on reporting the perceived benefits of the participants. However, little is known about why startup founders initially participate in hackathons, how they perceive the impact of participating on their entrepreneurial journey, and how different hackathon settings can affect their perception. To address this gap, we conducted an interview study with startup founders who have participated in hackathons. Our findings indicate that founders are mainly motivated to participate in hackathons in relation to their startups to learn about the topic of their startup and train the prototyping skills of their startup team. Moreover, we found that the initial intentions of startup founders could change during the hackathon.

Keywords: Hackathon · Startup · Entrepreneurship

1 Introduction

Hackathons are time-bounded, themed events where participants gather in teams and work on a project of their interest. They originated as weekend-long events in the early 2000s as an agile approach for corporations to foster innovation [37]. Nowadays, they are organized by, among others, by universities [15, 18, 33] hosting academic hackathons, and private corporations [14, 41] hosting corporate events. In addition, there are also entrepreneurial hackathons that are often organized as a means to promote entrepreneurial practices [6], such as networking [10, 18, 40], learning [7, 15], providing participants with early-stage entrepreneurship guidance [39], interdisciplinary collaboration [25], funding [10], the formation of a team [27], and the creation of a prototype or a minimum viable product (MVP) [10]. Such events are often perceived as the starting point for startup creation [40], as they allow for designing an initial product that can be validated by potential users, which is essential for startups [38]. Prior work provides indications that hackathons can also be useful for startups in the later stages of their development to find potential employees, acquire investment, and validate or

X. Wang et al. (Eds.): ICSOB 2021, LNBIP 434, pp. 107–121, 2021.
https://doi.org/10.1007/978-3-030-91983-2_9

promote their projects [31]. Most existing work has focused on the organizer perspective and the perception of participants during and after an event, instead, we focus on how startup founders have experienced hackathons as their means for supporting their startups, and if startup founders have indeed been motivated to attend entrepreneurial hackathons to foster their startups. Thus, we propose our first research question **(RQ1): Why have startup founders attended hackathons?** In addition to understanding the goals of startup founders for attending hackathons, we also aim to study whether and how they achieved them. Thus, we also propose our second research question **(RQ2): What are the perceived benefits of entrepreneurial hackathons to startup founders?** Finally, to understand how entrepreneurial hackathons have supported entrepreneurs, we aim to study how the hackathon setting has supported or hindered startup founders to achieve their goals. Thus, we propose as our third research question **(RQ3): How did participants perceive the hackathon setting to have influenced the achievement of their goals?** To answer these questions, we conducted an interview study with startup founders about their motivations to attend hackathons, their perceived benefits, and how the setting supported or hindered them. Our findings indicate that the startup founders we studied attended hackathons in relation to their startups to receive feedback about an idea related to their startup, learn technological skills, network with experts, develop the prototype of their startup, and develop the skills of the startup team.

2 Background

We perceive entrepreneurial hackathons as events that focus on turning an idea into a product, and later into a new, independent, and profitable startup [9]. Most of these events offer prizes that may include tools and resources, mentorship, or tickets to startup incubators [12, 32]. Prior work has identified various motivations for individuals to attend such events that include entrepreneurial goals, such as **building a product, finding a team to work with** [5], **networking** [4], **learning** [5], and **finding investors** [26]. There are also motivations unrelated to entrepreneurship though, such as free pizza [5], status and reputation [21], having fun [26], and career concerns [9]. Our research expands this line of research by focusing on the goals of startup founders and how these goals could be related to the development of their existing startups.

Prior work has established that startup founders are motivated to attend hackathons to receive feedback about an idea, promote their idea to the general public, attract funding, find suitable partners or employees, or construct an initial prototype [31]. We expand on these findings by addressing why startup founders have participated in hackathons and whether or not their expectations have been met.

Prior work in the context of start-ups discusses various stages of development. Some include three stages [11, 42], while others include four [22, 36, 45] and more than four stages [43]. We chose the model of four startup stages of development [22] as it describes specific challenges inherent to each stage. These four startup stages consist of inception, stabilization, growth, and maturity [22]. During the early stages, the main challenges consist of forming a team with the right skills to create the first version of the startup product, while in later stages, the focus is centered on business growth [2] in the market share [22]. While prior research about hackathons focuses on stage one of startup development, we aim to expand to other stages.

The perceived benefits of hackathon participants that have been addressed by previous research include the validation of ideas [19], startups [4], exercising entrepreneurial thinking, and learning entrepreneurial skills [3, 44]. The entrepreneurial skills participants have learned at hackathons involve *"leadership, negotiation, team working and communications skills"* [3], as well as *"the basic processes of assumption validation, stakeholder analysis, and root cause analyses"* [39], and *"a greater ability to come up with a viable business idea"* [44]. Team formation supports networking, as it presents an opportunity *"to make contacts and grow networks that would otherwise be difficult to achieve outside of hackathons"* [34]. Hackathons also allow participants to validate their ideas into prototypes and have *"proof of the potential market demonstrated with the first viable product"* [19]. Our research contributes to these findings by focusing on the perceived benefits of startup founders.

Certain aspects that make up the hackathon setting have been found to influence the achievement of the goals of the participants. These include the duration of the hackathon, its theme, team formation, ideation, additional feedback, and competition [27], and they have been found to be related to goal achievement. The presence of stakeholders at hackathons has also been found to positively influence [16, 28, 35] the quality of the final prototypes, as having stakeholders at hackathons allows participants to validate their prototypes. Certain aspects of the setting, however, have been found to affect the goals of participants negatively. Hackathons are often weekend-long events, and thus, *"too short of an event to generate lasting enthusiasm and progress"* [39]. The short duration of hackathons has also been found to hinder the quality of the final prototypes [27]. In addition, more often than not, the ideas, projects, teams, and connections made at the hackathon are not sustained after the hackathon ends [20].

3 Research Method

To answer the research questions, we conducted an interview study. We selected semi-structured interviews as our main research method as they are appropriate for describing the perspective of an individual of a situation or set of events [24]. Our aim is to study the perception of startup founders (**SF**) attending hackathons. We thus excluded hackathon participants who have not founded a startup because they would not be able to provide insight about their experiences at hackathons in relation to the development of their startup. We identified suitable study participants by intersecting a database [31] of hackathon events from 2010 to 2019 with a database about startup founders and contacted individuals within that intersection. From the responses obtained we selected six participants (**SF1–SF6**). Their startups had contrasting traits (see Table 1), such as focusing on either software (*"Soft"*) or hardware (*"Hard"*) products. While most startup founders are still working in their startups, two of the founders are no longer part of their startup (SF3, SF5). In Table 1, *"Y"* (*"Yes"*) indicates startup founders that are still part of their startups. At the time each founder attended the hackathons, their startups were in various degrees of development. Some went to hackathons before founding their startups (SF1, SF4, SF5), while others attended when the startups were at later stages (SF2, SF3, SF6).

The hackathons our study participants attended had a similar setting. With the exception of SF1, who attended an entrepreneurial hackathon that focused on business model

Table 1. Startup traits at the year 2020.

Startup traits	SF1	SF2	SF3	SF4	SF5	SF6
Startups founded	2	1	1	1	2	1
Active startup	Y/Y	Y	N	Y	N/Y	Y
Founder in startup	Y/Y	Y	N	Y	N/N	Y
Team size	7	3	0	4	7	25
Product type	Hard	Soft	Hard	Soft	Hard	Soft/Hard
Startup stage	3	3	0	3	0/3	3

development, all founders attended hackathons that were organized by the same north-eastern european institution that specializes in events related to entrepreneurship. They were all weekend-long events that followed the common hackathon schedule [29] where participants pitched their ideas for projects at the beginning and were free to join a team based on the ideas that interested them. To ensure that participants would stay on track the organizers provided access to mentors and held regular checkpoints. The hackathons were focused on the completion of a prototype, but the teams were also given mentorship about how to pitch their projects with a business-focused format, which included addressing how to monetize their prototype. We created an interview guide[1] before interviewing the participants. The guide covered questions related to their motivations to attend the hackathons (**RQ1**), their perceived benefits (**RQ2**), and their perception of how the setting has helped them achieve their goals (**RQ3**). Some of the questions included "*Tell me about why you went to the hackathon*" in reference to **RQ1**, and "*At the hackathon, what helped you to achieve (your aforementioned goals)?*" in relation to **RQ2** and **RQ3**. We analyzed the interview findings by coding and clustering the interview answers into themes. The clusters were based on the relationships between the hackathon settings and outcomes [27]. There were first-level clusters, such as "*hackathon outcomes*" that contained second-level clusters, such as "*networking*" and "*learning*".

4 Experiences of Startup Founders at Hackathons

In this section, we present a detailed description of the hackathon experience of each startup founder (Sects. 4.1, 4.2, 4.3, 4.4, 4.5 and 4.6) before comparing their findings (Sect. 5).

4.1 SF1 – Meeting a Temporary Startup Team Member at a Hackathon by Accident

The startup team of SF1 developed a hardware product and launched it in 2016. Since then, they have been producing and selling the product to clients. At the time SF1 attended a hackathon in 2015, however, this startup had not been founded. SF1 thus did

[1] The complete guide is accessible here: https://tinyurl.com/33krjvd9.

not participate in a hackathon with a motivation related to the startup but rather attended a hackathon as a mentor: "*I was actually asked [to participate] as a mentor*" (SF1). But soon after the hackathon started s/he talked to one of the teams, found their idea "*really interesting*" (SF1), and joined that team. S/he mentioned that s/he could switch roles at the hackathon because there were no restrictive participation guidelines: "*If there's [a] very strict guideline as to what the mentor should do or should not do, then perhaps this would not have happened*" (SF1). During the hackathon, s/he worked together with the team on a website for their project. They won the main prize of the hackathon: a mentoring program and "*a place in the top 100 [of a business accelerator competition]*" (SF1). The team took part in the competition, where SF1 made new contacts, but they did not become part of the top 30 finalists and eventually stopped working on their hackathon project. In addition, SF1 met one of the designers of their startup product at the hackathon: "*we got to know each other on this hackathon for the first time*" (SF1). SF1 also met the CEO of an enterprise and talked about a product which later got turned into a product: "*We had an initial agreement already on the hackathon [...] and then we went on to try to develop something*" (SF1). To develop the product, SF1 created a company: "*I still have the company. And that one carried on quite long*" (SF1). Overall, networking and the creation of a company were the main benefits for SF1: "*The main positive effect for me was the networking. That I made longtime friends from that. And also, yeah, just spinning a few startups*" (SF1).

4.2 SF2 – Learning Through Networking at a Hackathon

The startup of SF2 focuses on entry access technologies. It was founded eight months before the hackathon and consisted of a small team of people. The startup was at an early stage, where the main challenges related to "*how to finally make this prototype a product that is sustainable*" (SF2) and how to "*find a business model that works...because development is costly*" (SF2). But SF2 did not attend a hackathon to solve these challenges. Instead, SF2 attended a hackathon to have fun, receive feedback about an idea related to the field of her/his startup, and network and learn from people who are experts in that field. To SF2, these goals were connected, and s/he achieved them by pitching an idea that would allow her/him to meet and learn from experts in the field of the startup: "*That particular idea attracted the people we were interested in*" (SF2). Weeks before the hackathon took place, SF2 met with colleagues who would become part of her/his hackathon team: "*We had a meeting with our team members...[we] made some preliminary plans*" (SF2). S/he then sent the project idea and the pitching presentation to the hackathon organizers. At the hackathon, the different ideas that participants had sent were displayed on posters. Participants gathered around the posters with the ideas they were interested in to form teams. SF2 recruited team members, but s/he also took advantage of this setup to network. S/he stated that s/he approached the posters about ideas of her/his interest and talked with people who were also interested in those ideas: "*these ideas attract people who are knowledgeable in that field. So, when I go to meet this team... I can meet people who are really good at this*" (SF2). On the second day of the hackathon, s/he visited other teams to meet with people again and "*to see what they have done and just talk and hopefully it gives them good ideas... [and to] contribute and also learn by experience*" (SF2). Overall, SF2 was able to learn by meeting *"people who were very knowledgeable about access control systems and we got some ideas about how to develop our prototype"* (SF2). In addition to learning from participants from other teams, SF2 learned from the mentors and her/his team members, who were knowledgeable in the field related to the hackathon project: "*there were some good mentors, and also my team members that are very good on this field*" (SF2). S/he also learned new skills by working on their prototype: "*I learned also, from my own experience, building this mesh network, I learned some new skills*" (SF2).

4.3 SF3 – Participating in a Hackathon to Create a New Startup

The startup team of SF3 used to develop and sell hardware products to clients. However, at the time of the hackathon that SF3 recounted, the startup was not generating enough profit to become sustainable "*the startup I was already with was not getting traction fast enough*" (SF3), which motivated SF3 to attend a hackathon to create a new startup. In order to create a new startup at the hackathon, SF3 joined a team and worked on a project with people s/he did not know beforehand, and they won the main award of the hackathon: "*we won the first prize*" (SF3). The prize consisted of a team-building hike with the hackathon team: "*one of the prizes was a hike*" (SF3). After the hackathon ended, some team members left the team, but SF3 and the remaining members continued looking for funding, as "*developing hardware...costs awfully*" (SF3). They found financing with a "*public procurement thing*" (SF3) but eventually ceased working on their project, as the amount of funding they obtained was not enough to start production and keep the project afloat. The hackathon was thus helpful for SF3 to find a new startup team, although they did not continue working on their project afterwards. SF3 also recounted two other hackathon experiences. SF3 stated that s/he first took part in a hackathon for the first time because the hackathon "*seemed interesting to me*" (SF3). On another occasion, SF3 attended a hackathon to connect a topic of her/his interest with hackathons: "*I wanted to see what happens if I take [topic of interest] to a hackathon*" (SF3). S/he pitched an idea related to her/his job in a field of her/his interest, formed a team, and won a prize at that hackathon: "*for that, we won... 500 kg of processed steel*" (SF3). However, this prize has not been claimed yet: "*this is still valid, if I would want to, like, make something out of steel*" (SF3).

4.4 SF4 – Learning and Networking at a Hackathon

The startup team of SF4 developed an educational app that is currently active. The original prototype was developed at a hackathon. SF4 attended this hackathon in 2014 where s/he met the initial members of the startup team *"[I] met the initial teammates there. But basically, everybody has changed from that original team"* (SF4). At the hackathon, they developed and presented a prototype *"we got out a really ugly prototype"* (SF4). Albeit the team did not win any prizes at the hackathon, after the hackathon their prototype was uploaded to an app store and was downloaded at least a thousand times *"we could use this prototype to prove that there was need and demand on the market. So [the] prototype got 1000 downloads, which was nice*" (SF4). This motivated the team to continue working on their project: "*it proved to us that at least somebody is looking for it, and somebody wants to try this out*" (SF4). Albeit the startup of SF4 originated at a hackathon, there seems to be no further connection between the startup and hackathons. SF4 added that s/he would not attend a hackathon with her/his current startup because of potential problems that could arise concerning the ownership of intellectual property: "*if I have [an] already established startup, then everybody – all the new people who would join in another hackathon would have rights to the IP*" (SF4). After founding the startup, SF4 attended a hackathon that focused on a topic of her/his interest because s/he is currently working as a volunteer in that field "*I like [topic] and [topic] hackathons I've always enjoyed because they're really interesting*" (SF4). At the hackathon, SF4 learned by talking to experts in the field: "*I have contacts now I can turn to*" (SF4), including mentors and organizers. S/he learned "*some things about [topic] industry in [country], what companies are there and how they work together*" (SF4). SF4 also mentioned that s/he won the second prize at the hackathon, which consisted of "*hardware tools*" (SF4). But the prize did not contribute to the sustainability of the project, as the tools "*wouldn't have helped*" (SF4).

4.5 SF5 – Learning About Business Management at a Hackathon

SF5 has co-founded two startups. Less than six months after the foundation of a startup, SF5 and the startup team went to a hackathon to develop their startup product. Before the hackathon took place, SF5 organized a meeting with the team to discuss what they would do at the hackathon and answer questions such as "*Why are we going there?... What do we want to do?*" (SF5). S/he mentioned that the hackathon was "*an excuse to sit down with the team for two days and talk about stuff*" (SF5), and that s/he was also motivated to attend because of the tools and facilities provided at the hackathon: "*free stuff, free food, free equipment*" (SF5). Albeit SF5 took part in the hackathon to develop the prototype of their startup product, those plans soon changed: "*we built nothing, because we understood that building was not the problem*" (SF5). Soon after the hackathon started, SF5 learned that business management was a relevant aspect that could support the startup: "*we could have, like, a shelf full of the best product in the world, but we still wouldn't have a company*" (SF5). S/he learned this while preparing for the final pitching session: "*the thing that has taught me the most is preparing for the final pitch*" (SF5). In addition to learning from the feedback given by the mentors, SF5 also learned about business management from a document supplied by the organizers: "*in the end, you have to do a pitch. And it has to be it has to be structured. And there is a document that helps you to write this thing well*" (SF5). After the hackathon ended, SF5 stated that the startup team focused more on the business management of the startup: "*We... focused on another direction after that*" (SF5). The startup team of SF5 continued to share what they learned at the hackathon when they talked with "*some investors or potential clients*" (SF5). However, SF5 would not like to pitch again at hackathons because s/he perceived the feedback to be similar at different hackathons: "*I have done that pitch training a couple of times... and that gets repetitive*" (SF5).

Currently, learning a new technology is one of the main reasons SF5 attends hackathons: "*when I go to hackathons now I go because I want something that is technically challenging, but new*" (SF5). The second main reason SF5 currently attends hackathons is "*to network with everybody*" (SF5). SF5 attended another hackathon that a private company had funded. SF5 initially attended as a mentor but soon joined a hackathon team s/he was familiar with: "*a couple of my friends were doing a radio project [and] I helped them because I like radio stuff*" (SF5). The idea for the project originated from a client of the startup company that sponsored the hackathon: "*this idea was given to the startup by a big client*" (SF5). At the hackathon, s/he met with one of the project managers of the company with whom s/he had also worked beforehand: "*I had worked with her/him, like, for a couple of years*" (SF5). They talked about a potential job opportunity if their project obtained funding: "*I said...I need a good-paying job*" (SF5). A few months after the hackathon ended, the project manager contacted SF5, and s/he soon started working in his company: "*My now[sic] boss called me... [and said] we need somebody who can build this. Come and build this*" (SF5).

4.6 SF6 – Hackathons as a Means to Develop the Skills of the Startup Team

The startup of SF6 creates prototypes for clients and helps other companies build their hardware projects. Since the creation of the startup in 2013, SF6 and various members of the startup team have attended at least four hackathons together for at least three consecutive years. SF6 mentioned that s/he attended various hackathons with some startup team members to improve their prototyping skills "*we want... our team to grow their skills and see, like, a little bit more projects*" (SF4). SF6 also added that s/he was motivated to take part in the hackathon with the startup team to "*focus on working together with these different, smaller teams to just build their relationships*" (SF6). The startup team developed their skills at the various hackathons by working on projects "*we really developed our own skillset*" (SF6). They worked on any project that they considered interesting because the project itself was not of core interest to them because "*the hackathon itself is not that serious*" (SF6).

5 Comparison of the Hackathon Experiences of Startup Founders

In this section, we provide a comparison of the different experiences of startup founders we interviewed. We address their motivations to attend (Sect. 5.1), whether they reached their goals (Sect. 5.2), and the aspects of the hackathon setting that they perceived as beneficial to the achievement of their goals (Sect. 5.3).

5.1 Motivations of Startup Founders to Attend Hackathons (RQ1)

We found that startup founders attended hackathons for motivations related and unrelated to their startups (see Table 2). SF2 attended a hackathon to receive feedback about an idea related to the startup, SF5 attended a hackathon to develop the initial startup product, and SF6 attended to develop the skills of the startup team. This points towards hackathons being perceived as beneficial to startup founders not only in terms of supporting product development but mentoring and skills training as well.

Some startup founders, however, also attended hackathons based on personal interests unrelated to their startups: SF1 participated in a hackathon as a mentor, and SF3 participated in a hackathon to create a new startup in addition to an already existing startup. Moreover, some of the motivations of startup founders to attend hackathons

Table 2. Motivations of startup founders to attend hackathons.

SF1-6	Related to existing startup	Unrelated to existing startup
SF1	No	Participating as a mentor to provide feedback to teams
SF2	Learning/Networking/Getting feedback about an idea related to the startup	No
SF3	No	Creating a new startup
SF4	No	Developing a prototype/Learning about a topic of personal interest
SF5	Developing the prototype of the startup product	Participating as a mentor to provide feedback to teams
SF6	Developing the skills of the startup team	No

changed over time: SF4 developed the first prototype of their startup at a hackathon but currently attends hackathons to learn about topics of her/his interest. Similarly, SF5 once attended a hackathon to develop a startup prototype but since then has attended hackathons to network and meet new people. This may indicate that startup founders go to hackathons but do not necessarily work on their startup, and that building a product is only one of many motivations.

5.2 Perceived Benefits of Startup Founders (RQ2)

Most startup founders achieved their goals, both related and unrelated to their existing startups at the time of the hackathon (see Table 3). SF2, who attended a hackathon to receive feedback about an idea related to the startup and was able to do so by teaming up with people who were knowledgeable in that field. In addition, SF6, who attended hackathons to develop the skills of the startup team, was also able to create various prototypes with them. This points towards hackathon participants being able to achieve their goals related to entrepreneurship by taking their own initiative and using aspects of the hackathon setting in accordance with their own needs. However, not all the hackathon goals of the startup founders were achieved, e.g., SF3 took part in a hackathon to create a startup, but despite winning an award and obtaining funding, the team abandoned the project. In this case, despite benefiting from various aspects of the setting, the startup did not take off, as opposed to SF4, who continued developing a startup after the hackathon ended. In this case, to support a startup after the hackathon has ended, market validation appeared to be more valuable than awards.

Some of the perceived hackathon benefits were unexpected. SF1 did not attend a hackathon to support her/his startup, as it had not been founded yet, but at the hackathon s/he met a designer who would become a temporary startup team member. Similarly, SF5 attended a hackathon as a mentor to give teams feedback, but unexpectedly met with her/his future employer. On another occasion, SF5 attended a hackathon to develop the initial startup product, but focused on learning about business management instead. This points towards hackathons supporting networking by the presence of diverse participants

Table 3. Perceived benefits of startup founders.

SF1-6	Related to existing startup	Unrelated to existing startup
SF1	Meeting a temporary startup member	Networking, Creation of company
SF2	Learning, Networking, Getting feedback about an idea related to the startup	No
SF3	No	Developing a prototype
SF4	No	Startup prototype/ Learning about a topic of personal interest
SF5	No	Learning about product development/Career development
SF6	Developing the skills of the startup team	No

and team formation, as well as learning, that is supported by working on a project and mentoring.

5.3 Beneficial Aspects of the Hackathon Setting (RQ3)

Various aspects of the hackathon setting were perceived as beneficial to the achievement of the aforementioned goals of startup founders at hackathons (**RQ3**):

- **Participant presentations.** Pitching an idea related to the startup field allowed SF2 to meet new people who were knowledgeable in that field and that gave her/him expert advice.
- **Developing a project (Hacking).** SF2 also learned about a field related to the startup by working with the hackathon team on a prototype. Similarly, SF4 and her/his team practiced their prototyping skills by developing a prototype.
- **Information material.** SF5 received feedback from the mentors about the pitch for the final presentation. The organizers also gave participants a document that explained the format of the pitch and the topics that needed to be addressed. This document allowed SF5 to learn and explore various aspects of the startup that s/he had not thought of before, such as potential ways to monetize the prototype, which were helpful when discussing funding possibilities with potential investors.
- **Mentors.** Mentors helped startup founders to learn about topics related to the startup (SF2, SF5) and a personal topic of interest (SF4).
- **Changes of roles during the event.** SF1 and SF5 changed from their roles as mentors to hackathon participants. Switching roles allowed them to work with other participants in a team and win a prize (SF1) and obtain employment (SF5).
- **Team formation.** For SF1 and SF5, team formation allowed them to meet people they would work with after the hackathon ended. For SF2, working with a team was helpful for learning. Finally, for SF3, SF4, and SF6, team formation allowed them to create a prototype with the help of their teammates.
- **Awards.** For SF1, winning an award at the hackathon was considered useful as s/he networked with new people s/he met during the mentoring process after the hackathon

ended. However, SF3 mentioned that the type of award the hackathon team received did not offer the necessary support for the team to continue working on their project after the hackathon ended, and the other hackathon award that SF3 won has not been claimed yet. Similarly, SF4 won a hackathon award that s/he claimed was not useful for developing the hackathon project further.

6 Discussion

Some of our findings of the hackathon goals of startup founders (**RQ1**) match the findings from previous research (see Sect. 2). **Learning** as a hackathon motivation [5] was mentioned in our study by SF2 and SF4, who attended hackathons to learn about topics related (SF2) and unrelated to their startups (SF4). This points towards hackathons allowing for a multitude of learning opportunities, such as learning from working on a project [46] and learning from mentors [30]. Learning is also an essential factor for startups [1] to improve their business and product development. **Networking** was also a motivation to attend hackathons that was mentioned in our study by SF2, SF4, and SF5. It has also been addressed [5] as one of the most popular motivations to attend hackathons, and as a helpful aspect for startups [8] as founders can learn from experts and peers about how to solve startup problems. **Building a prototype** [26] was mentioned by almost all startup founders as a motivation to attend hackathons. It is evident why these findings match, as hackathons are events that focus essentially on the development of projects. However, in community settings or collegiate settings, the main focus of the participants and the organizers might differ [13]. Receiving feedback about an idea was mentioned by SF2 (both as a hackathon goal and a perceived benefit) and has also been addressed by previous research [31]. However, other motivations, such as promoting an idea to the public, finding suitable employees, achieving status and reputation, attracting investors, and winning prizes [21, 31], were not mentioned by startup founders in our study. One of the reasons this occurred was explained by SF4, who mentioned that there were issues concerning IP rights at hackathons that restrained her/him from sharing new startup ideas, which has also been addressed by previous research work [23].

Regarding how the motivations of founders matched the current challenges of their startups, we found that some of them attended hackathons in relation to those challenges. The startup of SF5 was at the inception stage, and SF5 went with the startup team to develop the first initial version of their product at a hackathon, which matches the main challenges of a startup at an initial stage [22]. Moreover, SF6, whose startup was at the growth stage, used the hackathon as a chance to improve the skills of the startup team. However, most startup founders did not attend hackathons to solve startup challenges in relation to their current stage (SF1, SF2, SF3, SF4).

We also found that the perceived benefits of entrepreneurial hackathons addressed in literature matched those addressed by the startup founders in our study (**RQ2**). **Learning** as a hackathon benefit [17] was mentioned in our study by SF2, SF4, SF5, although the latter had no learning expectations for the hackathon. **Networking** [28] was mentioned by most startup founders (SF1, SF2, SF4, SF5). However, **developing the skills of the startup team** was mentioned by SF4 in our study, but it has not been addressed by previous research. Startup founders mentioned other perceived benefits, such as the recruitment of a temporary startup team member and finding employment. These were unexpected hackathon benefits that might have been related to the startup founders (SF1, SF5) switching roles during the hackathon from mentors to participants. Changing roles during a hackathon and achieving unexpected benefits implies that organizers should, to a certain extent, allow participants to change their initial goals and develop their own strategies to achieve new goals. This unexpected behavior led to beneficial results for the startup founders.

Regarding the aspects of the setting that supported or hindered the achievement of the goals of participants (**RQ3**), we found that mentors, participant presentations, information material, energizing activities, and allowing for role changes were beneficial for startup founders. However, not all of these findings overlap with the connections found in previous research [27]. It has been found that the presence of mentors at hackathons is beneficial to the participants [30], but it is still unknown how allowing role changes could affect participants under other circumstances. Moreover, even when some of the hackathon teams won awards (SF1, SF3, SF4), the startup founders mentioned that it was not enough to continue working on their projects. This matches with the findings of previous research that points towards the lack of funding [39] being one of the major reasons hackathon teams stop working on their projects after the hackathon, and that awarding teams with more substantial prizes to ensure that they continue working on their projects [40] could be a way to solve this issue. Some research gaps remain about the experience of participants (including startup founders) at entrepreneurial hackathons. The connection between the goals of participants and their intention of continuing working on their projects after the hackathon ends is still unknown, but we took a first step towards covering this gap.

7 Implications

Based on our findings, we suggest that organizers of entrepreneurial hackathons consider the different motivations of participants for attending hackathons and apply the aspects of the setting the startup founders mentioned to be beneficial for their hackathon experience. Moreover, we suggest entrepreneurs who are thinking about attending a hackathon take into account all the benefits of hackathons beyond team formation and developing a prototype. One of those benefits is networking. Our findings indicated that networking at hackathons allowed startup founders to meet new people who became valuable to the development of their careers, and their startups.

8 Limitations

We involved a small sample of startup founders as only a few had been to a hackathon and addressed their individual experiences as opposed to the experiences of the various hackathon teams, which limits the generalizability of our findings regarding the connection between the hackathon setting and the perceived benefits. Future research work regarding the hackathon goals of startup founders featuring a larger sample size may also obtain different findings. Moreover, our findings were based on the perceptions of startup founders about hackathons that took place years ago in collocated spaces, thus, important nuances that could have changed the direction of our conclusions might have been omitted.

9 Conclusion

This paper contributes to our understanding of how entrepreneurial hackathons can support startups by presenting an overview of the motivations of startup founders for taking part in entrepreneurial hackathons, as well as their perceived benefits and how the setting helped them achieve their goals. We found that startup founders take part in hackathons motivated by reasons related to their startup. Those reasons can also change during the hackathon and lead to unexpected outcomes. These benefits are supported by certain aspects of the setting, such as team formation, participant presentations, and unrestrictive participation guidelines. These aspects can be applied to future hackathons that aim to encourage entrepreneurial behavior, create startups, and support the development of startups at various stages. We are currently in the progress of running a larger scale survey study with the aim to support the creation of guidelines about how startups at various stages can benefit from hackathons.

References

1. Afonso, P., Fernandes, J.M.: Determinants for the success of software startups: insights from a regional cluster. In: Wnuk, K., Brinkkemper, S. (eds.) ICSOB 2018. LNBIP, vol. 336, pp. 127–141. Springer, Cham (2018). https://doi.org/10.1007/978-3-030-04840-2_9
2. Assyne, N., Wiafe, I.: A dynamic software startup competency model. In: Hyrynsalmi, S., Suoranta, M., Nguyen-Duc, A., Tyrväinen, P., Abrahamsson, P. (eds.) ICSOB 2019. LNBIP, vol. 370, pp. 419–422. Springer, Cham (2019). https://doi.org/10.1007/978-3-030-33742-1_35
3. Avila-Merino, A.: Learning by doing in business education. Using hackathons to improve the teaching and learning of entrepreneurial skills. J. Entrep. Educ. **22**(1), 1–13 (2019)
4. Bazen, J.: Analysis of the effects of creative hackathons on participants, challenge providers and the entrepreneurial ecosystem (2018)
5. Briscoe, G.: Digital innovation: the hackathon phenomenon. Creativeworks London **6**, 1–13 (2014)
6. Bubbar, K., Shukla, D.S.: Promoting entrepreneurial practice by cramming a product development project over a weekend. PCEEA (2019)
7. Byrne, J.R., et al.: An IoT and wearable technology hackathon for promoting careers in computer science. IEEE Trans. Educ. **60**(1), 50–58 (2017)
8. Cico, O., Souza, R., Jaccheri, L., Nguyen Duc, A., Machado, I.: Startups transitioning from early to growth phase - a pilot study of technical debt perception. In: Klotins, E., Wnuk, K. (eds.) ICSOB 2020. LNBIP, vol. 407, pp. 102–117. Springer, Cham (2021). https://doi.org/10.1007/978-3-030-67292-8_8
9. Cobham, D., et al.: From appfest to entrepreneurs: using a hackathon event to seed a university student-led enterprise. Presented at the International Technology, Education and Development Conference, Valencia, Spain, March 2017
10. Cobham, D., et al.: From hackathon to student enterprise: an evaluation of creating successful and sustainable student entrepreneurial activity initiated by a university hackathon. Presented at the International Conference on Education and New Learning Technologies, Barcelona, Spain, March 2017

11. Crowne, M.: Why software product startups fail and what to do about it. Evolution of software product development in startup companies. In: IEEE International Engineering Management Conference, pp. 338–343. IEEE, Cambridge (2002)
12. DePasse, J.W., et al.: Less noise, more hacking: how to deploy principles from MIT'S hacking medicine to accelerate health care. Int. J. Technol. Assess. Health Care **30**(3), 260–264 (2014)
13. Drouhard, M., et al.: A typology of hackathon events. Presented at the Conference on Computer-Supported Cooperative Work and Social Media (2017)
14. Frey, F.J., Luks, M.: The innovation-driven hackathon: one means for accelerating innovation. In: Proceedings of the 21st European Conference on Pattern Languages of Programs - EuroPlop 2016, pp. 1–11. ACM Press, Kaufbeuren (2016)
15. Gama, K., et al.: Hackathons in the formal learning process. In: Proceedings of the 23rd Annual ACM Conference on Innovation and Technology in Computer Science Education - ITiCSE 2018, pp. 248–253. ACM Press, Larnaca (2018)
16. Gama, K., et al.: Mapathons and hackathons to crowdsource the generation and usage of geographic data. In: Proceedings of the International Conference on Game Jams, Hackathons and Game Creation Events 2019 - ICGJ 2019, pp. 1–5. ACM Press, San Francisco (2019)
17. Ghouila, A., et al.: Hackathons as a means of accelerating scientific discoveries and knowledge transfer. Genome Res. **28**(5), 759–765 (2018)
18. Guerrero, C., et al.: Analysis of the results of a hackathon in the context of service-learning involving students and professionals. In: 2016 International Symposium on Computers in Education (SIIE), pp. 1–6. IEEE, Salamanca (2016)
19. Hecht, B.A., et al.: The KumbhThon technical hackathon for Nashik: a model for STEM education and social entrepreneurship. In: 2014 IEEE Integrated STEM Education Conference, pp. 1–5. IEEE, Princeton (2014)
20. Irani, L.: Hackathons and the making of entrepreneurial citizenship. Sci. Technol. Hum. Values **40**(5), 799–824 (2015)
21. Juell-Skielse, G., Hjalmarsson, A., Johannesson, P., Rudmark, D.: Is the public motivated to engage in open data innovation? In: Janssen, M., Scholl, H.J., Wimmer, M.A., Bannister, F. (eds.) EGOV 2014. LNCS, vol. 8653, pp. 277–288. Springer, Heidelberg (2014). https://doi.org/10.1007/978-3-662-44426-9_23
22. Klotins, E., et al.: A progression model of software engineering goals, challenges, and practices in start-ups. IEEE Trans. Softw. Eng. **47**(3), 498–521 (2021)
23. Komssi, M., et al.: What are hackathons for? IEEE Softw. **32**, 60–67 (2015). https://doi.org/10.1109/MS.2014.78
24. Lazar, J., et al.: Research Methods in Human-Computer Interaction. Wiley Publishing, Hoboken (2010)
25. Lyndon, M.P., et al.: Hacking hackathons: preparing the next generation for the multidisciplinary world of healthcare technology. Int. J. Med. Inform. **112**, 1–5 (2018). https://doi.org/10.1016/j.ijmedinf.2017.12.020
26. Medina Angarita, M.A., Nolte, A.: Does it matter why we hack? – exploring the impact of goal alignment in hackathons. In: 17th European Conference on Computer-Supported Cooperative Work, p. 16 (2019)
27. Medina Angarita, M.A., Nolte, A.: What do we know about hackathon outcomes and how to support them? – a systematic literature review. In: Nolte, A., Alvarez, C., Hishiyama, R., Chounta, I.-A., Rodríguez-Triana, M.J., Inoue, T. (eds.) CollabTech 2020. LNCS, vol. 12324, pp. 50–64. Springer, Cham (2020). https://doi.org/10.1007/978-3-030-58157-2_4
28. Nandi, A., Mandernach, M.: Hackathons as an informal learning platform. In: Proceedings of the 47th ACM Technical Symposium on Computing Science Education - SIGCSE 2016, pp. 346–351. ACM Press, Memphis (2016)
29. Nolte, A., et al.: How to organize a hackathon – a planning kit. arXiv:2008.08025 [cs] (2020)

30. Nolte, A., et al.: How to support newcomers in scientific hackathons - an action research study on expert mentoring. Proc. ACM Hum.-Comput. Interact. **4**(CSCW1), 1–23 (2020)
31. Nolte, A.: Touched by the hackathon: a study on the connection between hackathon participants and start-up founders. In: Proceedings of the 2nd ACM SIGSOFT International Workshop on Software-Intensive Business: Start-ups, Platforms, and Ecosystems - IWSiB 2019, pp. 31–36. ACM Press, Tallinn (2019)
32. Olson, K.R., et al.: Health hackathons: theatre or substance? A survey assessment of outcomes from healthcare-focused hackathons in three countries. BMJ Innov. **3**(1), 37–44 (2017)
33. Page, F., et al.: The use of the "hackathon" in design education: an opportunistic exploration. Presented at the Engineering and Product Design Education (2016)
34. Perng, S.-Y., et al.: Hackathons, entrepreneurial life and the making of smart cities. Geoforum **97**, 189–197 (2018)
35. Pe-Than, E.P.P., et al.: Corporate hackathons, how and why? A multiple case study of motivation, projects proposal and selection, goal setting, coordination, and outcomes. Hum.–Comput. Interact. 1–33 (2020)
36. Picken, J.C.: From startup to scalable enterprise: laying the foundation. Bus. Horiz. **60**(5), 587–595 (2017)
37. de Toledo Piza, F.M., et al.: Assessing team effectiveness and affective learning in a datathon. Int. J. Med. Inf. **112**, 40–44 (2018)
38. Pompermaier, L., Chanin, R., Sales, A., Prikladnicki, R.: MVP development process for software startups. In: Hyrynsalmi, S., Suoranta, M., Nguyen-Duc, A., Tyrväinen, P., Abrahamsson, P. (eds.) ICSOB 2019. LNBIP, vol. 370, pp. 409–412. Springer, Cham (2019). https://doi.org/10.1007/978-3-030-33742-1_33
39. Ramadi, K.B., et al.: Health diplomacy through health entrepreneurship: using hackathons to address Palestinian-Israeli health concerns. BMJ Glob Health. **4**(4), e001548 (2019)
40. Richter, N., Dragoeva, D.: Digital entrepreneurship and agile methods—a hackathon case study. In: Soltanifar, M., Hughes, M., Göcke, L. (eds.) Digital Entrepreneurship. FBF, pp. 51–68. Springer, Cham (2021). https://doi.org/10.1007/978-3-030-53914-6_3
41. Rosell, B., et al.: Unleashing innovation through internal hackathons. In: 2014 IEEE Innovations in Technology Conference, pp. 1–8. IEEE, Warwick (2014)
42. Salamzadeh, A., Kawamorita Kesim, H.: Startup companies: life cycle and challenges. SSRN J. (2015)
43. Salamzadeh, A., Kesim, H.K.: The enterprising communities and startup ecosystem in Iran. JEC **11**(4), 456–479 (2017)
44. Szymanska, I., et al.: The effects of hackathons on the entrepreneurial skillset and perceived self-efficacy as factors shaping entrepreneurial intentions. Adm. Sci. **10**(3), 73 (2020)
45. Wang, X., Edison, H., Bajwa, S.S., Giardino, C., Abrahamsson, P.: Key challenges in software startups across life cycle stages. In: Sharp, H., Hall, T. (eds.) XP 2016. LNBIP, vol. 251, pp. 169–182. Springer, Cham (2016). https://doi.org/10.1007/978-3-319-33515-5_14
46. Warner, J., Guo, P.J.: Hack.edu: examining how college hackathons are perceived by student attendees and non-attendees. In: Proceedings of the 2017 ACM Conference on International Computing Education Research - ICER 2017, pp. 254–262. ACM Press, Tacoma (2017)

User Experience Practices in Early-Stage Software Startups - An Exploratory Study

Guilherme Corredato Guerino[1(✉)], Nayra Suellen Borges Cruz Dias[2], Rafael Chanin[3], Rafael Prikladnicki[3], Renato Balancieri[2], and Gislaine Camila Lapasini Leal[1]

[1] State University of Maringá, Maringá, Brazil
{gcguerino,gclleal}@uem.br
[2] State University of Paraná, Apucarana, Brazil
renato.balancieri@unespar.edu.br
[3] Pontifical Catholic University of Rio Grande do Sul, Porto Alegre, Brazil
{rafael.chanin,rafael.prikladnicki}@pucrs.br

Abstract. Early-stage software startups have specific challenges that need to be overcome to survive in the market, e.g., acquiring initial investment, managing multiple tasks, and delivering value to the customer. Thus, User Experience (UX) practices can leverage the product value creation of these startups. Although UX practices are consolidated in the literature and the industry, it is necessary to verify how early-stage software startups have applied these practices because of their challenges. Therefore, the goal of this paper was to investigate how early-stage software startups use UX practices. We interviewed five early-stage software startups, represented by six employees divided between UX designers and developers. After qualitative analysis of the responses obtained, we identified that the startups have some specific reasons for using the practices, such as support in building the minimum viable product and fostering mentoring programs. Besides, we observed that these software startups understand that UX practices can generate value for the customer, the product, and potential investors. Furthermore, we identified several challenges these startups face when using UX practices, linked to the small team, users participating in the practices, methodology, time, and investment. Finally, we synthesize the main findings of our research into a set of five recommendations for early-stage software startups when using UX practices, among them the use of the results of UX practices to generate value for investors and the development of strategies to identify and engage users.

Keywords: Software startups · Early-stage · User experience

1 Introduction

Software startups develop innovative products in a challenging context, operating with a small team, lack of resources, fast growth [11], besides have rapid evolution, thin margins of error, and goals that are often misaligned with the

X. Wang et al. (Eds.): ICSOB 2021, LNBIP 434, pp. 122–136, 2021.
https://doi.org/10.1007/978-3-030-91983-2_10

stakeholders [9]. In the early stages of a software startup, the main goal is to meet market demand by developing a business model for its products and services [2]. However, many startups fail in the early stages due to inconsistency between what the startup understands about the market problem and what it is proposing [4]. Thus, the literature addresses topics that can assist software startups in their development and growth process, such as technical debt management, risk management, and user experience (UX) [14].

According to ISO-9241 [8], UX is the "user's perceptions and responses that result from the use and/or anticipated use of a system, product or service." For the Nielsen Norman Group [10], UX "encompasses all aspects of the end-user's interaction with the company, its services, and its products." Both definitions show that UX, as the name implies, has a total focus on the user, and the opinions of that user impact the decisions the company will make regarding the product or service. Some scientific papers investigate the use of UX practices in software startups which, although challenging, generates value and competitive advantage [6,7,13].

However, early-stage software startups survive in an uncertain context and have specific challenges that may impact the use of UX practices, such as acquiring first paying customers, acquiring initial funding, managing multiple tasks, targeting a niche market, among others [3]. Therefore, our paper aims to investigate how early-stage software startups have applied UX practices in their development process. In this way, we formulated two research questions (RQ):

- RQ1: How do early-stage software startups use UX practices?
- RQ2: What benefits and challenges are associated with applying UX practices in startups?

To answer these two RQs, we conducted semi-structured interviews with five early-stage software startups, represented by six employees, among UX designers and developers. Our results show that startups have some reasons for using the practices, motivated mainly by mentoring programs. However, the startups reported some challenges when using UX practices, linked to the small team, time, users participating in the practices, and practice methodologies. Moreover, our results also show that, even though their use is challenging, startups in the early stages can see the value that UX practices generate for the product, investors, and users.

The results of the qualitative analysis were synthesized into five recommendations for UX work in early-stage software startups. These recommendations contribute to software startup professionals with insights on the use of UX practices from the moment of creation of the company. In this way, we intend to motivate these professionals by showing the benefits of using these practices and alerting them to the main challenges reported. Furthermore, UX researchers can benefit from our results to conduct further studies for the creation, adaptation, experimentation, or evolution of UX practices that benefit software startups in the early stages.

The remainder of this paper is divided as follows: Sect. 2 presents related work on UX and software startups. Section 3 shows the method used in this research. Section 4 presents the results found. Section 5 shows the discussion, recommendations, and threats to validity. Finally, Sect. 6 presents the conclusions and future work.

2 Related Work

Research involving UX practices at software startups is still scarce but has been growing in recent years. Hokkanen and Väänänen-Vainio-Mattila [6] conducted interviews with eight startups in Finland to understand the practices they used and future needs regarding UX work. From the results, the authors highlight some contributions for startups professionals, such as the need to be skilled at collecting and analyzing information from users, apply quick methods of interviews, surveys, and tests, strive to find users, prepare for the feedback and data they will receive, and create a UX strategy. The authors conclude the article by stating that further investigations of startups from different markets and locations are needed to generalize the results.

Hokkanen et al. [5] also interviewed eight startups from Finland to identify a UX strategy for these companies. As a result, the authors identified skills and practices that startups find helpful in creating UX for early product versions, which are: graphic design skills, collecting feedback, producing a minimal implementation that brings value to users, user testing, usability theories or heuristics, recognizing good interface solutions from other products and emulating them, social skills, and iterative process.

Another study by Hokkanen et al. [7] investigated the factors that affect UX work in startups through a survey with twenty participants. The strategy was one of the identified factors, divided into strategic choices in resource allocation and product quality. The quality of the team was also another factor, being divided into UX expertise, domain expertise, and the team's mindset. Also, the authors identified that user feedback and involvement impact the UX work, being part of the user interaction factor.

Silveira et al. [13] surveyed 88 startup professionals to identify how startups deal with UX work and how relevant UX is for these professionals. As a result, the authors suggest six challenges in UX work for startups: combine UX work with agile practices, make practices leaner for UX work, adjust the pace of UX work, align UX work with the business model and user needs, train and develop skills to perform UX activities, and conduct real user research. The authors conclude by highlighting the need to conduct further research in early-stage software startups and other ecosystems.

The research papers cited above are relevant to the literature encompassing UX in software startups. However, these works analyzed their data taking into account software startups of different life stages. Thus, our work aims to contribute to the literature by directing the analysis and results to software startups in the early stages to enable, through UX practices, greater chances for these companies to stabilize in the market and overcome the challenges they face.

3 Methodology

Our research method followed Runeson and Höst [12] guidelines for conducting and reporting case studies in Software Engineering. The semi-structured interview was developed seeking to answer the two RQs. First, *how do early-stage software startups use UX practices?* Second, *what benefits and challenges are associated with applying UX practices in startups?* In RQ1, we sought to identify characteristics of how the practices are used in the daily life of software startups in the early stages. In RQ2, we sought to verify the professionals' opinions and the vision that they (representing their startups) have about these practices.

Our target sample was composed of professionals from early-stage software startups who are in the ideation or validation phase. The participating professionals could be UX Designers, UX Researchers, developers, or professionals connected to the UX work in the startup. All the startups in our study are part of *Omitted*[1], a science and technology park of a *omitted* university. As a data collection method, we developed a semi-structured interview[2], divided between questions to answer demographic information, questions to answer RQ1, and questions to answer RQ2.

Even though the interview was semi-structured, the division into three parts helped in the conduction. The interviews with the professionals were done online in June 2021 through Google Meet and lasted an average of 35 min each. Before starting each interview, the responsible researcher explained the purpose and asked for permission to start recording. All participants agreed to the recording. To conduct the interviews, the first two authors attended the meetings.

To analyze the data, we used the thematic analysis approach [1] and the Atlas.ti[3] tool. This approach consists of identifying patterns and categories with the data obtained through the interviews. In this step, the first two authors performed the analysis, and the others reviewed the categories. The steps we followed to perform the analysis were:

- Transcription of the interviews: we transcribed the recorded audio of the interviews into text format so that it was possible to do the qualitative analysis. In this step, every care was taken to avoid possible errors. To assist in the transcription, we used the Transcriber Bot[4] tool in Telegram, which helped transform the recorded audios of the interviews into text.
- Reading the transcripts: in this step, we read the transcripts to correct possible errors in words or phrases.
- Coding: the goal of this step was to define codes to represent phrases and ideas that the interviewees provided.
- Creating the categories: after coding all the answers, we grouped the codes that were related into larger categories.

[1] omitted.
[2] https://bit.ly/3zh2MGu.
[3] https://atlasti.com/.
[4] https://telegram.me/Transcriber_Bot.

- Report of findings: after identifying the categories, we organized them to identify which category was related to responses for each of the RQs used in the study.

4 Results

We interviewed six professionals representing five early-stage software startups. All professionals have been at the startups since the moment of creation. Demographics about the startups and the UX practices used by each are shown in Table 1 and those of the interviewees are in Table 2.

Table 1. Demographics of software startups. Legend: **S**: Startup, **NE**: Number of Employees, **P/S**: Product/Service.

S	NE	Stage	P/S	Niche	UX practices
A	4	Validation	Mobile app	Food	Competitive analysis, interviews, user flow and high-fidelity prototype
B	5	Validation	Mobile app	Health	Interview, survey, wireframe, high-fidelity prototype, and usability test
C	6	Validation	Software House	Not specified	Paper prototyping, interviews, survey, wireframe and high-fidelity prototype
D	4	Validation	Mobile app	Health	Interview, high-fidelity prototype, survey, and wireframe
E	5	Validation	Software House	Education	Interview, benchmarking, market analysis, breadbording, wireframe, and high-level prototype

Table 2. Demographics of the interviewees.

Startup	Interviewees	Formation course	Role
A	I1	Graphical Design	UX Designer
B	I2	Graphical Design	UX Designer
	I3	Multimedia Production	UX Designer
C	I4	Multimedia Production	UX Designer
D	I5	Biomedical Informatics	Developer
E	I6	Information Systems	Developer

The demographic data show that early-stage software startups already have knowledge about some UX practices, mainly about high-fidelity prototyping and interviews, used by all startups. Besides, we highlight that the interviewees who work as UX Designers have degrees in graphical design or multimedia production, which are not computing courses.

The remaining data obtained with the answers from the interviews were analyzed, seeking to answer the two RQs proposed in this research. Therefore, the categories identified with the qualitative analysis were organized to assist in understanding each of the questions. For RQ1, the following categories were identified: reasons for using UX practices, working with the data obtained, and participation of other employees. For RQ2, the following categories were identified: value creation through UX practices and challenges faced. The main responses for each of these categories will be explored in the following subsections.

4.1 RQ1 - How Do Early-Stage Software Startups Use UX Practices?

The UX practices used by the startups interviewed are shown in Table 1. Despite being startups in early stages, the interviewed companies use UX practices since the moment of foundation. Thus, some **reasons for using UX practices (CAT1)** were identified. In startup B, the interviewee mentioned the use of a survey with the goal of first understanding the user profiles, the problem they were going to explore, the purpose, and the priorities to build the minimum viable product (quotation Q1 below). On the other hand, Startup A used competitive analysis to understand the design and flow of a competing app to gain insights for their solution (quotation Q2). In addition to these reasons, we noticed that all startups were created within the *Apple Developer Academy* program, an extension course that aims to foster innovation and teach programming. The creation of the startups in this program caused the startups to invest time and effort in understanding the needs of their potential users through UX practices. According to the interviewees, the program organizers encourage the use of the practices (quotation Q3 and Q4). Thus, it is possible to infer that the program that fostered the creation of the startups interviewed directly influences in the adoption of UX practices and understanding the needs of potential users. Thus, the participation of early-stage software startups in programs that encourage the use of these practices is a crucial factor for continuous UX work.

Q1: *"We applied an online questionnaire to understand about pregnant women and doctors. This was right at the beginning, in the phase of discovering our problem, our need. From these conversations, we were able to direct what our problem was, what the purpose was, what we needed to solve, and what the priorities were for defining an MVP."* (I2)

Q2: *"[...] I took screenshots (of the competitor app) to analyze the design, the layout, and I made a flow video [...]. Then I documented, separated what was more and less relevant, and started to build ours."* (I1)

Q3: *"It was from the beginning (the use of the practices). As we were born in the Apple Developer Academy program and there they already have the practice, we had a UX teacher who encouraged and taught us this."* (I2)

Q4: *"This project (Apple Developer Academy) has the intention to develop entrepreneurs within the Apple ecosystem, and they really appreciate this UX point. We have a series of classes about programming about UX, and we learn a lot about this. So from that root, we already had and valued these processes."* (I6)

Because they are companies with small teams, the interviewees reported a **participation of the other employees (CAT2)** that are not associated with the UX work in the use of the practices. In startup C, the interviewee reported that the developers actively participate in the interface design process, mentioning which elements they can develop or not (quotation Q5). In startup A, the interviewee mentioned that the entire team participated in the flow design of the app (quotation Q6). In startup D, the interviewee reported that she conducted the user interviews even though she is a developer because she has a background in the area in which the product is inserted. After analyzing the data, the interviewee synthesized and passed the results to the team (quotation Q7). We observed that the work with UX practices in early-stage software startups is decentralized, i.e., a large part of the employees, whether specialized in UX or not, participate directly or indirectly in the processes. On the one hand, this can be an advantage, since all employees share and discuss the same ideals, making decisions together. On the other hand, the results may contain the bias of people who are not experts in understanding the user or UX practices, and the decisions may incorporate these biased results.

Q5: *"We have our Discord group, so everybody joins in, and it is important that the developers are together because they can see what can be done and what cannot."* (I4)

Q6: *"So we started to build our (application). [...] We designed the flow together; the whole team designed it together."* (I1)

Q7: *"In these interviews, actually, I did it myself. I worked more on this part because I have a background in health. [...] So I processed this data to pass it on to the team, so we could see what other functionalities and other improvements we were going to make."* (I5)

Despite all the challenges that an early-stage software startup has, the **working with the data obtained by UX practices (CAT3)** is a step that the interviewees reported to be very important. In startup A, the interviewee mentioned the need to present this data in a way that generates value to stakeholders and investors (quotation Q8). In startup E, the interviewee mentioned that they spend one to two months interviewing and understanding the end-user to produce results that generate value for their customer (quotation Q9). According to the results obtained, we verified that startups also use the data obtained by UX practices to generate value for investors and customers. It is interesting to verify that the results of these practices go beyond the product experience itself and are also used to add external value.

Q8: *"If you can present this data in a way that is palatable and interesting, I think it brings value. You have to turn it into something commercial to bring value because investors and stakeholders see value in what gives them a return."* (I1)

Q9: *"We have a process before we start writing any line of code, where we spend one to two months just interviewing, talking to the target audience, and trying to understand more deeply how to create an experience that makes sense. This is our proposition, and when the clients accept this proposition, they usually accept to pay above market value to have this experience."* (I6)

4.2 RQ2 - What Benefits and Challenges Are Associated with Applying UX Practices in Startups?

Our results indicate that early-stage software startups can visualize the **value creation of UX practices (CAT4)**. Furthermore, the thematic analysis allowed us to classify this visualization into three groups: value creation for the product, value creation for the user, and financial value creation.

Regarding the value creation for the product (CAT4.1), the interviewee representing startup E mentioned that the UX practices make the developed application increase the possibility of positively impacting the user (quotation Q10). Moreover, even the practices are time-consuming to apply, the contact with the user allows knowing if the product is going in the correct direction (quotation Q11). Similarly, according to I1, the practices allow knowing if the startup will continue developing that way (quotation Q12). Also, for I4, UX practices can generate value to the product in processes that startups go through, such as building the minimum viable product and pitch presentations to investors (quotation Q13). Thus, we perceived that startups see UX practices as a "checkpoint" for the product idea, verifying, from the results of these practices, if the product is going in the right direction or if something needs to change. In addition, we found that the results of UX practices can also be used to prove the need for that product to investors, generating a value to the product that can help the startup get an investment.

Q10: *"We see that today technology has no boundaries. That feeling that at any moment, you can make an application that will go viral, reach as many people as you want. What returns this is the impact it generates on users. It's when you make something so cool, a user experience so cool for a person that they feel motivated to share it with other people. And the moment this happens tells us that we did our job well, we applied the right practices."* (I6)

Q11: *"It is essential to have contact with the user the whole time because even if it takes a little more time, at least you know that you are going in the right direction and not totally the other way around."* (I3)

Q12: *"I think UX comes very strongly with the research part. The impact it produces is to show if we are really going to keep making this product, if there is this pain, if there is this need."* (I1)

Q13: *"The benefit is that you can have a more precise MVP. You are not doing a project in the dark. You will have more basis when you make a pitch, for example, you will be able to base your decision making in a much more concrete and precise way."* (I4)

In value creation for the user (CAT4.2), I5 mentioned that the practices allow them to understand the user's "pain" and propose a solution for this pain, increasing the value for their user (quotation Q14). Furthermore, I2 mentioned that the practices improve the user experience when using the product created by the startup and consequently simplify people's lives (quotation Q15). Also, I5 mentioned that approaching their target audience and showing the solution made users more engaged in helping the proposal (quotation Q16). Thus, we can infer that the startups interviewed understand that this approach to the user also generates a positive result for the user. Therefore, using UX practices from the initial moments directs the development towards a solution that makes more sense to the user, facilitating their activities and generating value.

Q14: *"You must understand what the users' pain is, what they want, if it is a real need, and from there, think of possible solutions and also validate them. It is a cyclical process, and I think this will lead to your product having the value that the user expects."* (I5)

Q15: *"From the moment I improve the experiences, I simplify the person's life in some activity they do."* (I2)

Q16: *"The solution that we made excited the pediatricians. So they were people who were engaged in helping to improve the application."* (I5)

Regarding the financial value creation (CAT4.3), I1 mentioned that UX practices are tied to better costs since better experiences generate better results for the company (quotation Q17). Furthermore, I6 reported that the startup sells itself as a team focused on UX practices and that this has paid off financially (quotation Q18). Also, I2 mentioned that a good user experience increases brand value, citing companies that have invested in this approach (quotation Q19). Thus, we can conclude that the interviewees understand that getting closer to the user also has a financial value since the solution developed will make more sense to the user, who, in turn, will be willing to pay for the services.

Q17: *"You have to transform the results of the practices into something commercial, into money. You have to understand your user because then he will buy your product."* (I1)

Q18: *"We sell ourselves as a team focused on user experience and seeking to bring all these aspects to the technology that the person is developing. We can get an hourly rate above the market average we work with, and we also notice our clients' satisfaction and their feedback is very positive.* (I6)

Q19: *"I think the brand value influences a lot. The better my experience, the more my brand is worth. Apple is there to prove it. It is an extremely valuable brand, not only for this reason, but it is one factor that makes it very well seen in the market. Google is also a very practical example of this."* (I2)

Moreover, the thematic analysis also allowed us to identify several **challenges faced (CAT5)** by early-stage software startups when applying (or trying to apply) UX practices. As a way of organization, we divided the challenges into four subcategories: small team, users participating in the practices, methodological aspects, and time and finances.

Regarding the challenges faced by having a small team (CAT5.1), I1 mentioned that having few collaborators requires the same person to perform several different functions (quotation Q20). Furthermore, I1 mentioned that she made the decisions alone in the design process because she was the only one who had design knowledge while the other collaborators were all developers (quotation Q21). According to the results, we observed that the number of employees that the startup has could impact the use of UX practices, even if it has a specialized employee for the job. This impact is because employees, in general, can perform more than one function besides their specialty. Moreover, working alone with UX practices can overload the employee because (s)he will have to make all the decisions alone. Therefore, the employees must remain united and support the team/person responsible for applying the practices.

Q20: *"My role in the startup is UX Designer, but since we don't have enough employees, I do a little bit of marketing and commercial. [...] We have to be commercial, marketing, research, and it gets a little bit overwhelming."* (I1)

Q211: *"But when it came time to make the screens, they (the developers) didn't decide with me, mostly I did. Because we kind of have a certain view that "the [Anonymous] knows design, let's allow her to do it."* (I1)

Another challenge identified through the analysis involves engaging users who participate in UX practices (CAT5.2). First, the startups reported that it is difficult to find and recruit potential users to participate in their research and testing (quotations Q22 and Q23). Moreover, they have difficulty engaging and extracting information from users (quotation Q24 and Q25). According to these results, we can infer that these difficulties can hinder startups when using UX practices since it is necessary to approach potential users for the results to be interesting. Therefore, startups must have strategies, networks, or external influences to attract these users. In addition, it is interesting that the employees responsible for applying these practices become familiar with existing methodologies to perform suitable data extraction from users who are willing to participate in the studies.

Q22: *"We don't have financial support to do the research; we don't get contacts with people to do research, sometimes we don't get enough people to do an effective test."* (I4)

Q23: *"[...] another challenge is people. Because you are dealing with people, and people are challenging to deal with, difficult to access. I think that within research, it is very difficult to recruit whom I'm going to interview."* (I1)

Q24: *"We could not engage the person in many interviews, and we did not get a good result. Or, many times, we prepared questions that made the person inclined to a type of answer that we wanted to receive."* (I6)

Q25: *"I think the biggest challenge is to get engagement. From the moment I have to do research, and I need to talk to people, be close to people, be engaged, and have contact."* (I2)

Also concerning challenges, the results showed that startups have methodological challenges when applying UX practices (CAT5.3). For example, interviewee I6 mentioned that it is challenging for employees to prepare and conduct an interview without inducing or pressuring the user (quotation Q26). As for I1, the methodology of UX practices is a challenge because the study of UX is not inserted in the curriculum of the Graphical Design course (quotation Q27). In addition, I5 mentioned that she has difficulties treating the results obtained by the practices and focuses on understanding the main problem (quotation Q28). Thus, we can conclude that although the interviewed startups were born into a program that encourages UX practices, they still have methodological challenges when using these practices. As shown in Table 2, the interviewees working as UX Designers are graduated in courses such as Graphical Design and Multimedia Production, courses that generally focus on digital content production and interface design. However, the employee who works with UX goes beyond design and also uses research and validation methodologies. Thus, there is a gap between what they learned in the courses and what they are applying in practice, which justifies these methodological flaws.

Q26: *"Because it is at that moment of the interview, the user wants to help, and he gives an answer that many times is not what he would give in his real life. So this is a very fine line that the person conducting the interview has to cross. And this is something that we still don't know how to deal with."* (I6)

Q27: *"I think the methodology is a challenge because it is all very new, and things are constantly changing. It is not content that is in my college curriculum. So, for those who had the training that I had, we are not prepared for this."* (I1)

Q28: *"Handling this information is a challenge because if you interview many people, you have to know how to focus to understand what the main problem is, so you do not get lost and want to solve everything."* (I5)

Also, early-stage software startups go through a very challenging context that usually involves time and money (CAT5.4). According to the analysis, this context also impacts the use of UX practices. For example, I1 mentioned that if they had a larger investment, they could spend more time on UX practices (quotation Q29). Also, we observed that because there is pressure to get the product to market as soon as possible, startups accelerate the process of UX practices (quotations 30 and 31). Thus, we can conclude that this pressure directly impacts the UX practices' processes. For example, research practices usually take a few weeks or even months to design, execute, and analyze. However, startups need to get their product in the market as soon as possible, either to have a financial return or to meet the deadline of investors or the program to which they belong. Thus, they accelerate some crucial stages of the practices, which could generate significant results for the product.

Q29: *"If we had outside investment, we would be able to put more time into our lives, more dedication, and then we would have more UX practices."* (I1)

Q30: *"We do wireframe if we have a little more time; otherwise, sometimes, we start making interfaces, look for visual references and see what can fit the project."* (I4)

Q31: *"We had very tight deadlines and had to accelerate. At first, we interviewed only one person, but it worked out well because it was someone who has been in the area for a long time and has also discussed this with other colleagues."* (I5)

5 Discussion

5.1 Recommendations for UX Work in Early-Stage Software Startups

UX practices have the potential to leverage the product value of a software startup. However, using these practices has been a challenge for these companies, and the literature attempts to map ways to assist practitioners in using these practices, listing the difficulties and providing recommendations [5–7,13]. Nevertheless, the results covered in the literature to date do not direct their guidelines to early-stage software startups, focusing on the processes of startups as a whole. Through a thematic analysis of interviews conducted with early-stage startups, we identify important characteristics related to how these startups have used these practices and what the views of these startups are about these practices. Our results highlight characteristics that favor and characteristics that challenge UX practices in early-stage software startups. Thus, we analyzed the extracted categories and arrived at five key recommendations that can assist practitioners at early-stage software startups in using UX practices. The categories that based each recommendation are in Table 3 and the recommendations are detailed below.

Table 3. Recommendations for UX work in early-stage software startups derived from the identified categories.

Categories	Recommendations
CAT1 - Reasons to use UX practices	1 - Participate in mentoring programs that encourage the use of UX practices
CAT4.1 - Product value creation CAT2 - Participation of the other employees CAT5.1 - Small team challenge	2 - Integrate all employees in the results achieved by the practices
CAT3 - Working with the data obtained by UX practices CAT5.4 - Time and money challenges CAT4.3 - Financial value creation	3 - Use the results of UX practices to generate value for investors
CAT4.2 - User value creation CAT5.2 - User engagement challenge	4 - Develop strategies to identify and engage users
CAT5.2 - User engagement challenge CAT5.3 - Methodological challenges	5 - Encourage technical training of the team on UX practices

Recommendation 1 - Participate in Mentoring Programs that Encourage the Use of UX Practices. The reasons for using UX practices, category presented in Sect. 4.1, shows that the interviewed startups, in their majority, use UX practices because they were encouraged in the program in which they were created. These programs aim at performing mentoring and directing the product proposed by the startup, fostering innovation and entrepreneurship. Therefore, if possible, being part of this type of program is a kick-start in UX practices for early-stage software startups.

Recommendation 2 - Integrate all Employees in the Results Achieved by the Practices. Early-stage software startups usually have few employees. Through the categories "participation of other collaborators" and "small team challenges," our results showed that collaborators actively participate in the process of UX practices while having several tasks. However, the mindset of these employees may influence the use of UX practices, as many of them are generally focused on product programming [7]. Thus, it is essential to take advantage of this small-team characteristic to show all employees the results that the practices generate since this is an outcome evidenced in the "value creation to the product" category. Nevertheless, it is necessary to be careful that decisions about the use and methodologies of UX practices are not influenced by people who do not have expertise. In addition, it is necessary to pay attention to the overload of work and information provided to these employees, since they usually perform multiple tasks [3]. Using this recommendation, we believe that the startup's mindset about using UX practices can benefit.

Recommendation 3 - Use the Results of UX Practices to Generate Value for Investors. Acquiring initial funding is one of the main challenges faced by early-stage software startups [3]. As shown in the "time and money challenges" category, lack of funding also impacts UX practices. Thus, we recommend that early-stage software startups work with the data generated by UX practices to make decisions about the product and sell the idea to potential investors, a result evidenced from the "generating value to the financier" category. Thus, the data must be analyzed and interpreted in a way that demonstrates to investors the need to develop the idea (category "working with the data obtained by UX practices"). We believe that by better selling the results and the user's need, the possibility of getting an investment is higher.

Recommendation 4 - Develop Strategies to Identify and Engage Users. Conducting end-user research is a challenge faced by startups in general when using UX practices [6,13]. Furthermore, through the "challenge to engage user" category, our results evidenced a difficulty for early-stage software startups in identifying and engaging users when conducting research. Therefore, the UX team must develop strategies to meet this challenge. These strategies can be developed in several ways, involving contact networks of employees, customers (if the product developed is a customer's idea), social networking, personal contacts, participation in events, or partnerships with educational institutions. The important thing here is that the team plans this strategy and puts the execution to identify users to participate in the UX research and generate value to these users (category "create value to users").

Recommendation 5 - Encourage Technical Training of the Team on UX Practices. Hokkanen et al. [7] show that UX expertise is one of the factors that influence UX work in startups. Moreover, according to Silveira et al. [13], startups do not have specialized professionals to perform UX work. According to the categories "methodological challenges" and "challenges to engage users," our results corroborate these literature findings. Most of the interviews in our study who work with UX have a specialty in graphical design. In addition, the methodological difficulties that early-stage software startups have in using the practices were evident. Thus, we recommend that CEOs or those responsible for managing the startup encourage the specialization of these employees through courses that teach the philosophy and methodology behind UX practices.

5.2 Threats to Validity

The threats to the validity of our study were categorized according to Runeson and Höst [12] definitions:

- Construct validity: to mitigate threats that could influence construct validity, we developed our questions based on related previously published work on the

[6,7,13] research topics. In addition, we adopted the interview structure used in [2], divided into demographic data, questions to answer RQ1, and questions to answer RQ2. Therefore, we believe that threats to construct validity were adequately controlled.
- Internal validity: this aspect is related to the analysis of the data and the way it was analyzed. We tried to mitigate the threats of this aspect by using the theme analysis guidelines proposed by [1], a qualitative analysis methodology well known in the literature.
- External validity: this aspect is related to the generalizability of the results achieved by the study. To mitigate this threat, we selected startups that are at a specific stage, in early stages. However, we admit that our study is initial, and further, more extensive studies are necessary for the results to be generalized. We plan to conduct further interviews with more startups so that the results can be augmented.

6 Conclusions and Future Work

Early-stage software startups have several challenges that need to be overcome to stay in the market. In this way, the use of UX practices by these startups can contribute to the product's success and, consequently, of the company. In this paper, we checked how early-stage software startups have used UX practices and what is the view of these startups when using these practices. We interviewed five early-stage software startups, represented by six employees.

From the qualitative analysis of the interviews conducted, we identified some categories that characterize UX practices in early-stage startups, such as the reasons, the generation of value, and the challenges faced. From this analysis, we proposed five recommendations that can help professionals at early-stage startups with UX practices. We hope that practitioners can benefit from these recommendations. Furthermore, we hope that researchers in the field of UX and software startups will use our results as a beginning to create new recommendations, propositions, adaptations, or evolutions of UX practices that benefit early-stage software startups.

As future work, we plan to collect more data about UX work in early-stage software startups through interviews and surveys. We hope that the augmentation of the results of this paper with the results of future research will provide a basis for proposing solid guidelines that will benefit the scientific community and software startups.

References

1. Braun, V., Clarke, V.: Using thematic analysis in psychology. Qual. Res. Psychol. **3**(2), 77–101 (2006). https://doi.org/10.1191/1478088706qp063oa
2. Cico, O., Souza, R., Jaccheri, L., Nguyen Duc, A., Machado, I.: Startups transitioning from early to growth phase - a pilot study of technical debt perception. In: Klotins, E., Wnuk, K. (eds.) ICSOB 2020. LNBIP, vol. 407, pp. 102–117. Springer, Cham (2021). https://doi.org/10.1007/978-3-030-67292-8_8

3. Giardino, C., Bajwa, S.S., Wang, X., Abrahamsson, P.: Key challenges in early-stage software startups. In: Lassenius, C., Dingsøyr, T., Paasivaara, M. (eds.) XP 2015. LNBIP, vol. 212, pp. 52–63. Springer, Cham (2015). https://doi.org/10.1007/978-3-319-18612-2_5
4. Giardino, C., Wang, X., Abrahamsson, P.: Why early-stage software startups fail: a behavioral framework. In: Lassenius, C., Smolander, K. (eds.) ICSOB 2014. LNBIP, vol. 182, pp. 27–41. Springer, Cham (2014). https://doi.org/10.1007/978-3-319-08738-2_3
5. Hokkanen, L., Kuusinen, K., Väänänen, K.: Early product design in startups: towards a UX strategy. In: Abrahamsson, P., Corral, L., Oivo, M., Russo, B. (eds.) PROFES 2015. LNCS, vol. 9459, pp. 217–224. Springer, Cham (2015). https://doi.org/10.1007/978-3-319-26844-6_16
6. Hokkanen, L., Väänänen-Vainio-Mattila, K.: UX work in startups: current practices and future needs. In: Lassenius, C., Dingsøyr, T., Paasivaara, M. (eds.) XP 2015. LNBIP, vol. 212, pp. 81–92. Springer, Cham (2015). https://doi.org/10.1007/978-3-319-18612-2_7
7. Hokkanen, L., Xu, Y., Väänänen, K.: Focusing on user experience and business models in startups: investigation of two-dimensional value creation. In: Proceedings of the 20th International Academic Mindtrek Conference, AcademicMindtrek '16, pp. 59–67. Association for Computing Machinery, New York (2016). https://doi.org/10.1145/2994310.2994371
8. ISO 9241-210: Ergonomics of human-system interaction—part 210: human-centred design for interactive systems (2019). https://www.iso.org/obp/ui/#iso:std:iso:9241:-210:ed-2:v1:en. Accessed 02 Aug 2021
9. Klotins, E.: Software start-ups through an empirical lens: are start-ups snowflakes? In: Proceeding of the 1st International Workshop on Software-Intensive Business: Start-Ups, Ecosystems and Platforms, pp. 1–14. CEUR-WS, Finland (2018)
10. Norman, D., Nielsen, J.: The definition of user experience (UX) (2016). https://www.nngroup.com/articles/definition-user-experience/. Accessed 02 Aug 2021
11. Paternoster, N., Giardino, C., Unterkalmsteiner, M., Gorschek, T., Abrahamsson, P.: Software development in startup companies: a systematic mapping study. Inf. Softw. Technol. **56**(10), 1200–1218 (2014). https://doi.org/10.1016/j.infsof.2014.04.014
12. Runeson, P., Höst, M.: Guidelines for conducting and reporting case study research in software engineering. Empir. Softw. Eng. **14**(2), 131–164 (2009). https://doi.org/10.1007/s10664-008-9102-8
13. Silveira, S.A.M., Choma, J., Pereira, R., Guerra, E.M., Zaina, L.A.M.: UX work in software start-ups: challenges from the current state of practice. In: Gregory, P., Lassenius, C., Wang, X., Kruchten, P. (eds.) XP 2021. LNBIP, vol. 419, pp. 19–35. Springer, Cham (2021). https://doi.org/10.1007/978-3-030-78098-2_2
14. Unterkalmsteiner, M., et al.: Software startups - a research agenda. e-Informatica Softw. Eng. J. **10**(1), 89–123 (2016). https://doi.org/10.5277/e-Inf160105

A Study of Factors on Women from the Tech Sector and Entrepreneurship

Yekaterina Kovaleva, Sonja Hyrynsalmi, Andrey Saltan, and Jussi Kasurinen(✉)

School of Engineering Science, LUT University, Yliopistokatu 34, 53850 Lappeenranta, Finland
{sonja.hyrynsalmi,andrey.saltan,jussi.kasurinen}@lut.fi

Abstract. The gender imbalance on the science, technology, engineering and medical domains commonly referred as STEM fields is a problem in the high-tech society. Furthermore, as women has been underrepresented in the field for decades, most success stories are usually male-driven. To study the factors affecting the women interest to-wards entrepreneurship and tech sector, we conducted a series of surveys and interviews to understand the problems and the underlying phenomena better. Based on our results, the most common factors limiting the interests towards entrepreneurship such as financial risks or leadership skills might not be gender-related, but there are also aspects such as social acceptance, inequality, and lack of role models, which affect especially the women interested in the possibilities on be-coming an entrepreneur in STEM fields. Even if the younger generations seem to be more interested on becoming entrepreneurs, easy fixes such as adding positive examples of success could have a meaningful impact of fixing the gender imbalance on STEM field, and in technology entrepreneurship in general.

Keywords: Women in tech · Entrepreneurship · Affecting factors · Equality · Gender bias

1 Introduction

Building inclusive higher education system does not require equal, but equitable treatment. This implies, that the differences between students should be acknowledged and the barriers hindering participation should be identified and removed. There is evidence [1] on the trend, that women do not choose entrepreneurship as their career path as commonly as men do, and that entrepreneurship in general is considered a masculine [2] line of work. There are also similar observations from the selection of science, technology, engineering and medical (STEM) disciplines [3] as a higher education major, with varying reasons such as lack of universal role models for women interested in STEM field education.

In this paper, we aim to study and identify the factors and topics of interest, which affect the decision for women to select the STEM fields, engineering in specific, as their profession in the context of Finland and the Finnish higher education system. We also study the decisions and reasons on what skills women perceive as important for a career as

X. Wang et al. (Eds.): ICSOB 2021, LNBIP 434, pp. 137–151, 2021.
https://doi.org/10.1007/978-3-030-91983-2_11

an entrepreneur, with an objective to define a set of areas for improvement to understand the barriers and enhance inclusiveness in the engineering and entrepreneurship education. Overall, our objective was to identify and understand *what factors influence the decision for women to select tech sector as their profession*, and further *what factors influence the women of tech sector on their decision to become entrepreneurs?*

Our research group conducted several data collection rounds, consisting of two data collection surveys via participation to a trade fair event focusing on women interested in programming and computer science careers, and supplemented this with an open online survey aimed towards women in, or interested in, the technology sector. In addition, we conducted two rounds of interviews with women entrepreneurs to discuss the theme of women entrepreneurship in technology sector in more detail. In total, we collected 104 survey submissions and 16 interviews describing the barriers and areas of interest in technology sector and entrepreneurship. The collected submission represented different age groups, career stages and varied amount of people already working as an entrepreneur, or potentially being interested in becoming one in a near future.

Based on the results, it is apparent that there are trends such as ability to innovate or solve humanity's problems with the scientific approach, which seem to be general areas of interest for women in the tech sector. There also are some clear divisions between the younger and older age groups of women, for example in the attractiveness of the entrepreneurship as a career. More interestingly, there also seems to be significant gender-based barriers for women to become entrepreneurs, even in Finland, a country which for the last fourteen years have ranked to the World Top-5 countries on the European Institute for Gender Equality's gender equality index [4]; only one third of the respondents considered that there are no meaningful differences between men and women becoming entrepreneurs. On the in-depth interviews, further observations were also made on the feasibility or likelihood of becoming an entrepreneur, and driving factors behind this decision. Some of these were universal, but some affecting especially women were also identified.

2 Related Works and Motivation

The underpresentation of women in the science, technology, engineering and mathematical fields is well-known phenomena. In fact, a study by Griffith [3] observe that the gender differences in engagement of the STEM fields is not only global problem, but a problem that seems persists from decade to another: the underrepresentation has not changed much between the 1980's and the turn of the century, with the gender gap growing wider the higher the level of education was observed. Few possible offered explanations could be the lack of role models and related to that, the general gender composition of the faculty, or the mental investment towards the selected major during the initial studies. Women are not less likely to switch away from the STEM topics during their university studies than men, but significantly less likely to switch into STEM topics from another major.

A study by Wang & Decol [5] proposes a model of expectancy-value perspective model to explain the problems with the attractiveness towards STEM fields; in countries with high overall equality the students are able to choose their education based on their own interests and steer their career towards topics they consider themselves most capable for. In this sense, several other factors, such as lifestyle values and the perception of own abilities play role in the selection of future career paths. Similarly, the Wang & Decol [5] study points out that the nations with high overall gender equality tend to have also lower personal economical risks factors due to social systems, enabling people to pursue careers which cater more to their personal interests, not only the ones that offer them better economical security.

On the selection process towards engineering, a study by Powell et al. [6] identifies prior research and discusses their own observations on factors leading to the students selecting an engineering discipline as their profession. One of the most influential factors identified were technology-oriented childhood hobbies; students who were doing something 'hands on' with technology were more likely to select engineering as their future career. Similarly, the effect of encouragement from the school teachers towards pursuing a career in technology and engineering was considered a major influence. On the gender differences, Powell et al. identify that stereotypical marketing of the different opportunities related to engineering combined with a very limited knowledge related to engineering disciplines drives a believe that there is a 'certain type of women' who choose engineering and science as their profession, and that they 'want to be different' from the general population and expectations towards their career paths. In fact, some of the interviewed women perceived equality as a negative aspect for their career, since it would mean that capable women engineers would no longer have a novelty factor associated with them.

Besides selecting a career path in engineering, science or technology, a career as an entrepreneur is also factor which has been studied and is an area of interest for this study. Similarly to engineering, entrepreneurship is also considered generally masculine career path according to study by Stoet & Geary [5]. Their findings over the dataset covering more than 400 000 student records discovered, that women are underrepresented in the science and technology sector, even from the initial amount of applicants, and this phenomena gets only worse if we take into account the startup companies, and the general willingness to become an entrepreneur. This phenomena is also observed by Poggesi et al. [8], adding that for the STEM fields specifically, the academic women are not very keen to pursue a career of entrepreneurship in general, and non-academic women tend to adopt the viewpoints of masculine culture to "fit in". On differences against male entrepreneurs, the Poggesi paper mentions as an example the trust between the stakeholders, which tends to be emphasized in women-lead start up teams.

A study by Cukier and Chavoushi [8] discusses the women from the STEM fields and their general attitudes towards entrepreneurship in their case study concerning Canada. In this study, they observe that the underrepresentation is not only a problem of the degree programs at universities, it is also a larger issue of the society: business incubators, accelerators and venture investors seem to also avoid women entrepreneurs, causing fewer opportunities for success. In their study, the startup culture is considered "bro culture of alpha males", furthering the problem of women not becoming entrepreneurs, or having to adopt the masculine viewpoints and culture mentioned by Poggesi et al. [7].

3 Research Method

To study women entrepreneurship in the technology sector and the factors affecting the interests and views towards entrepreneurship, we organized a set of data collection rounds to study the phenomena in detail. The data collection consisted of four rounds; rounds 1 and 3 being implemented as quantitative surveys, and rounds 2 and 4 implemented as qualitative interviews. The objective was to first gather general themes and areas of interest from a larger audience, and discuss these observations with the more in-depth interviews with women entrepreneurs in the technology sector, and then conduct the same study to assess the accuracy of our results.

The first and third round were organized as quantitative online surveys, with the general guidelines on structuring the data collection instruments designed by following the principles set by Fink [9]. The design of both questionnaires was to collect feelings, considerations and ideas from our target audience; in the first round the focus was on the areas of interest in technology and entrepreneurship, whereas in the second round the focus was on the obstacles, hindrances and topics identified in the first survey, and the 1st interview round. In general, we wanted to keep our data collection tools and the questions exploratory [10] in nature, to be able to dig deeper into the phenomena in the interview rounds, which followed the surveys (Table 1).

Table 1. Data collection rounds related to this study

Data collection round	Description	Amount of participants
1; 1st Survey	First survey data collected from a general population participating a trade fair on computer science and information technology	55
2; 1st Interview round	First interview round with women CEO's or company founders, discussing the different aspects of women entrepreneurship in technology	10
3; 2nd Survey	Second survey conducted online with women interested in the technology sector, or already working in the technology sector	49
4; 2nd Interview round	Follow-up interviews with women CEO's and company founders on topics of interest	6

The data collection rounds two and four where conducted as qualitative interviews, with the data analysis step using the open and axial coding principle common for example from Straussian Grounded Theory approach [11]. Straussian approach was used, since it promotes active data collection over passive observation, and due to restrictions of access to our interviewees, we needed to organize the interview sessions over online connections. Overall, the interviews provided about ten hours of recordings, and 33 observed factors in seven categories.

The interview population was collected from suitable volunteers identified during the data collection round 1, and later supplemented with assistance from our partnering organizations. The population criteria was that the interviewed person was either the current CEO, founder or one of the founders, or a partner in a new or recent startup that operated on the technology, science, engineering or medicine (STEM) business. In total we carried out 16 interview sessions, 10 for the first interview round, and 6 for the second. All of the interviews were collected by the same interviewer with the intent to keep the context between the interviews similar, and ensure that all interviewees understood the questions similarly. During the first interview, the themes were focused on topics such as personal values, personal background, business practices, management style and known problems, with the theme on the second interview round switching towards more confirmatory topics such as support networks, risk management and tolerance, and stereotypes associated to women entrepreneurship.

4 Results

In this chapter we discuss the observations, starting with the quantitative survey data, and comparing our findings against the interviews with women who are entrepreneurs in the technology sector.

4.1 Results from the 1st Survey

The initial survey was conducted with a general public, consisting of women of all ages collected from a trade fair aiming to attract women towards information technology sector, and supplemented with an online survey distributed via social networks and interest groups for women in the technology sector. On the online survey, also a number of men answered to the survey, but the amount was statistically insignificant so they were removed from the dataset since they could not be used as a point of comparison. Overall, we got 55 answers, with 56% coming from women from the age group 36 or older, 38% from 25 to 35 year olds, and 6% from 18 to 24. For statistical purposes, we combined the groups 18–24 and 25–35 to one group, when comparing age groups against each other.

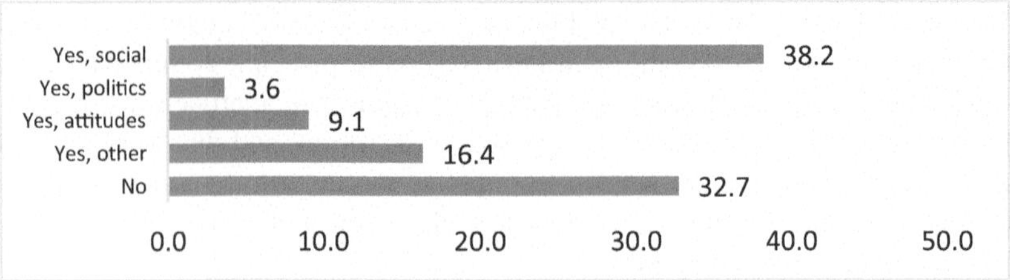

Fig. 1. "Do you think that for women it is more difficult to take an entrepreneurial path", answers in percentages (N = 55)

The first survey questions were about was about entrepreneurship. Overall, 22% (12) of the respondents were entrepreneurs, with additional 18% (10) being already an entrepreneur in technology sector. 40% (22) of respondents had an interest towards becoming one in the future and the rest, 20% (11) of the respondents did not have interest towards being entrepreneurs, at least right now. In addition, the division of the answers were also divided in the age groups: 8 out of the 10 technology entrepreneurs were women in the group 36+, while majority of the interest in becoming an entrepreneur were in the 18–35 group.

The second figure on the entrepreneurial question set was about difficulty of becoming an entrepreneur (Fig. 1). A majority of the responses identified that they feel that it is more difficult for women to become an entrepreneur than men, with the social acceptance and other social aspects being the most common consideration. On age differences, the younger respondent groups emphasize the attitudes toward women (71.4% from 18–35), with 36+ emphasizing "other reasons" such as "lack of networks and connections", "old women are not respected" and "lower risk tolerance" being named separately on the open options. With the "No" -option there as no clear differences between age groups.

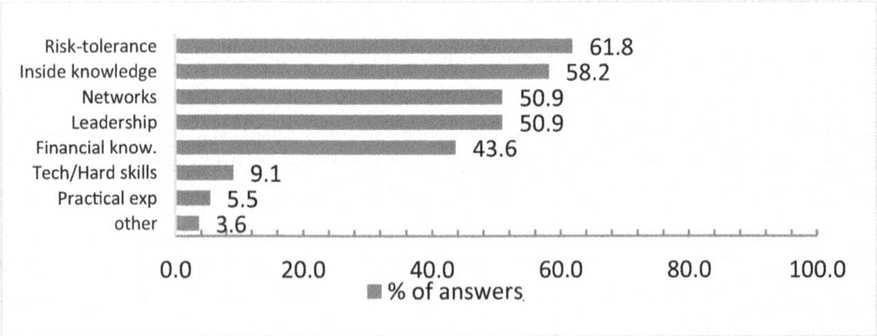

Fig. 2. Characteristics expected from an entrepreneur (pick max 3, no order, N = 55)

Finally, the last item on entrepreneurship was about expected characteristics required to become an entrepreneur. As illustrated in Fig. 2, the most common characteristics were Risk-tolerance (62%) and Insider knowledge (58%). Overall, "Soft" skills were very much emphasized in the answers; "Hard" skills such as technical knowledge or practical experience both got less than 10% of votes. Comparing age groups, the main differences are that 18–35 promoted leadership, while the 36+ group selected financial knowledge more commonly than the others.

Table 2. Areas of interest in technology codified (Total 129 codes, individual codes might be classified to more than 1 category)

Areas of interest in technology	1st priority	2nd prioritory	3rd prioritory	Total
Future/innovation	10	7	5	22
Specific tech/domain	9	7	5	21
Education/pedagogy/research	7	4	5	16
Help people/Solve problems	9	3	2	14
Creativity	7	3	4	14
Programming work /SE	5	5	3	13
Games/UX	3	3	3	9
Machine learning/AI	5	0	1	6
Equal/Fairness	3	2	1	6
Sustainable	2	2	1	5

The final item of the survey was a question regarding the most interesting areas of technology. The respondents were asked to name three most interesting technologies or areas of interest they find appealing in the order of their personal preference. For the analysis these submissions were abstracted and combined to larger categories to assess the topics that interest women in the technology sector. The three most interesting areas were future and new innovative technologies, some specific technology, or educational technology and research. Accounting only 1st priority answers, also "technology that helps people or solved real-world problems" was also considered one of the areas of high interest. On more concrete topics, games and user interface design, and machine learning and AI were ranked the most interesting singular areas of technology. The full list of identified areas of interest if available in Table 2.

4.2 Results from the 2nd Survey

The second survey was conducted fully online, and it collected responses from 49 women from the tech industry, or studying towards degree in technology or science. 61.2% of the respondents had a or were studying for a degree in information technology-related field, 12.2% on other science or engineering discipline, and 26.5% were from other areas.

In the second survey, we focused on the aspects of becoming an entrepreneur. As observable from Fig. 3A and 3B, the respondent opinions divided almost equally between those who are considering building their own business and are not interested in it, with only 4% of respondents certain that they would not be interested in an entrepreneurial career. Interestingly, even if 73% of the respondents were graduates or students, in a STEM field, only 41% of the respondents were interested in entrepreneurship in a technology sector.

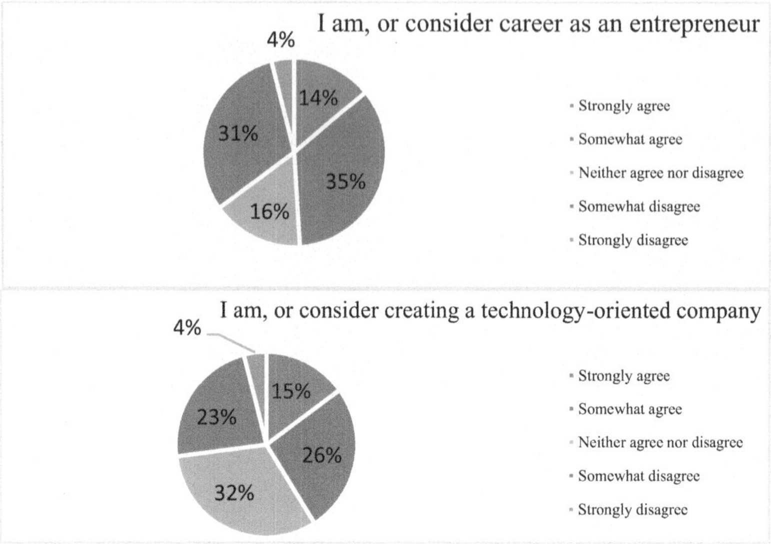

Fig. 3. A – (up) Intention to be an entrepreneur, 3B(bottom) – if agree to A, Intention of founding a technology-oriented startup

Based on our earlier observations on the aversion of risk-taking and other areas that inhibit women entrepreneurship, in this survey we studied these reason in more detail. First of all, as illustrated in Fig. 4, majority (74%) of the respondents considered working as an employee would be preferred to working as an entrepreneur. Interestingly, no respondent selected "Strongly disagree" on this question, and only 12% found out life as an entrepreneur preferable to salaried position as an employee.

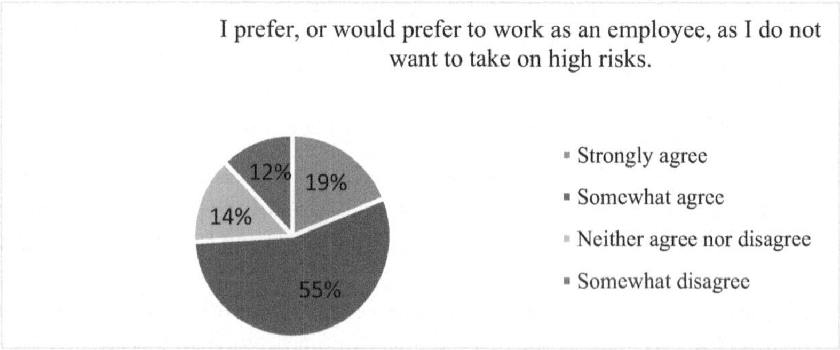

Fig. 4. Risk-based work preferences.

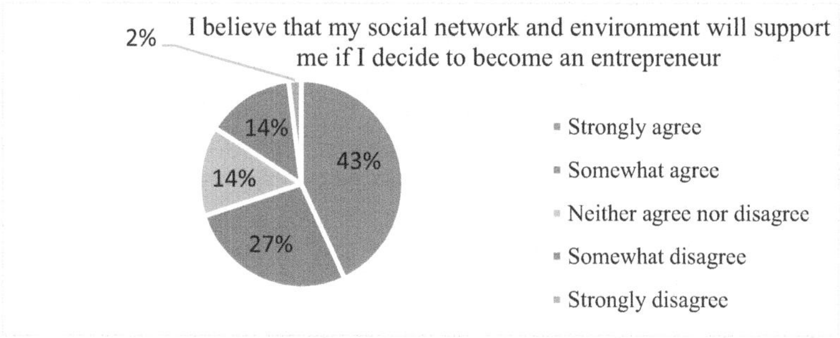

Fig. 5. Environment support

The next question involved social networks, connections and in general the perceived equality of women entrepreneurs. Unlike the first survey, where 32% of respondents mentioned social networks and pressure to be a roadblock for the women to become entrepreneurs, in this survey only 14% believed that their social networks or working environments would not support them. As illustrated in the Fig. 5, in this item not a single responded selected the "Strongly disagree". For a more detailed analysis of the relationship between the various factors, statistical coefficients were also considered by using Webropol analysis tool. The correlation coefficient shows the presence of a relationship between two factors with its value equal to 0.3 and higher. There was a correlation (correlation coefficient equal to 0.3) between the respondents' responses regarding the support of the environment and their desire to build their business from the Fig. 3A. This indicates that there is a connection between the support and approval from the social environment in building business activities or becoming an women entrepreneur.

The second survey also included further questions regarding the background and equality of the respondents in their earlier life. As illustrated in Fig. 6, there were some unequal opportunities reported by women, as 37% of respondents reported that they had been treated in selection of educational programs unfairly because of gender, and 20% reported that they have had at least some pressure on their future career expectations because they are women. Almost half, 43% reported that they were not allowed, or were pressured to select certain hobbies because of their gender.

As a follow up-question on the observations from the first survey and interviews, the second survey also included a question regarding enabling factors for women to become entrepreneurs. The respondents chose the "coming from the families of entrepreneurs" as the most significant factor increasing the likelihood of a woman to choose an entrepreneurial career, while the second most important factor women chose was "rich and varying work experience". These both factors were also present in the interviews, and mentioned several times as enabling factors. From the list of items identified, the least important aspect that was considered is state support. Although the interviewees confirmed the importance of government involvement, it does not have that large impact in practice. The rest of the items can be seen in Fig. 7.

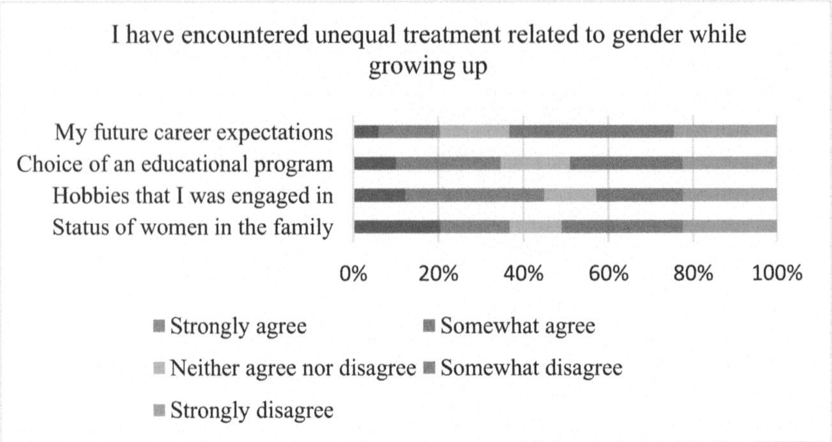

Fig. 6. Unequal treatment in different areas of life

The last survey questions focused on actually becoming an entrepreneur. From the survey respondents, 73% reported that there is a lack of women role models in the business world. As a follow-up, 60% reported that they would be willing to consider entrepreneurship as an option, if they had women role models who to follow, or examples on how women have been successful in the technology sector. Interestingly there was also a correlation between the women who had been allowed to choose their own hobbies, and women who strongly agreed that the technology sector needs more women as an example to others.

As the last item in the survey, the respondents answered whether they considered entrepreneurial activity more advantageous or not. A large number of respondents (39%) answered that business is at least somewhat attractive direction, but similar group did not have a strong preference or opinion if the entrepreneurship is better or worse than working for hire as an employee. The correlation analysis also shows the relationship between this question and the consideration of an entrepreneurial career (the coefficient is 0.44) and the desire to work for hire (the coefficient is 0.55). These correlations indicate that the reluctance to be an entrepreneur is not only gender issue as such, but the lack of resources to withstand potential failure in a business venture, or reliance on the guaranteed monthly income are most likely also important factors beyond equality and gender.

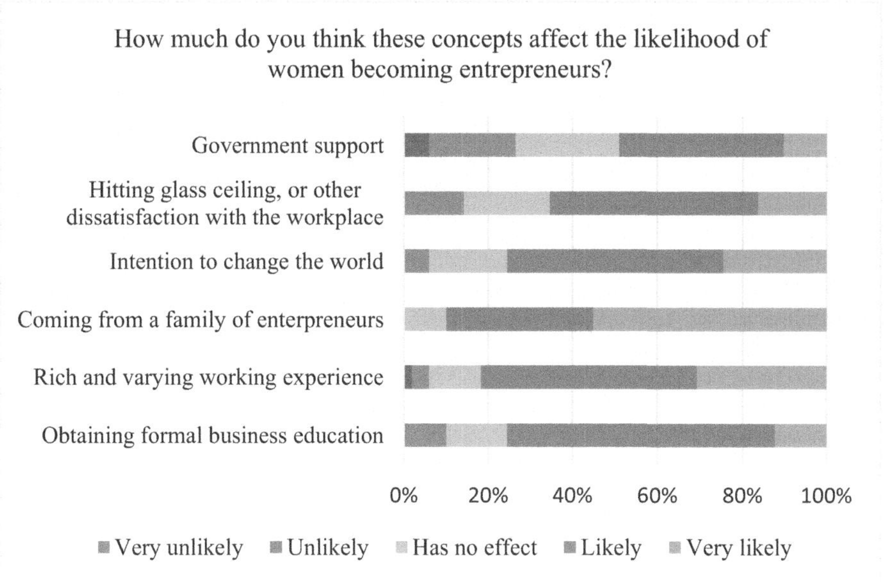

Fig. 7. Concepts that affect the likelihood of women becoming entrepreneurs

4.3 Interview Observations on Entrepreneurship

As a part of the study, 16 women CEOs or company founders were interviewed on their considerations over the topic of entrepreneurship. Over the analysis of the interviews, we came up with a categorized codification of all the observed problems and concepts mentioned by the interviewees, these categorizations are presented in the Table 3.

On topics related to entrepreneurship, we came up with four major observations, which either explain or confirm our observations from the survey, or provide further insight into the results:

1. **Support from the environment is more important than indicated.** All interviewees mentioned that they received some form of support from their environment, government, social connections or family. Especially family support was emphasized as a critical success factor along with support programs or funding opportunities for business start-ups.
2. **Success stories do matter.** Most interviewees agreed that there really are no women success stories, or that basically all well-known ones are from male-driven startups. This is emphasized by the observation that most interviewees came from a family of entrepreneurs, where their parents also served as their role model for entrepreneurship.
3. **Internal motivations** attracted all interviewees towards entrepreneurship; development of a new technology, attract to the possibility to make the world a better place, or possibility to decide freely your next projects were mentioned regularly. Several of the interviewees also ranked the desire to constantly learn new things as an affecting factor, although in these interviews all participants had degree from higher education

Table 3. Categorized observations and discussed items from the interviews

Codes	Main category
Innovation	High values
Intention to make the world a better place	
Social impact	
Building a team	
Making changes	
Impact thinking	
Feeling the need	Business idea
Dream	
Constant search for ideas	
Idea	
Inability to influence something	Leadership potential
Lack of freedom	
Need of bigger challenges	
Intention to build a legacy	
Self-affirmation	
Decision-making	
Network	Solid background
The natural course of things	
Higher (master+) education	
Rich field experience	
Male assertiveness	Networking problems
Difficulties in getting support	
Disrespect	
Biased attitude to appearance	
Customer bias	
Stereotypes	
Quotas	Quotas
Media interest	
Perfectionism	Perfectionism
Pressure of expectations	
Imposed self-doubt	

institute. No-one from the interviews became an entrepreneur "because they had to", nor considered such scenario a viable way of becoming one.

4. **Self-doubt is a limit.** On the hindering factors, several interviewees also mentioned that tendency to self-doubt and drive to perfectionism were usually considered their most limiting factors on their personal success. The general opinion was that especially technology sector needs experience and deeper knowledge on the domain, which is something that other more traditional business sectors do not necessarily require and which might seem daunting since there are only so few success stories.

5 Discussion and Implications

The initial findings from all the collected data indicates, that our observations are in line with prior studies, for example Griffith [3] and Poggesi et al. [7]. There are only limited amount of success stories and well-known examples, and almost all of them are male-dominated. The interviews with women CEOs and business founders emphasized several times that while the women do not necessarily need to become "one of the guys", it seems to make things sometimes easier. In general, the main problems of becoming an entrepreneur are social connections or the lack of them, ability to mitigate economical risks, and having an insider knowledge on how and where to find customers and contacts to run the business operations. Interestingly, even though the surveys and interviews were aimed towards women working on the technology sector, the need of having very high technological skills was not considered very meaningful aspect on becoming and tech entrepreneur. Similarly interesting was the fact that even though the surveys were aimed towards women interested in the tech sector, only 41% of those expressing any interested in becoming entrepreneurs were interested in founding a startup company at the technology sector.

Both the surveys and interviews mention risk-tolerance, financial security from the day job and social connections as leading aspects on why women choose not to become entrepreneurs, with leadership skills also mentioned in the survey. While these are not strictly gender issues, the results also emphasize the social acceptance and support of being an entrepreneur as a social aspect, which is considered important problem especially with the women entrepreneurs. On the required skills, the survey results offer an interesting insight; younger women emphasize leadership skills, while older women emphasize practical aspects of running a business. Regardless, the interest towards new technology and possibility to lead the change, and larger creative freedom were considered the lead motivators towards entrepreneurship, both on the surveys, and based on the interviews.

On the terms of inequal treatment, the "traditional" problems such as glass sealings or other unfair treatment leading to dissatisfaction over working as an employee, wasn't considered a strong driving force; in fact becoming an entrepreneur without strong internal drive to become one was considered unfeasible and unrealistic. This phenomenon was also earlier observed by Wang & Decol [5]; countries with high equality and good social support systems such as Finland people are free to seek employment from things that interest them, so the need to become an entrepreneur out of practicality, or increased income, is not necessary. However, it should be acknowledged that even in Finland, more than 40% of survey respondents answered that they had been at some point of their life treated unequally because of their gender, most usually on their selection of hobbies and interests as a child, and more than one third said that their choices in education were also affected. Overall, the results implicate that the best actions points would be to kindle the entrepreneurial spirits with examples and success stories from women in the tech industry, which would drive those interested to reject their self-doubts, and take the "leap of faith" towards entrepreneurship.

There are threats that should be acknowledged when addressing the validity of our findings and the overall results [12]. For example, validity or data reliability in qualitative research are not the same as in quantitative research such as surveys, so the results we presented in this paper should be explained in more detail to put the results and observations presented in the study into a context. For example, Onwuegbuzie and Leech list several threats in qualitative studies and approaches to qualitative data analysis that can affect the results [13]. According to their study, the most common and severe threat is personal bias meaning that the researchers apply their personal opinions, knowledge, and believes in the data analysis, disregarding the patterns and observations which do not fit or support their own theories. Obviously, this can affect the data collection and analysis, and in worst case scenario make the study unreliable [13]. In this study these risks have been taken into account when planning and implementing the study with several actions. First of all, the surveys are exploratory in nature, with no intention to seek only strong correlations from the dataset, and the data collection and analysis was done by several researchers. In addition, as always with the qualitative data, the interview observations should be only regarded as recommendations arising from that particular set of interviews. Outside this ecosystem, they might not be generalizable, but could be used as a guideline for further research considerations. For example in our interviews, we acknowledge the fact that all of the interviewees were academically educated women, so the interview observations and identified factors may not be relevant on business domains outside tech sector, of the most common problems faced by the non-academic entrepreneurs, as suggested by Poggesi et al. [7] or Cukier and Chavoushi [9]. In this area, further investigation is needed.

6 Conclusions

In this study we focus on the aspect of entrepreneurship from the viewpoint of women in the technology sector. We conducted two online surveys and interviews with the intention of understanding the factors of two things; what are the main motivations for women in technology sector to seek entrepreneurship, and what are the most common hindrances or reasons why women are less reluctant than men to seek self-employment.

The most common motivators for women to become interested in the tech sector and to become entrepreneurs were both related to be able to make something new, innovate, and gain creative freedom to do whatever you wanted. In addition, the most common reasons why according to survey women chose not to try entrepreneurship was related to financial risks, social networks, support from social environment and lack of suitable examples and success stories. Other interesting observation was that even women in the tech sector do not consider the tech skills to be very important for tech startup, and that only 41% of women who considered founding a new business, were interested in tech startup. Reflecting on the results collected from the survey and interviews, it seems that the best practical action to promote interest towards entrepreneurship amongst the women in tech sector would be to offer examples, success stories and support from the environment; all of the interviewed women CEOs mentioned the practical support from their family, friends and the support networks from the government. Similarly, almost all interviewees were from a family of entrepreneurs, where their parents or close relatives acted as their role models. While not a silver bullet, this would promote the interest amongst those who have the drive and personal interests towards entrepreneurship.

As for the future research, we identified that all our interviewees ended up being women with an academic background. To assess the hindrances and factors affecting the decision-making process of becoming an entrepreneur in more general terms, we are planning to extend this survey to the general population, and possibly do comparisons against the different cultural regions, or countries, in our future projects.

References

1. Minniti, M.: Gender issues in entrepreneurship. Found. Trends® Entrep. **5**(7–8), 497–621 (2009). http://dx.doi.org/10.1561/0300000021
2. Bruni, A., Gherardi, S., Poggio, B.: Doing gender, doing entrepreneurship: an ethnographic account of intertwined practices. Gend. Work Organ. **11**(4), 406–429 (2004)
3. Griffith, A.L.: Persistence of women and minorities in STEM field majors: is it the school that matters? Econ. Educ. Rev. **29**(6), 911–922 (2010)
4. Gender Equality Index, European Institute for Gender Equality. https://eige.europa.eu/gender-equality-index/2019. Accessed 9 Apr 2020
5. Wang, M.-T., Degol, J.: Motivational pathways to STEM career choices: using expectancy–value perspective to understand individual and gender differences in STEM fields. Dev. Rev. **33**(4), 304–340 (2013). https://doi.org/10.1016/j.dr.2013.08.001
6. Powell, A., Dainty, A., Bagilhole, B.: Gender stereotypes among women engineering and technology students in the UK: lessons from career choice narratives. Eur. J. Eng. Educ. **37**(6), 541–556 (2012). https://doi.org/10.1080/03043797.2012.724052
7. Poggesi, S., Mari, M., De Vita, L., Foss, L.: Women entrepreneurship in STEM fields: literature review and future research avenues. Int. Entrep. Manag. J. **16**(1), 17–41 (2019). https://doi.org/10.1007/s11365-019-00599-0
8. Cukier, W., Chavoushi, Z.H.: Facilitating women entrepreneurship in Canada: the case of WEKH. Gend. Manag. Int. J. (2020)
9. Fink, A.: How to Conduct Surveys: A Step-by-Step Guide. Sage Publications, Thousand Oaks (2012)
10. Kitchenham, B.A., et al.: Preliminary guidelines for empirical research in software engineering. IEEE Trans. Softw. Eng. **28**(8), 721–734 (2002)
11. Corbin, J., Strauss, A.: Basics of Qualitative Research: Techniques and Procedures for Developing Grounded Theory. Sage Publications, Thousand Oaks (2014)
12. Whittemore, R., Chase, S.K., Mandle, C.L.: Validity in qualitative research. Qual. Health Res. **11**, 522–537 (2001). https://doi.org/10.1177/104973201129119299
13. Onwuegbuzie, A.J., Leech, N.L.: Validity and qualitative research: an oxymoron? Qual. Quant. **41**(2), 233–249 (2007). https://doi.org/10.1007/s11135-006-9000-3

Making Internal Software Startups Work: How to Innovate Like a Venture Builder?

Anastasiia Tkalich(✉), Nils Brede Moe, and Rasmus Ulfsnes

SINTEF Digital, 7034 Trondheim, Norway
{anastasiia.tkalich,nils.b.moe,rasmus.ulfsnes}@sintef.no

Abstract. With the increasing availability of software usage and the influence of the Lean Startup mindset, more and more companies choose to innovate through internal software startups. Such startups aim at developing new business models while at the same time relying on the resources from the companies where they emerged. The evidence from both researchers and practitioners indicates that driving internal software startups is challenging. This paper seeks to address this problem by asking the research question: *how to make internal software startups work?* We examined a unique case of a venture builder – a company primarily focusing on building internal software startups and launching them as independent companies. Applying a Grounded Theory approach, we analyzed data on four internal software startups at the case company. The results suggest that four strategies drive the examined startups: *cultural, financial, personnel,* and *venture arrangement*. We interpret our results by drawing on earlier literature on intrapreneurship and internal ventures and suggest four recommendations to succeed with internal software startups: 1) establish shared arenas for the employees; 2) provide necessary resources for experimentation in the initial phase and increase them incrementally; 3) build up in-house product management competence through coaching, and 4) harness employees' own motivation to develop their own ideas.

Keywords: Intrapreneurship · Internal venture · Internal software startup · Internal startup · Lean startup · Innovation strategy · Venture builder

1 Introduction

Innovation is seen as the most critical company capability for company performance[1], which is clearly seen in startups that even with limited resources and capabilities are often able to outperform established organizations. Anthony et al. [2] demonstrated that the average lifespan of a large company is continuously decreasing (based on the S&P500 index of the 500 largest companies). The short lifespan makes innovation not only essential but vital for many companies. At the same time, innovation through traditional R&D units that are primarily used to improve and modify the existing products is not always a solution for innovation because R&Ds have not been sufficiently productive in the last two decades [3]. Creating space, allocating resources, and systematically fostering an innovation culture have thus been solutions for many companies. Giving a set percentage of time for employees to work on projects of their choosing has been

X. Wang et al. (Eds.): ICSOB 2021, LNBIP 434, pp. 152–167, 2021.
https://doi.org/10.1007/978-3-030-91983-2_12

implemented by companies such as Google, 3M, Atlassian [4, 5]. Another strategy is to allocate dedicated days (hackathons) where developers work together to develop new products and services [4, 6]. Lastly, an *internal startup* is yet another approach that utilizes the startup concept to foster innovation. For example, Lean startup is a popular way for established companies to create innovative software products [7, 8]. Given that software, data, and AI are becoming increasingly common instruments to innovate, it makes sense to differentiate *internal software startup* as a concept on its own, as we do in this study.

Implementing the Lean startup approach in an established company is more challenging than in a stand-alone startup. This is because internal startups, including *internal software startups*, are bound to the current business strategy of the parent company, which is often supported by rigid bureaucratic structures [9]. Bureaucracy and authoritarian aspects of the parent company constrain the internal startups and deprive them of autonomy, which is their fundamental need. When the startup depends too much on the parent company regarding decisions and resources, the startup's speed and flexibility are reduced [10, 11]. Therefore, many internal startups fail or transition outside the parent companies, as in Lokki, an internal software startup in F-secure [12].

Nevertheless, internal software startups remain a tempting approach for numerous companies who seek practical advice on succeeding. The goal of this study is thus twofold: 1) to provide insight into how to best operate internal software startups and 2) to acquire knowledge and vocabulary to better understand internal software startups. Therefore, we in this study ask the research question:

What makes internal software startups work?

To answer this research question, we analyze practical experience from a company specializing in creating and developing internal software startups. This is an extension of the earlier preliminary results [10] that builds on additional data and more rigorous data analysis. We believe this unique case can provide valuable insight for companies that need to grow, nurture, and coordinate several internal software startups; and researchers studying internal startups. The paper is structured in the following way. The next chapter gives an overview of the literature that sheds light on internal software startups. Section 3 outlines our research approach and the case context. We present the findings of the study in Sect. 4 and discuss the research question in Sect. 5.

2 Related Work

Internal software startup as we understand it in this paper is built upon the concepts of a standalone *software startup* and extrapolated to the context of entrepreneurship within an established company (*internal startups*). We will now elaborate on this view by drawing on earlier literature. *Startups* are generally seen as temporary organizations with little or no operative history that intend to develop scalable and repeatable business models [13]. According to Eric Reis, a startup is a human institution designed to create new products and services under extreme uncertainty [14]. Since software with an increased focus on data and AI are key innovative differentiators [15], it is important to distinguish *software startup* as a concept on its own. *Software startups* are risk-taking and proactive initiatives that develop *software products* under highly uncertain conditions by constantly searching for repeatable and scalable business models [16, 17]. Such startups utilize software-enabled technologies to rapidly grow and disrupt markets relying on continuous and agile processes. While having the edge over established companies in agility and speed, software startups also suffer from challenges in their own right. For example, in the early stages, the startups may struggle to develop the features that interest customers, build the entrepreneurial team, and find financial resources [18].

Although the notion of an *internal startup* is relatively new in software engineering, the issue of entrepreneurship within existing companies has been scrutinized by management literature for decades. In her comprehensive literature review Lengnick-Hall [19] outlined four different routes to corporate entrepreneurship:

- *Formal research and development* – units consisting of specialists who focus on innovation and the creation of knowledge as their primary objective;
- *Intrapreneurship and internal venture* – individual employees/teams of employees working beyond their normal responsibilities to develop a specific product or process;
- *External joint ventures* – two or more firms pooling their resources to achieve innovation;
- *Acquisition* – innovation through the purchase or stock merger of existing firms.

There are several important distinctions between R&D and internal venture, according to Bart [20]. First, an internal venture is dedicated to the outcome of the venture (e.g. a product) and not to innovation in general. Further, participants in the internal venture are responsible for all phases of the innovation process while at the same time continuing to fulfill their other responsibilities in the company. Gradually, such employees can be fully reassigned to the ventures.

By combining the concepts of *software startups* and *internal ventures/intrapreneurship*, one can define *internal software startups.* These are initiatives that are developed inside of parent companies to achieve software product innovation [11]. Within software development, it is crucial to reduce the uncertainty related to developing a new software product, which gave rise to the concept of Lean startup. Lean startup [21] was suggested as an approach to iteratively develop both the customer problem and its solution through the build-measure-learn loop. A startup should build a product, measure how the customers respond, and learn whether to pivot or continue, which all together allows to better formulate and solve the customer problem. Internal startups do not have to remain in the company, for example, a *spin-off* is an internal startup developed by an employee and with technology from the parent company and later launched as an independent firm [22].

Building upon the summarized above, we suggest the following definition of an *internal software startup*:

- a temporary organization with short or no operative history
- that searches for scalable and repeatable business model
- and develops new *software* products or services under extreme uncertainty
- while relying on technology developed by individual employees/teams of employees working beyond their normal responsibilities in the parent firm.

Some companies specialize in building up internal software startups and are thus known as *venture builders* (aka venture factories, company builders, or venture studios) [23, 24]. Venture builders provide support to their startups, such as identifying business ideas, building teams, finding capital, and governing [24]. In return, they receive equity and certain control over the stakes in the emerging startups [23]. Unlike incubators and accelerators, venture builders operate as permanent organizations and are deeply involved with their startups up until they exit [24]. These traits make venture builders a valuable source of knowledge on how to best initiate and operate internal software startups. However, research on *intrapreneurship/internal ventures* in the context of *internal software startups* driven by *venture-building* companies seems scarce. Our study seeks to address this gap of knowledge.

3 Research Approach

To answer the research question, we collected data from four internal software startups at Iterate, which can be described as a *venture builder* [23]. This section describes our case context and our research approach.

3.1 Case Context

Iterate is a technology and investment company in digital product development. The 80 employees are software engineers, designers, product managers business developers. Iterate's approach to development and innovation is continuous experimentation. For the past ten years, the company has been named Norway's top three best workplaces (Great Place to Work), and in 2020 Iterate was listed among the 100 best workplaces for innovators in the world [25].

Iterate has three business areas: 1). **Investments:** incubation of employees' own ideas or helping external startups build their product, where Iterate enters as an investor and technologist/design partner. 2). **Consulting:** System development and design on behalf of others (combinations of Java, JavaScript, Clojure, and Scala with DevOps and Continuous Deployment), including corporate ventures. 3). **Software as a Service:** Software tools for innovators, built on insights gained in the other business areas. Iterate builds what they call an ecosystem for innovation, where employees can alternate between working in client assignments and developing their own ideas. In such a way the company acts as an investment fund, technology partner, and employer. Many of the internal startups (ventures) have an environmental profile and cover many domains, such as artificial intelligence for maritime surveillance (Vake), locally produced clothing (Woolit), sustainable food production (Dagens,) and rehabilitation in healthcare (Flow Technologies). Table 1 shows an overview of the startups that we examined. All of these startups completely relied on software for their value creation, which allows them to categorize them as *software ubiquity* [26].

3.2 Data Collection and Data Analysis

Iterate was familiar to us, as we had studied them for five years concerning other innovation topics and found them interesting and suitable for this study. Iterate was part of a

Table 1. Profiles of the internal startups

	Startup 1	Startup 2	Startup 3	Startup 4
Current/maximum team size	5 (executive team)	5	4	5
Composition	CTO, CEO, CFO, developer, DPO, excl. a sales team	Developers and designers	Founder, developers, designer	CEOs and developers
Product type	Application for rehabilitation of people with chronic diseases	Online calculation tool	Application for household management	Artificial intelligence for maritime surveillance
Timeframe	2017 - nowadays	2020 - nowadays	2020–2021	2018 - nowadays

research project on software development and innovation in turbulent contexts. The data collection on the internal software startups (the embedded units of analysis) was performed between October 2020 and August 2021. We conducted 7 interviews with a total of 9 participants (see Table 2), and collected documents and notes from several meetings with the company's representatives (e.g. kick-off meetings on the research project, feedback sessions on the emerging results). For the semi-structured interviews, we used interview guides that slightly differed for the startup founders and the executives. We asked the startup founders questions like *Please, tell us the story of your startup, what was important for succeeding? Which support do you receive from Iterate? What are the plans for the startup now?* We asked the executives about their view on the case startups (*How are the startups supported by Iterate, what is important for the startups to succeed? What are the obstacles that you encounter?*).

In this paper, we present results from the data analysis that was based on the procedures suggested by Hoda [27] in her Socio-Technical Grounded Theory (STGT) for Software Engineering. These procedures are recommended for the studies applying the Grounded Theory approach but are also described as suitable for other types of studies, e.g. case studies as the current one [27]. The purpose of STGT is to set a methodological ground for studying both social and technological aspects of software engineering. This was crucial for our study because understanding internal software startups implies both understanding the technology under development and the social aspects (such as interaction within the startup teams or with the parent company). *Literature review, Open coding, constant comparison, basic memoing*, and *axial coding* with the use of a pre-defined theoretical template, are the procedures that we applied, as we proceed to describe. *Literature review* should be performed both early in the study (*lean literature review*) and periodically as the results mature (*targeted literature review)* [27]. We performed a *lean literature review* prior to the data analysis to identify the research gaps. The *targeted review* was conducted during the preparation of this manuscript to position the results within the existing research on internal startups and intrapreneurship. *Open*

Table 2. Data sources

Startup	Source ID	Source(s) description	Participant ID	Source type	Length of the interview (min)
1	I1	Startup founder	S1P1	Semi-structured interview	60
2	I2	Startup founder	S2P1	Semi-structured group interview	85
N/A		Senior Executive	E1		
3	I3	Senior Designer in a startup team	S3P1	Semi-structured interview	75
	I4	External program manager	S3P2	Informal interview	40
	I5	External program manager	S3P3	Informal interview	30
4	I6	Startup founder	S4P1	Semi-structured interview	55
N/A	I7	Senior Executive	E1	Semi-structured group interview with the executives	85
		Senior Executive	E2		
N/A	M1	Kick-off of the research project	E1	Meeting notes	120
N/A	M2	Presentation of the preliminary results from the data analysis	E1, E2	Meeting notes	30
N/A	M3	Presentation of the first paper draft	E1, E2	Transcript of the video recording	67

Documents: Status emails, pitching slides, and webpages related to the startups

coding is a process of representing textual raw data into a condensed format and where all the data is covered [27]. To perform open coding, we inserted all the interview transcripts into the analytical tool NVivo 12 and coded all instances in relation to our research question (see Table 3). The codes represented a phrase, and each phrase summarized an abstract or several sentences. Following the *constant comparison* technique, the codes were continuously compared within and across the data sources, to identify meaningful patterns [27]. *Concepts* are patterns of codes at a lower level of abstraction, whereas *sub-categories* and *categories* – at higher levels of abstraction [28]. To reflect on the emerging data structure, the first author applied *basic memoing*, which is a technique to document the researcher's thoughts on the emerging concepts and categories [27]. Small texts (memos) were written down and updated throughout the analysis process to describe the concepts and why they include the particular codes. The data collection was carried out in parallel with the data analysis, which allowed for iterative data analysis when the emerging concepts and categories informed the latest data collection.

A pre-defined theoretical template from Masood et al. [28] was applied as an analytical tool to map the relationships between the emerging concepts and categories. Such templates are recommended by STGT to guide the theory development when the examined phenomena are relatively narrow (as in our case "How does a venture builder make internal startups work?") [27]. The template is one way to systematically relate categories and sub-categories, which is the essence of *axial coding* [28]. The application of the template allowed us to map the emerging concepts and categories to the pre-defined fields, e.g. strategies, intervening conditions, facilitating conditions, consequences, etc. This paper reports mainly from the category identified as *strategies* and partly from the category *consequences* that together reflect how the case company makes its internal startups work. In doing so we followed the recommendations by Hoda [27] to report parts of an emerging grounded theory (e.g. individual categories) throughout the process of the theory development. The purpose of this is to acquire feedback from practitioners and the research community to guide further theory development.

Table 3. Examples of applying the STGT analytical procedures

Interview transcript	Open coding	Concepts	Category
"We have what we call Iterate Time. We can use a certain number of hours per month to learn something new or to do something one is really excited about. So we decided to use this time to work until the next sprint" - S1P1	Using Iterate Time to finance work in the startup teams	Iterate Time, Startup teams	Strategies; **sub-category:** financial
"We are a highly autonomous team [...], we take responsibility for the tasks that we choose and never must ask each other "Now you should remember to do this". This culture has everything to do with the culture at Iterate" – S1P1	Culture in the startup team has everything to do with the culture in the parent company	Shared culture, Autonomy, Startup teams	Consequences; **sub-category:** startup teams

(*continued*)

Table 3. (*continued*)

Interview transcript	Open coding	Concepts	Category
"*The fact that the employees own the company as a whole, makes us all wanting to help each other*" – E2	All employees have a share in the parent company to motivate everyone to help each other	Employees and investors and shareholders	Strategies; sub-category: financial

4 Results

We will now present the seven identified strategies that appeared crucial for the internal software startups to work (identified consequences) at Iterate (Table 4). The strategies were grouped into four sub-categories (cultural, financial, personnel, and venture arrangement).

Table 4. Overview of the strategies

Strategy type	Description	Identified consequences
Cultural	**S1:** Exposing employees to each other	Motivation to formulate new ideas, source of feedback for the initial startup ideas, networking among the employees, a lower threshold to ask for help Employees become capable of starting up their own businesses
	S2: Creating implicit norms of taking initiative	Autonomy and responsibility in the startup team
Financial	**S3:** Incremental funding	Employees have time to explore their ideas, the possibility to recruit others to the startup teams, time squeeze
	S4: Shared incentives	Willingness to collaborate, committed startup teams over time
Personnel	**S5:** Highly selective recruitment	Employees' readiness for entrepreneurship
	S6: Executives as coaches	Startups receive support, executives make informed decisions on further investment
Venture arrangement	**S7:** Postponing distribution of shares	Extended experimentation period, the equity is shared among the most committed team members

4.1 Cultural Strategies

The two identified cultural strategies reflect how Iterate promotes a climate meant to create favorable conditions for internal startups.

S1: Exposing Employees to Each Other. The idea behind Iterate is to create new ventures based on the ideas of the employees. Therefore, it is essential to promote an environment where ideas emerge and grow. Iterate has established arenas where employees pitch ideas, give and receive feedback on ideas and collaborate on developing new ideas. The company does it by promoting social events that expose employees to each other and stimulate networking. The executives emphasized that they strive to lighten up the company through several common events that happen on a regular basis (see Table 5). One of them said: "*We make sure that these events are the beating heart of the company. We offer a diversity of meeting places where people can get together, learn from each other, and get inspired […] We do not manage the content in this, but we make sure that this happens*" - E2, *executive.* The employees described these arenas as engaging, motivating, and a useful source of feedback on their ideas. It appeared that the events led the employees to be well-acquainted with each other, which lowered the threshold for asking for help, as one startup founder described: "*Due to all the social stuff that we have at Iterate, we have met everyone that works at Iterate, so we know whom to ask if we wonder about something, and they help because they know us*" - S4P1, *Startup founder.*

S2: Creating Implicit Norms of Taking Initiative. Being initially an IT consultancy company, the transition to becoming a venture builder required a cultural shift for people from solving technical problems to being entrepreneurs. To promote this shift, Iterate trains people at making independent decisions and taking initiative, which people also call "actionocracy". One of the executives explained that if employees ask to purchase new furniture or other things for the office, he encourages them to do it themselves. He said: "*If you cannot buy new furniture for the office, then you cannot build a new company, either*" – E1, *executive.* The norms have an implicit nature, because they stem from people's behaviors and unspoken assumptions, not from written guidelines. Different participants referred to these norms as "invisible principles" (S2P1), "Iterate DNA" (S1P1), and "Iterate culture" that all point out to this implicit nature.

The norms are promoted by numerous means. Even before the actual employment, the norms are shared through student meetings, summer internships, and even through informal networks of the current employees. The norms are reinforced through the social events (see S1) and supported by the close interaction with the executives (S7) who themselves serve as good examples of taking initiative. Arrangements such as Ship-It Day (Table 5) and Iterate Time (S3) also nudge the employees towards initiating and completing the tasks that they themselves find meaningful. Ultimately, the norms support employees in becoming startup founders. In addition, they promote a high level of both autonomy and responsibility in the startup teams, as indicated by this quote: "*We are a highly autonomous team […], we take responsibility for the tasks that we choose and never must ask each other "Now you should remember to do this". This culture has everything to do with the culture at Iterate*" – S1P1, *startup founder.*

Table 5. Overview of the main events

Event	Description	Purpose	Frequency
Ship-it day	Hackathon where people have 24 h to work with totally new ideas or solve a complicated problem. The result should be a finalized prototype or a solution	Take a break from the routine, develop a somewhat finalized product	Annually
Breakfast meetings	An informal 30-min presentation around a breakfast table (before the pandemic) or digitally (during the pandemic). The presenter is randomly chosen at the beginning of the meeting	People get insight into what others are working with, training in spontaneous presentation, an arena for new startup teams to emerge	Flexible
Pitch night	Everyone is encouraged to pitch all kinds of ideas, no matter how good or bad	Lower the threshold for how good a new idea can be, have fun, share inspiration and ideas, an arena for new startup teams to emerge	Monthly
While-we-wait	A mini-conference where people with product management experience share it with the others	Increase people's competence in product management	Weekly

4.2 Financial Strategies

The two financial strategies create conditions for financing the startups in the initial phase and attracting investors for the future.

S3: Incremental Funding. The IT consultancy is a crucial source of revenue for Iterate, but it is also important to allow people to explore their own ideas. To balance these two, Iterate has established flexible mechanisms for funding to increase incrementally as ideas mature. The initial funding is enabled through about 10–20% work time that the employees are free to use for everything they find interesting, important, and meaningful. At Iterate it is known as "Iterate Time" and can in principle be used for absolutely anything. Many startup founders (such as S1P1, S2P1) used Iterate Time to work on ideation and initial user testing of their startup ideas. When 10–20% work time becomes insufficient for running a startup, the founders may request additional funding in form of hours paid for a month of work for the startup team or renting other resources from Iterate (e.g. UX-designer, additional developers). An executive, who is involved in decisions on the funding, commented: "*These are very easy and minor decisions for me because I don't fund the whole course, but just the time that costs much less. And we do this all the way*", - E2, executive.

Incremental funding allows the startup teams to finance their members' work up until (and if) they manage to acquire external funding at later stages. Iterate Time increased the number of startup ideas because many employees had resources to initiate their startups. It also created opportunities for other employees to contribute to the emerging ideas as they could "donate" their Iterate Time by working in other startup teams. On the other hand, some founders struggled in the initial phase because Iterate Time was not always sufficient to perform all the work that the startup founders would like to do, which made some of them squeezed between the startup and the consultant tasks, as shown in this excerpt: "*I would like to have an extra day to do all the things that I prioritize [in the startup] and rather go down 20% in salary to make up for it [...] but I would also like to continue in my daily consultant work*" - S2P1, *startup founder*.

S4: Shared Incentives. The business model of creating new ventures is directly dependent on the employees' willingness to become venture builders. To motivate them, Iterate promotes shared incentives for employees to avoid the competition created by individual bonuses. Being an employee-owned organization Iterate encourages its employees to also be its shareholders so that if Iterate's market value increases, everyone will benefit. According to the executives, this creates incentives for mutual collaboration, as indicated in this quote: *"The fact that the employees own the company as a whole, makes us all wanting to help each other. No individual bonuses at any level, because this creates conflicts"* – E2, *executive*. Apart from being shareholders of the parent company, the employees can also invest money in individual startups. This is mutually beneficial, because the startups acquire additional funding, whereas the internal investors acquire potential financial benefits. When people invest in the startups of others, they may also be motivated to help "their" startup team succeed.

Further, the startup founders own the majority of shares in their own startups, whereas Iterate holds the rest of the shares. This secures the commitment and responsibility of the startup team over time. One of the executives expressed: "*Owning shares gives the feeling of responsibility for caring about the startup over time, and this should belong to the team. Therefore, Iterate owns only 30%, and the team owns 70%*» - F2, *executive*. Since the startup teams own most of the startup many team members are willing to put extra work into the startups. Many startup founders were committed and worked in their spare time, as illustrated in this quote: "*I do not see the startup job as a job. I mean, there is some work in your spare time because it is fun to be able to build your own future*" - S2P1, *startup founder*.

4.3 Strategies Related to Personnel

The following two strategies reflect how the company recruits people and how people are supported in being entrepreneurs.

S5: Highly Selective Recruitment. People employed at Iterate should collectively possess skills that make them capable of developing new products internally. However, having technical skills, such as programming or designing, is not sufficient. Therefore, Iterate invests a lot in the recruitment process to find people who are both technically strong, as well as open to becoming entrepreneurs. A lot of today's recruitment happens among the students through a Summer internship. The highly competitive process (only 9 candidates of 200 receive the internship offer) takes up to 2 years until the candidate receives a permanent job offer. According to the executives, it is extremely important to find people that have an open mindset (e.g., among newly-graduated) and are robust in the face of uncertainty and effort of the entrepreneurship. One of them said: "*The type of people who aspire to be entrepreneurs but also understand how much effort it takes. These are the perfect candidates for us*" - E2, executive.

S6: Executives as Coaches and Co-founders. The majority of employees lack experience in establishing a new business/startup. Therefore, the executives offer coaching to those who work with new ideas. The coaching addresses issues as finding matching venture capitalists (S2P1, E1), distribution of shares between the members of the startup team (E2), and general product management (E2). A lot of coaching and feedback is informal since the executives often are also board members in the emerging startups, which allows them to participate in the decision-making process together with the startup teams. The startup founders themselves decide whether and when to ask for the coaching. One of the executives pointed out: "*If people feel that they need to validate things with us before they start, it will go too slowly. But when things are starting to become interesting, we are happy to be in the dialog*" – E1, *executive.*

The coaching is beneficial for both the startup founders who receive guidance and support and the executives who are thus continuously updated on the startups' progress and challenges. Working closely with the startups helps the executives to calibrate the startup's funding if necessary (see S3: Incremental funding). Further, the level of personal engagement in the startups is a good indicator of future success; one executive said: "*The more we coach them, the more we know them, whether they are passionate and whether they learn. And these are passion and learning we look for when we take bigger decisions on investment*" – E1, *executive.* The startup founders regarded the coaches as important, available, and motivating. One of them described: "*Our manager is very adept at showing how he can help. He's a busy man but always seems to have time for us [...] He is also a great motivator*" – S4P1, *startup founder.*

4.4 Strategies Related to Venture Arrangement

In this category, we describe one strategy that explains how Iterate deals with internal startups during the transition to a spin-off phase.

S7: Postponing Distribution of Shares. Since the team members work on the startup as long as they find it meaningful, they can leave at any time, whereas other members can come in. Besides, different team members contribute to the startups differently. To account for this, Iterate advises the startup teams to postpone the official registration of the new companies until the team has been stable for about 1–3 years. One executive noted: "*Those who want to start up together must date each other so long that they feel like getting married. [...] Also, it is very important to continuously discuss how the shares should be distributed, it is very important*" – E2, *executive.* Postponing the distribution of shares enables the startup teams to extend the prototyping phase while at the same time having flexibility in the team composition. A startup founder explained: "*When we missed people from the team, we still had not distributed the shares. Since we had not registered the company by then, we did not have to do emissions, to buy and sell again. We had only oral agreements until a certain point, it was an advantage for us*" - S1P1, *startup founder.*

5 Discussion and Practical Implications

We will now discuss our findings to answer the study's research question '*What makes internal startups work'?* The overall contribution of our study is an insight into intrapreneurship/internal venture [19] in the context of internal software startups in a venture building company.

Earlier research has demonstrated that intrapreneurship culture predicts the market performance of IT-enabled firms [29]. Our findings also show that intrapreneurship culture is a key for establishing internal software startups. We also found which exactly cultural strategies were beneficial for the startups in a venture builder environment. For example, by *exposing employees to each other* (S1), the case company strengthened networks among the employees, eventually enabling mutual collaboration, trust, and a shared spirit of entrepreneurship. Our findings indicate that when employees know each other well, they are likely to reach out for help thus acquiring access to the in-house expertise and resources. Moreover, informal networks facilitate the self-organization of the employees in the startup teams. Earlier research has indicated that access to the existing networks of experts internally in the company has a positive effect on internal startups [7]. Networking is also crucial for stand-alone software startups because it gives the founders access to people with different expertise and resources [18]. Therefore, establishing arenas for sharing ideas in an informal way (such as the Pitch Night) can be recommended to enable internal software startups.

From before, we know that internal venture and intrapreneurship activities are often financially constrained [19], which is why it is necessary to provide internal startups with sufficient funding. As appears from our results, financial strategies such as *incremental funding* (S3), is a good way to solve the problem of funding while at the same time keeping the startups' autonomy. The startup founders that used Iterate Time could dedicate some hours to work with the idea without any control from the executives. Moreover, the founders could convince others to join their team by "donating" their Iterate Time, which gave autonomy in designing the team. However, merely providing employees with extra hours to experiment does not have to result in internal software startups. Therefore, the startup teams at Iterate received *incremental funding* (S3), which conveyed their responsibility over time and created continuity and commitment. Strategies similar to Iterate Time are used under different names also in other companies (e.g. "15% Time" in Atlassian [4] and M3 [5]) and have two main benefits: 1) contribute to capturing, developing, and testing novel ideas 2) reduce the risks for the parent companies to invest in ideas that may not work. Our findings suggest that x% time strategies should be combined with incremental funding to extract the most potential out of internal software startups.

Further, earlier research suggests that intrapreneurs can be less assertive than a typical top manager, which might create problems as the products grow [19]. Our data also indicated that startups founders might need support from someone more experienced in business, particularly, the executives who functioned as coaches (S6). Apart from being business mentoring, coaching also functioned as a motivational incentive and continuous informal monitoring and feedback. This strategy also helped the executives make case-by-case decisions on how the startups should be funded, in collaboration with the startup teams. Earlier research has indicated that top management support, such as that of the Iterate executives/coaches, speeds up the developments process of the internal startups [7]. We, therefore, recommend the coaching of the startup teams to be performed by experienced entrepreneurs with authority at the top level of the company.

Finally, increased personal commitment and emotional investment are common with intrapreneurship and internal ventures [19]. In line with this, we discovered that harnessing peoples' own motivation to develop their ideas, was crucial to make the internal software startups work. Our results demonstrate that several strategies at the case company aimed at increasing the employees' personal stake in the outcome of the startup. Through *highly selective recruitment* (S5), Iterate was selecting people that were motivated to develop their own business. By creating *shared incentives* (S4) of their startups and of Iterate, the company built up peoples' financial interest in the outcome of the startups while at the same time fostering collaboration. Since the employees through *incremental funding* (S3) had room to work with what they were really dedicated to, they were gradually becoming emotionally engaged in their own projects to the extent that they were willing to work without being paid. *Postponing distribution of shares* (S7) ensured that the equity was distributed among those startup team members that had shown the most commitment over time. Earlier findings indicate that personal stake in the outcome strengthens the motivation of the internal software startup teams [7]. It is further proposed that equity offers both financial and emotional motivation to the startup team members [18]. Our results support these propositions also for internal software startups, indicating that personal stake in the outcome (e.g. making your own business succeed) is the main motivation of the startup founders and team members. Therefore, we recommend parent companies identify the people motivated for entrepreneurship and support their motivation by various means (e.g. financial incentives, work hours, recognition of effort) while at the same time promoting collaboration. The desire to make one's own idea work should be recognized as the main driver behind internal software startups.

6 Limitations, Conclusions, and Further Work

This study provides several insights into how the internal software startups are enabled at a venture building company Iterate, which is a particular type of company. The findings should therefore not be generalized to other contexts without precautions. What works in a relatively small venture-building company like Iterate does not necessarily work in a large-scale environment.

Taking the limitations into account, we conclude that the strategies that companies might apply to make internal software startups work, contribute to 1) more autonomous and collaborative organizational culture, 2) continuous financial resources for the startups 3) in-house competence in product management, and 4) flexible ownership of the emerging startups. Based on the findings, we recommend that organizations who wish to succeed with internal software startups 1) establish arenas where employees can share ideas and build informal networks, 2) provide incremental funding to experiment and establish self-managing startup teams, 3) arrange the startup teams to be coached by experienced entrepreneurs with authority in the company, and 4) identify people motivated for entrepreneurship and harness their motivation.

Further research should address the question of which innovation strategies are/should be used in contexts other than those of venture builders (e.g. in large-scale companies). We also aim to develop a more refined grounded theory that explains how the strategies for promoting internal software startups vary depending on their context and level of maturity. Finally, there is a need for a more theoretically grounded approach to understanding internal software startups.

References

1. Crossan, M.M., Apaydin, M.: A Multi-dimensional framework of organizational innovation: a systematic review of the literature. J. Manag. Stud. **47**, 1154–1191 (2010). https://doi.org/10.1111/j.1467-6486.2009.00880.x
2. Anthony, S.D., Viguerie, P., Waldeck, A.: Corporate longevity: turbulence ahead for large organizations (2016)
3. Cooper, R.G.: Perspective: the innovation dilemma: how to innovate when the market is mature. J. Prod. Innov. Manag. **28**, 2–27 (2011). https://doi.org/10.1111/j.1540-5885.2011.00858.x
4. Moe, N.B., et al.: Fostering and sustaining innovation in a fast growing agile company. In: Dieste, O., Jedlitschka, A., Juristo, N. (eds.) PROFES 2012. LNCS, vol. 7343, pp. 160–174. Springer, Heidelberg (2012). https://doi.org/10.1007/978-3-642-31063-8_13
5. Leppänen, M., Hokkanen, L.: Four patterns for internal startups. In: Proceedings of the 20th European Conference on Pattern Languages of Programs, pp. 1–10 (2015)
6. Ulfsnes, R., Stray, V., Moe, N.B., Šmite, D.: Innovation in large-scale agile - benefits and challenges of Hackathons when hacking from home. In: Gregory, P., Kruchten, P. (eds.) Agile Processes in Software Engineering and Extreme Programming – Workshops. XP 2021. Lecture Notes in Business Information Processing, vol. 426. Springer, Cham (2021)
7. Edison, H., Smørsgård, N.M., Wang, X., Abrahamsson, P.: Lean internal startups for software product innovation in large companies: enablers and inhibitors. J. Syst. Softw. **135**, 69–87 (2018). https://doi.org/10.1016/j.jss.2017.09.034
8. Sporsem, T., Tkalich, A., Moe, N.B., Mikalsen, M., Rygh, N.: Using guilds to foster internal startups in large organizations: a case study. In: International Conference on Agile Software Development, pp. 135–144. Springer, Cham, 14 June 2021
9. Thornberry, N.: Corporate entrepreneurship: antidote or oxymoron? Eur. Manag. J. **19**, 526–533 (2001)
10. Tkalich, A., Moe, N.B., Sporsem, T.: Employee-driven innovation to fuel internal software startups: preliminary findings. In: International Conference on Agile Software Development, pp. 145–154. Springer, Cham, 14 June 2021
11. Sporsem, T., Moe, N.B., Tkalich, A., Mikalsen, M.: Understanding barriers to internal startups in large organizations: evidence from a globally distributed company. Presented at the Preprint 2021 ACM/IEEE 16th International Conference on Global Software Engineering (ICGSE) (2021)

12. Kiljander, H.: Case: Lokki by F-secure. In: The Cookbook for Successful Internal Startups, pp. 68–71 (2016)
13. Blank, S., Dorf, B.: The Startup Owner's Manual: The Step-by-Step Guide for Building a Great Company. Wiley, Hoboken (2020)
14. Ries, E.: The lean startup: how today's entrepreneurs use continuous innovation to create radically successful businesses. Currency (2011)
15. Olsson, H.H., Bosch, J.: Going digital: disruption and transformation in software-intensive embedded systems ecosystems. J. Softw.: Evol. Process **32**, 1–24 (2020)
16. Paternoster, N., Giardino, C., Unterkalmsteiner, M., Gorschek, T., Abrahamsson, P.: Software development in startup companies: a systematic mapping study. Inf. Softw. Technol. **56**, 1200–1218 (2014). https://doi.org/10.1016/j.infsof.2014.04.014
17. Melegati, J., Guerra, E., Wang, X.: Understanding hypotheses engineering in software startups through a gray literature review. Inf. Softw. Technol. **133**, 106465 (2021). https://doi.org/10.1016/j.infsof.2020.106465
18. Melegati, J., Kon, F.: Early-stage software startups: main challenges and possible answers. In: Nguyen-Duc, A., Münch, J., Prikladnicki, R., Wang, X., Abrahamsson, P. (eds.) Fundamentals of Software Startups, pp. 129–143. Springer, Cham (2020). https://doi.org/10.1007/978-3-030-35983-6_8
19. Lengnick-Hall, C.A.: Innovation and competitive advantage: what we know and what we need to learn. J. Manag. **18**, 399–429 (1992). https://doi.org/10.1177/014920639201800209
20. Bart, C.K.: New venture units: use them wisely to manage innovation. MIT Sloan Manag. Rev. **29**, 35 (1988)
21. Reis, E.: The Lean Startup, vol. 27. Crown Business, New York (2011)
22. Edison, H., Wang, X., Jabangwe, R., Abrahamsson, P.: Innovation initiatives in large software companies: a systematic mapping study. Inf. Softw. Technol. **95**, 1–14 (2018). https://doi.org/10.1016/j.infsof.2017.12.007
23. Köhler, R., Baumann, O.: Organizing a venture factory: company builder incubators and the case of rocket internet. In: Social Science Research Network, Rochester, NY (2016). https://doi.org/10.2139/ssrn.2700098
24. McDermott, J.: What is a venture builder and what do they do? https://www.linkedin.com/pulse/what-venture-builder-do-jeff-mcdermott/. Accessed 05 Aug 2021
25. Fast Company: Best Workplaces for Innovators 2020. https://www.fastcompany.com/90527870/best-workplaces-for-innovators-2020. Accessed 08 July 2021
26. Nguyen-Duc, A., Münch, J., Prikladnicki, R., Wang, X., Abrahamsson, P. (eds.): Preface. In: Fundamentals of Software Startups (2020)
27. Hoda, R.: Socio-technical grounded theory for software engineering. arXiv preprint arXiv:2103.14235 (2021)
28. Masood, Z., Hoda, R., Blincoe, K.: How agile teams make self-assignment work: a grounded theory study. Empir. Softw. Eng. **25**(6), 4962–5005 (2020). https://doi.org/10.1007/s10664-020-09876-x
29. Benitez-Amado, J., Llorens-Montes, F.J., Nieves Perez-Arostegui, M.: Information technology-enabled intrapreneurship culture and firm performance. Ind. Manag. Data Syst. **110**, 550–566 (2010). https://doi.org/10.1108/02635571011039025

Software Platforms and Ecosystems

The Economic Anatomy of Paid Crowdsourcing Platforms

Egor Iankov[1,3] and Andrey Saltan[2,3](✉)

[1] CERGE-EI, Prague, Czech Republic
Egor.Iankov@cerge-ei.cz
[2] LUT University, Lappeenranta, Finland
andrey.saltan@lut.fi
[3] HSE University, St. Petersburg, Russia

Abstract. The discovery and dissemination of crowdsourcing have led to the emergence of platforms that offer the infrastructure for implementing crowdsourcing projects on a commercial basis. In this study, we investigate the economic structures of such paid crowdsourcing platforms. We develop an integrated Crowdsourcing Platform Economic Design framework based on existing studies on crowdsourcing and platform design. The framework incorporates a wide range of mechanisms available for the economic structure of paid crowdsourcing platforms grouped into three areas: Search and Matching, Pricing and Rewarding, and Control and Assembling. We further use the resulting framework to systematically compare and classify the economic structures of 45 paid crowdsourcing platforms. As a result, we provide a taxonomy of paid crowdsourcing platforms based on the economic mechanisms and their usage dependencies. The presented study of paid crowdsourcing platforms complements and extends the existing literature on crowdsourcing and platform economy; it also creates an appropriate basis for further research in these directions.

Keywords: Platforms · Crowdsourcing · Business model · Pricing

1 Introduction

Information and communication technologies (ICT) are transforming the business and societal landscape at an ever-increasing rate. One of the most noticeable effects is the fast growth of digital platforms and marketplaces that facilitate the provision of services and the exchange of goods. This growth is primarily determined by the increasing usage of the Internet and new frontiers in software development that allow the efficient and effective online collaboration of market participants. Another prominent example of ICT-enabled innovation is the emergence and expansion of crowdsourcing as a problem-solving approach.

Immediately after first crowdsourcing projects were introduced, they received attention from both academia and industry [12,23]. Scholars and practitioners

X. Wang et al. (Eds.): ICSOB 2021, LNBIP 434, pp. 171–186, 2021.
https://doi.org/10.1007/978-3-030-91983-2_13

investigated and evaluated crowdsourcing as a phenomenon with far-reaching developmental prospects. Despite all the benefits of crowdsourcing, few companies can, by themselves, build the infrastructure required to implement crowdsourcing projects and attract the necessary number of crowdworkers in a reasonable timeframe and within budget constraints. This led to the emergence of a particular category of digital platform, called paid crowdsourcing platforms, designed to implement commercial crowdsourcing projects. The very first and a well-studied example of paid crowdsourcing platforms is Amazon MTurk [9,13]. However, the growing demand for such paid crowdsourcing services has intensified the competition as more and more platforms are challenging Amazon's incumbent position in the market. These new platforms experiment with different business models and employ different economic structures to cope with the competition and capture market share.

Multiple studies in information technologies, economics, and sociology investigate and evaluate the momentum of the crowdsourcing phenomenon [11,14]. However, crowdsourcing platforms, by themselves, have not received much attention in academic literature. To the best of our knowledge, there has been no comprehensive study of the economic mechanisms used by paid crowdsourcing platforms, and existing studies do not provide convincing grounds for managing paid crowdsourcing platforms. Using both quantitative and qualitative research approaches, this study addresses the issues of designing the internal economic structure of paid crowdsourcing platforms.

The research presented in this paper is two-fold. First, we reveal the analytical Crowdsourcing Platform Economic Design (CPED) framework for the analysis of the economic structure of these platforms. This framework is grounded in a literature review and a survey of paid crowdsourcing platforms. Second, within the proposed framework, we compare and classify the set of 45 platforms. The patterns of mechanisms employed allowed us to draw conclusions on the interdependencies across various dimensions and mechanisms used and to derive a taxonomy of the generic economic structures of paid crowdsourcing platforms.

2 Background

The term "crowdsourcing", first coined in 2006 by Howe in a magazine article "The Rise of Crowdsourcing", is defined as "the act of a company or institution taking a function once performed by employees and outsourcing it to an undefined (and generally large) network of people in the form of an open call" [17]. For Howe, crowdsourcing is mainly a problem-solving approach for organizations with the roots in the concept of outsourcing: "[crowdsourcing] assumes splitting a problem into a large number of small tasks and involves a large and diverse number of participants usually outside the initiated organization" [17].

Crowdsourcing assumes the involvement of a large number of participants—the crowd—wishing to contribute to an extensive and complex project or initiative. ICT provides the infrastructure for effective and efficient communication, task allocation, and the assembly of completed parts into a ready-made solution. While participants of notable social, political, and ecological crowdsourcing projects contribute voluntarily, commercial projects initiated by organizations (contractors) provide monetary compensation for participants (crowdworkers). Such commercial projects involve routine data collection and verification tasks from open sources, sampling and data categorization for machine learning models, the classification of textual and graphical objects, and updating information in web-mapping services.

The first crowdsourcing projects confirm that engaging and effectively coordinating the collaborative work of participants was among the prime challenges of this approach to solving business problems. This led to the emergence of companies that have taken on the work of creating the necessary technological and social infrastructure in a form of a platform for the interaction between contractors and crowdworkers. However, the value provided by crowdsourcing platforms goes further than providing access to infrastructure. First, platform managers can help contractors effectively break down the tasks into Human intelligent tasks (HITs) and ensure the crowdworkers can deliver acceptable results. HITs are the minor parts of the task and can be defined more formally as: "small, simple tasks that are difficult for computers but relatively easy for humans" [14]. Secondly, through managing a community of crowdworkers, the platform ensures that each task gets sufficient involvement of crowdworkers and the required number of HITs will be performed. Thirdly, the platform can enforce quality and fraud control systems to fight against dishonest behavior and cheating.

The following four pillars of crowdsourcing are usually identified: the contractor, the crowdworkers, the task, and the platform [15]. The contractor is the entity that has a set of tasks to crowdsource. The task is the activity to be done by the crowdworkers, who are willing to participate with or without financial incentive. The crowdsourcing platform is the system used by contractors to publish tasks and by crowdworkers to complete them. The design of the workflow for paid crowdsourcing platforms usually follows a standard path. A contractor can run a few projects—campaigns—at once. Each campaign might include multiple tasks depending on its goal. One task consists of multiple HITs. All such HITs are easy to perform and can be done by almost anyone. The platform is responsible for dividing projects into a large number of HITs, assigning them to the crowdworkers, and assembling completed HITs into a ready-made solution provided to the contractor.

The economic design of paid crowdsourcing platforms has never been systematically analyzed in the academic literature. Still, a couple of studies tried to overview principles and practices of designing platforms regarding economic mechanisms. The idea of finding a balance between different mechanisms while designing a self-sustainable or viable platform is a central idea of the typology proposed in [4]. The authors suggest distinguishing between three core areas that define the platform business models: (1) Matching, (2) Assembling, and (3) Knowledge management. This initial triangle was further augmented with six dimensions: (1) Bundling of Coordination Services Provision, (2) Intermediation Market Structure, (3) Marketing Method, (4) Range of Packages, (5) Information Extraction & Use, and (6) Knowledge Distribution. Another attempt to provide a taxonomy of platform governance mechanisms across several dimensions was proposed in [25]. The authors identified six dimensions: (1) Governance structure, (2) Resources and documentation, (3) Accessibility and control, (4) Trust and perceived risk, (5) Pricing, and (6) External Relationship. An example of another approach used to analyze the pricing structures of products and services was proposed in [18]. The authors present the SBIFT framework with the following dimensions: (1) Scope, (2) Base, (3) Influence, (4) Formula, and (5) Temporal rights. This framework was further modified into a seven-dimensional one to assess pricing structures of cloud services [21].

The frameworks proposed in [4,25] reveal the complexity of the economic structure of platforms and classify economic mechanisms. However, they lack the necessary detail in the mechanisms used, which does not allow them to be employed for a systematic comparative analysis of the economic structures of platforms. Extending the SBIFT framework [18], taking into account the identified functional zones of the platforms, seems to be a suitable way to develop a framework that allows a comparison of the economic structures of paid crowdsourcing platforms.

3 Methodology

The study assesses the economic structure of paid crowdsourcing platforms and explores the essence and usage of the various economic mechanisms employed. More formally, to achieve this aim, we set the following two goals:

- to identify the economic mechanisms employed by paid crowdsourcing platforms and systemize them in the form of a framework,
- to study their interdependencies to determine the typical configuration and usage patterns of the mechanisms and provide a typology of the economic structures crowdsourcing platforms employ.

The exploratory nature of the research explains the methodology used, which was performed in two steps. First, we performed a literature review to reveal the characteristics of the economic structure of paid crowdsourcing platforms and the mechanisms available while designing this structure. These findings were used to develop the framework that will incorporate these mechanisms. The review of the literature is done following the guidelines from [2,20,24]. The search engines Google Scholar and Scopus were used to find publications that discuss characteristics of crowdsourcing and crowdsourcing platforms or platform design structures and principles in general. The literature identifies many mechanisms employed in platform operations. The relevant economic mechanisms available were further classified and structured in the CPED framework. The typologies mentioned above of mechanisms classified across several areas follow the examples of [4,18,21,25].

Secondly, we performed a comparative analysis of existing paid crowdsourcing platforms using the derived framework. We used the search engine Google, the Q&A forum Quora, and academic publications to find active paid crowdsourcing platforms. We used the following criteria for including a platform or service: (1) Provide paid services to contractors, (2) Crowdworkers receive payment for their involvement, (3) The unit of transaction is a HIT. In total, we found 45 paid crowdsourcing platforms eligible for further analysis and comparison. While the total number is not large, the sample coincides with the whole population. These platforms were analyzed using the following three quantitative research approaches: (1) Frequency analysis, (2) Comparison analysis, and (3) Clustering analysis. Hierarchical clustering was used to explore the natural division of the data set. The main reason for using it was that it supports categorical variables. We counted the frequencies for all variables, described below, to explore the distribution of platforms. It allowed us to distinguish patterns in the CPED framework. Essentially, differences in the patterns or "traces" capture differences between platforms for our purposes.

4 The Crowdsourcing Platform Economic Design Framework

The development of the CPED framework was based on an extensive literature review of publications on crowdsourcing and platform economic design. This classification summarises platform characteristics and mechanisms across the following three areas: *Search and Matching*, *Pricing and Rewarding*, and *Control and Assembling*. This classification is depicted as a triangle of platform economic design trade-offs in Fig. 1.

All the identified mechanisms were divided into groups, depending on whether they can be assessed by reviewing the platforms without surveying platform managers and whether they are essential in the economic structures of paid crowdsourcing platforms. As a result, we settled upon the framework that summarises all mechanisms into 12 dimensions within the three identified trade-off areas (see Fig. 2[1]).

4.1 Search and Matching

To fulfill the role of a mediator, the platform should have a transparent matching system, which will successfully match crowdworkers (supply) and the tasks given by contractors (demand). Search and Matching covers a vast area of methods and techniques employed to ensure the consistency of matching and its "quality" defined as the probability of completing a HIT correctly.

Complexity of Tasks. This scale measures to what extent contractors can influence HIT configuration (e.g., design, level of complexity, difficulty). At one extreme, contractors have no access to HIT design settings, at the other extreme, settings are fully customizable, or a contractor can provide their own specification.

[1] The framework is shown already with traces and mechanisms usage frequencies discussed in Sect. 5.

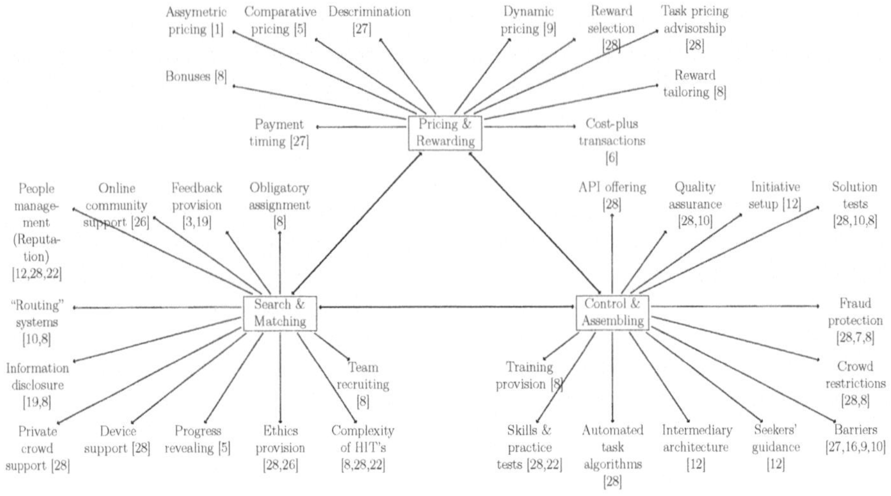

Fig. 1. Platform economic design trade-offs with corresponding mechanisms

Matching Automation. This variable describes the complexity of the matching process by the number of iterations both sides need to go through to find a match: from no automation when a party is presented with a listing of potential matches to complete automation when the system matches the parties using specific algorithms.

Reputation Management. To differentiate crowdworkers based on the quality of their work, platforms often employ reputation measurements. This can be done either on a purely algorithmic and automated basis, or platform managers can perform the ratings. For example, a platform can rank all crowdworkers according to the number of completed HITs, or employ more advanced criteria.

Online Community Support. The organization of an online community can provide positive effects to platforms. We measure whether these are used by platform management, by comparing the numbers of platforms with and without such a community. However, it also matters how much support is provided: whether there is an open forum or whether rules and behaviour guidelines are imposed on participants. Therefore, the scale measures the degree of complexity of community support which increases to the right.

4.2 Pricing and Rewarding

Pricing and Rewarding mainly refers to designing the reward structure for HIT completion and does not deal with the price contractors are charged. Therefore, there is a minor connection with platform revenue, insofar as it can get a higher share of cash flows from contractors to crowdworkers. This area accounts for different techniques of reward change or tailoring (e.g., dynamic pricing). Other

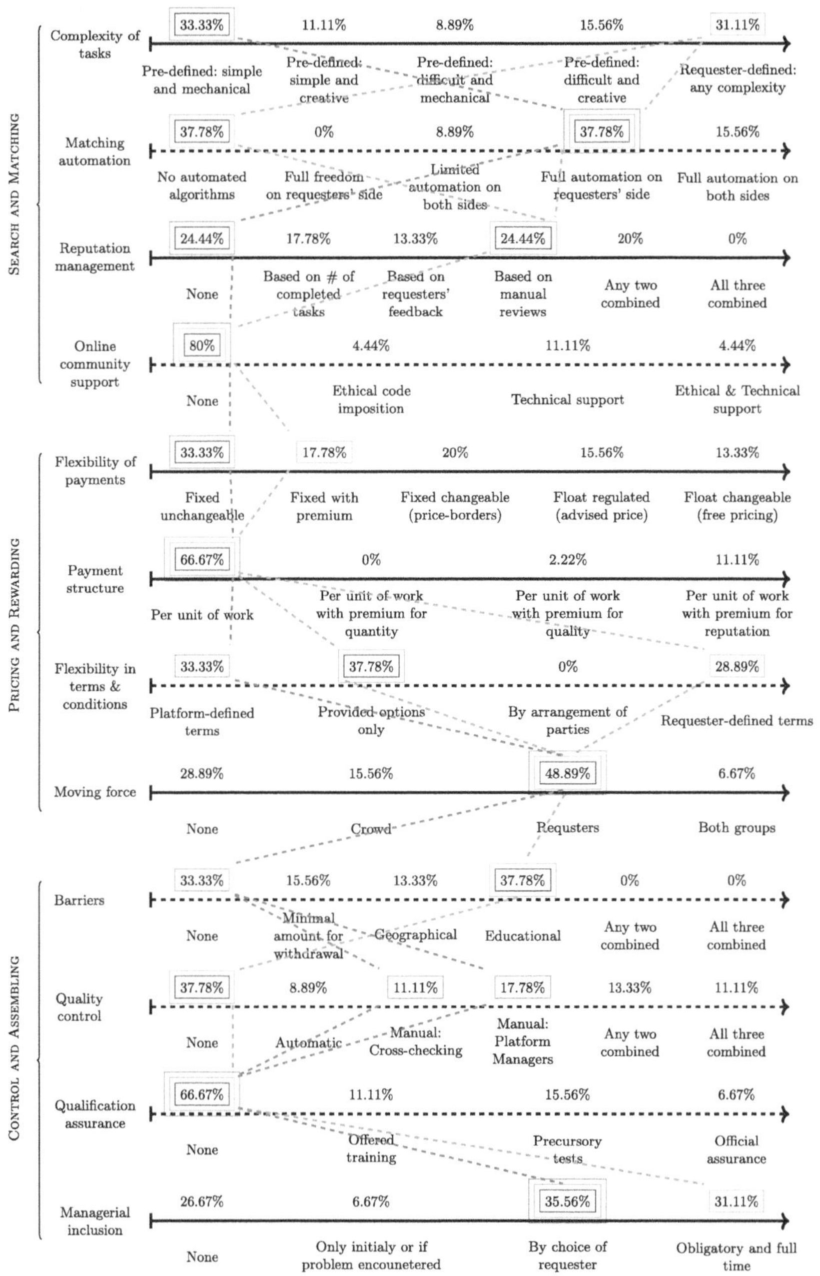

Fig. 2. CPED framework with traces for clusters of corresponding color. (Color figure online)

mechanisms also refer to various reward setting techniques, which, in theory, can be applied and related to ensuring fair compensation for crowdworkers.

Flexibility of Payments. HIT rewarding is an essential instrument. Therefore, functionality that allows the contractor to set up the reward structure and amount is crucial to success. Placing the "right" reward can incentivize crowdworkers to accept certain HITs and, thus, lead to a more successful campaign. Platforms on the right end of the axis provide this functionality, while left-end platforms employ a fixed reward structure.

Flexibility of Terms and Conditions. This dimension categorizes platforms in terms of the flexibility structure of "wage" bills. How much the contractor can tailor the reward to their own needs. For instance, the platform can set the reward for all HITs, or the contractor can issue premiums or change rewards within some borders. In the extreme case, the reward is set by the contractor freely.

Payment Structure. The payment to crowdworkers can consist of two parts: a basic reward for work completion and a bonus for quality, for example. Another example is an experience premium. The platform can promote incentives for a higher level of effort or spending more time on the platform.

Moving Force. While most of the platforms tend to look for growth opportunities, there is a high degree of diversity in this development. While some platforms choose not to emphasise any crucial elements, others display the sources of their development. For instance, a platform's management can suppose that they need to increase the number of crowdworkers. Another natural source of growth is the number of contractors.

4.3 Control and Assembling

Control and Assembling covers mechanisms available for platforms to ensure better control over crowdworkers and task performance. The inability of contractors to present tasks accurately makes the platform operate with unified versions of the contractors' requirements. At the same time, platforms have to ensure the required level of quality for the contractors. As a result, platforms need to balance the level of openness and certainty they can provide for crowdworkers and contractors.

Barriers. To manage and control crowdworkers, various measures can be employed. The relative complexity of the barrier increases to the right of the axis with the difficulty of checking a candidate's eligibility. For instance, a minimal amount for withdrawal does not need one at all, and the location can be tested via the Internet. Confirmation of education, however, can require sending a query to the awarding institution.

Quality Control. Essential issue with crowdsourcing is controlling the quality of the results produced by crowdworkers. Some platforms choose to deny any related liability, but others employ relatively advanced computer and human-based methods. The scale goes from the absence of quality control to a combination of computers and humans, assuming that machine verification is cheaper than using humans.

Qualification Assurance. Another problem related to control is the crowdworker's initial qualification or "quality", which can be relatively crucial for crowdsourcing. Therefore, platforms can require some form of skill confirmation. As in previous cases, the right side corresponds to more complex measures. The platform can provide online tests or conduct interviews with potential crowdworkers.

Managerial Inclusion. This variable measures the extent to which platform management is included in platform operations in cooperation with crowdworkers and contractors. An important issue is whether managers provide only initial support or come whenever a problem is encountered. They can provide support to either side or directly intervene if a problem appears. Another case is to have managers leading projects from the beginning to the end, and which requires more attention and resources from the platform.

5 An Analysis of Paid Crowdsourcing Platforms

5.1 Classification Parameters and Descriptive Statistics

We evaluated the 45 platforms across different dimensions grouped into the three CPED areas: Search and Matching, Pricing and Rewarding, Control and Assembling. This section gives an overview of the descriptive statistics (see Fig. 3) and discusses the peculiarities of platform positioning.

Search and Matching. Most platforms use pre-defined, simple, and mechanical (33%) or contractor-defined tasks of any complexity (31%). The same pattern with the two most popular options also holds for Matching automation: 38% of the platforms opt for the absence of automation and 38% for full automation on the contractor's side. Reputation management is distributed more equally: the minimum number (13%) of the platforms use contractor's feedback, and the maximal number (24%) do not employ this mechanism or use a combination of the two. Regarding community support, most of the platforms do not provide any support at all (80%), the second most popular option is providing only technical support, which is an expected result given the technical specialization of the platforms.

Pricing and Rewarding. Flexibility of payments is characterized by nearly the same number of results across all potential options within the variable. The maximal number is on the first level—fixed, unchangeable payments—33%. All other levels have from 13 to 20% of platforms. However, not all options we operationalized the dimension into were observed. Additionally, the number of platforms decreases constantly with the increasing complexity of "tariffs": 67% of platforms reward per unit of work without a premium and only 11% add a premium for reputation. The same applies to Flexibility in terms and conditions: not all levels present in the CPED framework were used by the platforms. However, the number of the platforms is nearly the same for all levels: from 29% to 38%. The most frequent is the provision of options for flexibility. It should be noted that most of the platforms (49%) see contractors as a crucial side of the market. This might indicate that the platforms encounter a shortage of contractors relatively more often than crowdworkers. Hence, platform management is focused on finding new contractors. Only 16% perceive crowdworkers as their moving force. This provides additional evidence in favor of the importance of contractors.

Control and Assembling. We did not identify any platforms that use more than one type of barrier. The two most popular options are the total absence of barriers (33%) and barriers related to educational level (38%). Only 28% of the platforms use technical barriers such as the minimal amount for withdrawal and location. 38% of the platforms take no responsibility for the quality of the performed tasks, and it is up to the contractors to solve any issues which might arise in this regard. However, 60% of platforms employ quality control, with 24% offering more than one mechanism for this purpose. Regarding the Quality assurance dimension, most of the platforms do not use any of the mechanisms. However, for those who do credential checks, the most popular form is verification of crowdworkers' skills. The majority of the platforms provide managerial support by default with all projects (31%), or this is the contractor's choice (36%). Only around 7% choose to implement on-demand help. This can mean that such a dynamic system would be complex or impractical. Thus, the platforms move to either of the extremes.

5.2 Hierarchical Clustering

Our data set consists of 45 platforms. The hierarchical clustering method was applied to identify a "natural" division of the data set into the following clusters (see Fig. 4):

- Blue cluster (23 platforms) consists of traditional paid micro-task crowdsourcing platforms.
- Red cluster (13 platforms), conversely, corresponds to the macro-task platforms.
- Green cluster (9 platforms) is made up of intermediary platforms, which tend to have characteristics of blue and red clusters.

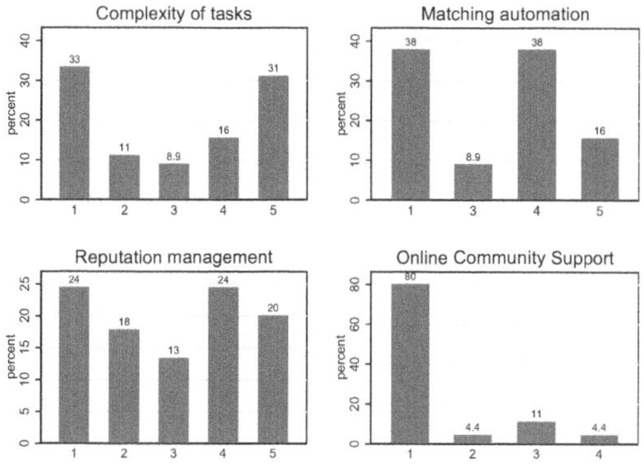

(a) Search and Matching mechanisms

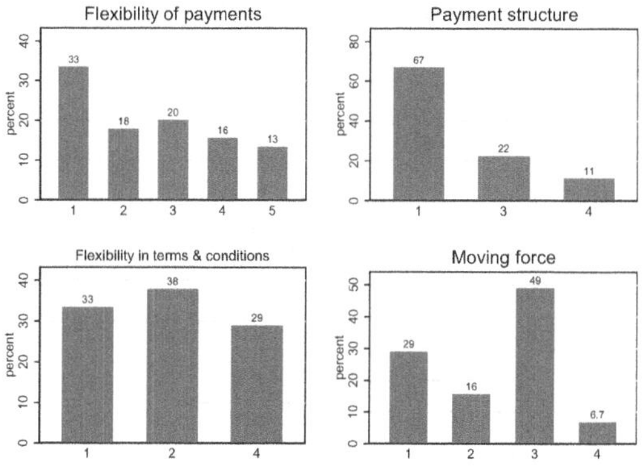

(b) Pricing and Rewarding mechanisms

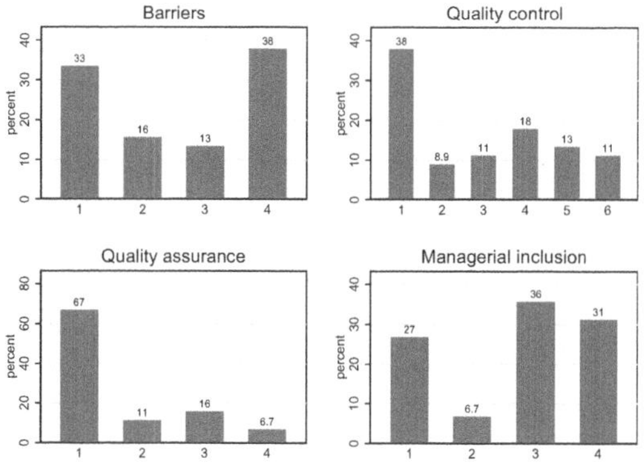

(c) Control and Assembling mechanisms

Fig. 3. Platforms distribution across CPED framework mechanisms

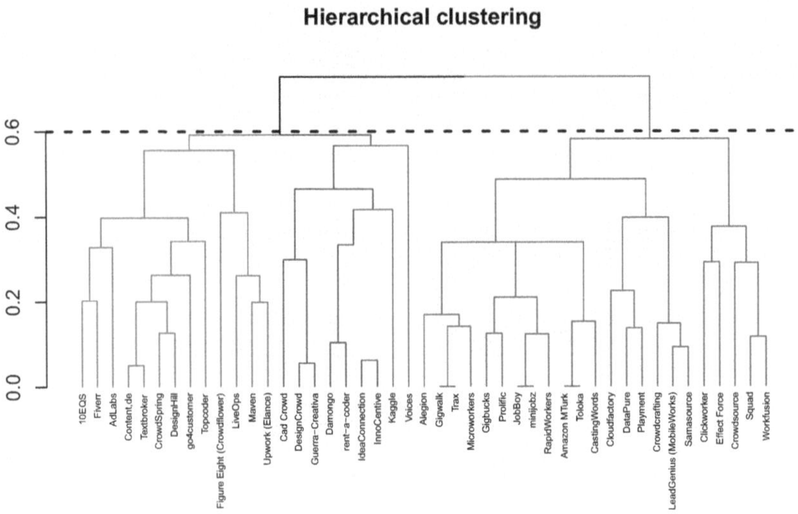

Fig. 4. Three clusters of platforms: macro-task, transitional, micro-task

One of the possible explanations for this might be that the units differ significantly in terms of the mechanisms used, as proposed earlier. It can, therefore, be assumed that different types (or clusters) of platforms have different baselines, or most frequently, mechanism choice trajectories. This provides additional reasoning behind our aim to analyze these traces.

The cluster analysis proves our assumption that paid crowdsourcing platforms exhibit different but steady patterns regarding strategic business choices and thus can be analyzed in strategic groups. Moreover, the highlighted division is essential as it follows the nature of crowdsourcing. While there are platforms of pure crowdsourcing (micro-task crowdsourcing), there are platforms that try to apply the approach to more complex tasks (macro-task crowdsourcing). Such platforms have much in common with freelance platforms. Thus, they are driven by the reasoning of classical crowdsourcing theory as more focus is put on the crowdworker. The heterogeneity of the data is the primary motivation for exploring multiple traces in the CPED framework.

5.3 Dependencies in the CPED Framework

We tested the variables for independence for each pair of the variables using χ^2 test statistics. The tests reveal how "orthogonal" the CPED framework is. If the system shows no dependencies within the area, each variable characterizes a platform from that perspective. However, if there are dependencies within any area, the number of variables should be reviewed. Independence tests show that the "inner" independence does not hold in all areas. However, this might be evidence of the existence of a trajectory, which is typical for the platforms. This trajectory connects all variables and, thus, leads to the presence of interdependencies within the area. It is considered evidence in favor of the existence of traces in the CPED framework.

The trajectories for macro- and micro-task crowdsourcing platforms differ significantly. The trace contains the most frequently observed options in each cluster. The platforms dealing with more complicated tasks tend to employ relatively more advanced mechanisms. While, in some cases, they use the same instruments, the differences can be explained as paid micro-task crowdsourcing platforms offer simple tasks but operate in high volumes. Therefore, they need to provide a high level of automation and do not necessarily require discriminating between crowdworkers. Such platforms provide little or no flexibility regarding payments and terms but still employ robust quality control mechanisms. The explanation might be as follows: simple and small tasks do not demand much effort from crowdworkers, which gives incentives to sacrifice quality for quantity. Macro-task platforms choose an alternative trajectory, possibly due to the complexity of their tasks. They cannot find a perfect match automatically and assess the result thoroughly. However, it allows and forces them to provide a better ranking of crowdworkers. This is also the reason behind the greater degree of freedom given to contractors in defining their terms.

To sum up, the difference we observe among the platforms lies in the mechanisms they employ to run their operations. The measurement of such mechanisms allows a comparison of the platforms and the identification of different types of platforms. Paid micro- and macro-task crowdsourcing have different approaches to their activities. A possible explanation for these results may be the difference in the tasks offered on these platforms. While anyone can do micro-tasks, macro-tasks often require specific skills and knowledge. This allows a traditional micro-task crowdsourcing platform to simplify matching and rewarding aspects but enforces a higher level of quality control.

6 Conclusion

The extended use of the Internet and ICT resulted in the fast growth of digital platforms and marketplaces that facilitate the exchange of goods, services, and labor resources. Combining the concept of crowdsourcing with platform thinking led to the emergence of a particular category of digital platforms—paid crowdsourcing platforms—designed to implement commercial crowdsourcing projects. We developed an economic framework of paid crowdsourcing and determined whether the employed mechanisms highlight and partially explain the differences in platforms. The findings reported here shed new light on the organization of crowdsourcing platforms and provide a new classification. Patterns of the most frequently used options were highlighted based on the data set of 45 platforms further divided into three clusters. Clustering shows that there is a "natural" division of paid crowdsourcing platforms. A business analysis of their choice of mechanism explains this differentiation. From our point of view, the main reason lies in the types of tasks they crowdsource. However, the study gives no grounds to build causal relations between mechanisms and does not evaluate performance or any other characteristics of the mechanisms identified. Our task was to provide grounds for questions and descriptions of the current situation rather than answers. Being, to the best of our knowledge, the first study of this kind, it contributes to the field in the following ways:

- the creation of theoretical grounds for future research on paid crowdsourcing platforms via the introduction of the CPED framework that can be used as a typology construction approach,
- the provision of guidelines on the basis for the decision-making of platform managers. The creation of guidelines from the identified "baseline" solution as a basis for decision-making.

The importance of the first contribution comes from the fact that paid crowdsourcing still lacks systematization—there is no common typology, at least known to us. Therefore, to increase the understanding of these entities, we decided to find elements allowing the categorization and highlighting of differences between platforms. The proposed framework fills this theoretical gap. The second contribution is relevant in the business area, as the categorization can also assist companies in designing and managing crowdsourcing platforms. It improves the perception of platform operations and highlights essential elements. Crowdsourcing is a relatively recent business model, so there are still no established business approaches in terms of the patterns of strategic choices. We provide some insights into the rationale behind such choices. This new understanding should help to improve the predictions and decision-making process of platform management. The reason for that is the provision of baseline solutions, which are the highlighted traces. Thus, managers can find a starting point and tailor the solution to their specific needs and desires.

This study also has limitations. The most important of them lies in the fact that we collected data by hand and, thus, the dataset is relatively subjective. Hence, another research opportunity lies in acquiring a more extensive and objective data set, which can shed light on other features and issues. It should be noted that there was no intent here to evaluate the mechanisms as good or bad. We do not analyze the engineering and economic mechanisms themselves. The study is also limited to a comparative analysis of website characteristics rather than exploring the economic or engineering mechanisms behind the website's crowdsourcing service. It effectively prevents considering all possible mechanisms due to their infeasibility: websites do not provide information about all employed mechanisms.

The limitations reveal several possibilities to extend the research. First, a larger, more representative sample of the platforms can be analyzed, resulting in more accurate and refined findings. An extended and modified CPED framework can be applied to the analysis of other platform types as many characteristics are not specific to paid crowdsourcing. The framework could be of even greater value for a more heterogeneous set of platforms. Second, the CPED framework can be extended and modified to incorporate mechanisms not included due to data collection limitations. A series of in-depth interviews with platform managers should provide a better understanding of the platforms' economic structures and evaluate mechanisms that cannot be assessed by exploring platform websites.

References

1. Bakos, Y., Katsamakas, E.: Design and ownership of two-sided networks: implications for internet platforms. J. Manag. Inf. Syst. **25**(2), 171–202 (2008)
2. Baskerville, R., Baiyere, A., Gergor, S., Hevner, A., Rossi, M.: Design science research contributions: finding a balance between artifact and theory. J. Assoc. Inf. Syst. **19**(5), 358–376 (2018)
3. Baumann, C., Gewald, H.: What motivates crowdsourcing contributors? A cross-platform comparative analysis, p. 14 (2018)
4. Brousseau, E., Penard, T.: The economics of digital business models: a framework for analyzing the economics of platforms. Rev. Netw. Econ. **6**(2), 81–114 (2007)
5. Chandler, D., Horton, J.: Labor allocation in paid crowdsourcing: experimental evidence on positioning, nudges and prices. In: Association for the Advancement of Artificial Intelligence Workshop, pp. 14–19 (2011)
6. Chen, D.L.: The economics of crowdsourcing: a theory of disaggregated labor markets (2017)
7. Cullen, Z., Farronato, C.: Outsourcing tasks online: matching supply and demand on peer-to-peer internet platforms. Manag. Sci. **67**, 3985–4003 (2020)
8. Daniel, F., Kucherbaev, P., Cappiello, C., Benatallah, B., Allahbakhsh, M.: Quality control in crowdsourcing: a survey of quality attributes, assessment techniques and assurance actions. ACM Comput. Surv. **51**(1), 1–40 (2018)
9. Difallah, D.E., Catasta, M., Demartini, G., Ipeirotis, P.G., Cudré-Mauroux, P.: The dynamics of micro-task crowdsourcing: the case of Amazon MTurk. In: Proceedings of the 24th International Conference on World Wide Web, pp. 238–247 (2015)
10. Gadiraju, U., Demartini, G., Kawase, R., Dietze, S.: Human beyond the machine: challenges and opportunities of microtask crowdsourcing. IEEE Intell. Syst. **30**(4), 81–85 (2015)
11. Ghazawneh, A., Henfridsson, O.: A paradigmatic analysis of digital application marketplaces. J. Inf. Technol. **30**(3), 198–208 (2015)
12. Ghezzi, A., Gabelloni, D., Martini, A., Natalicchio, A.: Crowdsourcing: a review and suggestions for future research: crowdsourcing. Int. J. Manag. Rev. **20**(2), 343–363 (2018)
13. Hauser, D., Paolacci, G., Chandler, J.: Common concerns with MTurk as a participant pool: evidence and solutions (2019)
14. Horton, J.J., Chilton, L.B.: The labor economics of paid crowdsourcing. In: 11th ACM Conference on Electronic Commerce, EC 2910, p. 209 (2010)
15. Hosseini, M., Shahri, A., Phalp, K., Taylor, J., Ali, R.: Crowdsourcing: a taxonomy and systematic mapping study. Comput. Sci. Rev. **17**, 43–69 (2015)
16. Howcroft, D., Bergvall-Kåreborn, B.: A typology of crowdwork platforms. Work Employ Soc. **33**(1), 21–38 (2019)
17. Howe, J.: The rise of crowdsourcing. Wired, 5 (2006). http://www.wired.com/wired/archive/14.06/crowds.html
18. Iveroth, E., Westelius, A., Petri, C.J., Olve, N.G., Cöster, M., Nilsson, F.: How to differentiate by price: Proposal for a five-dimensional model. Eur. Manag. J. **31**(2), 109–123 (2013)

19. Jiang, Z.Z., Huang, Y.: The role of feedback in dynamic crowdsourcing contests: a structural empirical analysis (2016)
20. Kitchenham, B., Pearl Brereton, O., Budgen, D., Turner, M., Bailey, J., Linkman, S.: Systematic literature reviews in software engineering - a systematic literature review. Inf. Softw. Technol. **51**(1), 7–15 (2009)
21. Laatikainen, G., Ojala, A., Mazhelis, O.: Cloud services pricing models. In: Herzwurm, G., Margaria, T. (eds.) ICSOB 2013. LNBIP, vol. 150, pp. 117–129. Springer, Heidelberg (2013). https://doi.org/10.1007/978-3-642-39336-5_12
22. Mourelatos, E., Frarakis, N., Tzagarakis, M.: A study on the evolution of crowdsourcing websites. Eur. J. Soc. Sci. Educ. Res. **11**(1), 29 (2017)
23. Neto, F.R.A., Santos, C.A.: Understanding crowdsourcing projects: a systematic review of tendencies, workflow, and quality management. Inf. Process. Manag. **54**(4), 490–506 (2018)
24. Rowe, F.: What literature review is not: diversity, boundaries and recommendations. Eur. J. Inf. Syst. **23**(3), 241–255 (2014)
25. Schreieck, M., Hein, A., Wiesche, M., Krcmar, H.: The challenge of governing digital platform ecosystems. In: Linnhoff-Popien, C., Schneider, R., Zaddach, M. (eds.) Digital Marketplaces Unleashed, pp. 527–538. Springer, Heidelberg (2018). https://doi.org/10.1007/978-3-662-49275-8_47
26. Stanoevska-Slabeva, K., Schmid, B.: A typology of online communities and community supporting platforms. In: Proceedings of the 34th Annual Hawaii International Conference on System Sciences, p. 10 (2001)
27. Strausz, R.: A theory of crowdfunding: a mechanism design approach with demand uncertainty and moral hazard. Am. Econ. Rev. **107**(6), 1430–1476 (2017)
28. Vakharia, D., Lease, M.: Beyond mechanical turk: an analysis of paid crowd work platforms, p. 18 (2015)

Power Relations Within an Open Source Software Ecosystem

Victor Farias[1(✉)], Igor Wiese[2], and Rodrigo Santos[1]

[1] Federal University of the State of Rio de Janeiro, Rio de Janeiro, Brazil
victor.farias@edu.unirio.br, rps@uniriotec.br
[2] Federal University of Technology - Parana, Campo Mourão, Brazil
igor@utfpr.edu.br

Abstract. Context: Relationships within open-source software ecosystems (OSSECO) emerge from the collaboration within the ecosystem. Power relations are present in this context whenever an entity has the power of making other entities act as it wants them to act. Therefore, these power relations could affect collaboration within an OSSECO. Objective: This research aims at investigating power relations, their benefits and challenges, and providing an understanding of them within OSSECO. The goal is to provide power relations forms description together with the power relations dynamics associated with them. Method: A systematic mapping study was conducted to extract information about power relations (forms, dynamics, benefits, and challenges) from previous studies. At the end, 10 studies reporting power relations within OSSECO were selected. Next, the data extracted from those was analyzed to understand what power relations affect the OSSECO and how this happens. Based on the results, the power relation forms and dynamics within OSSECO are defined. Results: The systematic mapping study show that power relations are present and affect relationships and interactions within an OSSECO. Moreover, 5 power relations forms and 7 power relations dynamics within OSSECO are presented. Implications: Identifying power relations that might be present within an OSSECO would enable those who study or are members of the ecosystem's community to enhance power relations that support collaboration and to avoid those who can lead developers to leave the OSSECO.

Keywords: Open source software · Software ecosystem · Power relations · Systematic mapping study

1 Introduction

In open-source software (OSS), a group of developers gets together in a project to solve common problems or because they share common needs [1]. When several OSS projects share their developers, artifacts and build relationships, creating a knowledge and collaboration network between them over a common technological platform (e.g., a programming language), we have an open-source software

X. Wang et al. (Eds.): ICSOB 2021, LNBIP 434, pp. 187–193, 2021.
https://doi.org/10.1007/978-3-030-91983-2_14

ecosystem (OSSECO) [2]. In the OSS development, power is usually referred to as decentralized and spread within the OSS community. This is highly related to the early years of OSS when the contribution was mostly voluntary [1]. The motivations to contribute with OSS have been changing recently, focusing more on learning, career, and payment motivations [3].

Power relations would be defined as asymmetric relations between an individual who has something to offer and some other individual who desires this something [4]. This concept has been deeply investigated in some areas of interest, such as Economics [5] and Sociology [6]. In Computer Science, other studies investigated different ecosystems' contexts and discussed benefits such as goals achievement [8] and collaboration support [9], through power relations management [10]. However, in the OSSECO context, the power relations have not been investigated yet.

This research aims to investigate power relations within an OSSECO and provide an understanding of how such relations affect developers, artifacts, and relationships within the ecosystem. This understanding must rely on how the power relations happen within the OSSECO. It must also clarify what benefits and challenges power relations can bring into the OSSECO. The research question that guides this work is *"What are the power relations and their dynamics within the OSSECO context and how they affect the ecosystem?"*. To answer this question, a systematic mapping study was conducted.

2 Systematic Mapping Study

This work investigates what power relations are present within an OSSECO and how their dynamics can affect the ecosystem, its actors and artifacts. Considering that power relations within an OSSECO have not been deeply investigated so far, the best option to gather information from the literature is performing a systematic mapping study (SMS) [11].

2.1 Planning

One inclusion criterion (IC) and four exclusion criteria (EC) were defined. The study selection process was divided into six steps (Fig. 1) and comprised from the search execution until the filtering of the returned studies. Next, a manual insertion of studies previously known as compliant to the IC and that did not present any problems regarding EC was executed. After the fifth step, the data extraction process was conducted aiming at answering the research questions. A search string was created combining terms that would relate to the studied topic. Since power relations could affect the interactions within an OSSECO, the term "interaction" was added to the string. The search string defined was: (("open source software ecosystem" OR "software ecosystem") AND ("power relation*" OR "relation*" OR "interaction*")).

2.2 Execution

The execution was intended to retrieve as many studies as possible reporting power relations within an OSSECO. The search engines used for the research were ACM, IEEE Xplore, ScienceDirect, Scopus, and SpringerLink. In the first step, 1,068 studies were found. At the end of the fifth step, 8 studies were selected. The manual insertion added 2 new studies to the list of selected studies. Therefore, at the beginning of the data extraction phase, 10 studies were enabled to be used to retrieve information about power relations within an OSSECO (Fig. 1).

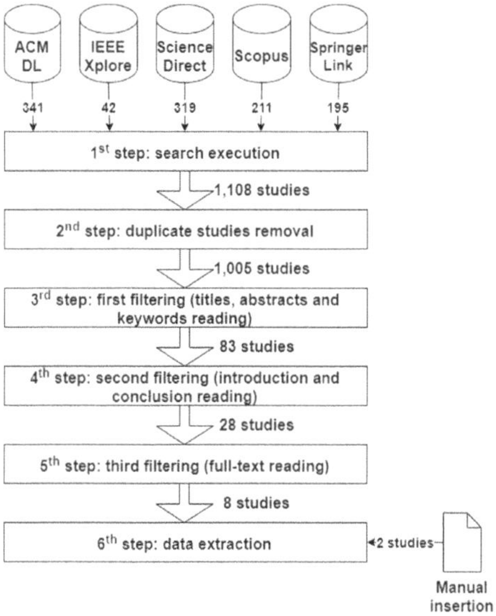

Fig. 1. Studies selection steps.

2.3 Results

The studies that were selected during this SMS were published from 2007 to 2021. From the 10 studies that were selected, none of them cited "power relations within OSSECO" directly. Were found studies that described situations in which it was possible to identify the occurrence of power relations within an OSSECO. Therefore, adding "interaction" as one of the search string's terms was determinant to retrieve those studies.

Data extraction was manually performed while reading the full text. It was important to consider the power relations implicitly reported by the studies. Those power relations were identified mostly because situations - called power relations dynamics - were described in those studies along with the actors or artifacts that would have the power and those that would be affected by the power. To help in the identification of the forms of power relations found in the SMS, Leonidou et al.'s [7] power form classification was adapted to the OSSECO context, as seen in Table 1. The benefits that can be brought into the OSSECO rely on the possibility that the power relations can motivate the actors to keep contributing to the OSSECO and to maintain the OSSECO's health (S04 [12], S05 [13], and S08 [14]). However, the power relations could bring some challenges, especially for those who are newcomers and might have to transpose some barriers to have their contribution accepted and could decide to abandon the OSSECO. The power relations, their dynamics and the source studies in which they were found can be seen in Table 2.

Table 1. Power relations forms [7] and the adaption to the OSSECO context.

Power relation form	Leonidou et al. [7] definition	Definition within OSSECO context
Referent power	Source of power based on the identification of one firm with another firm, or the former's wish for being closely associated with the latter	The belief that one actor - due to his/her identification with another actor - would be more likely to collaborate and act according to another actor's desires
Expert power	Source of power based on the belief that one firm has specific knowledge needed by another firm	The belief that an actor has knowledge about something related to an OSSECO (e.g., he/she has skills that very few actors have) and that it might share this knowledge and help other actors if they act as the first one's desires
Legalistic power	Source of power based on the belief that one firm retains a legitimate right based on formal processes to influence another	The belief that an actor - due to legal processes and contracts - has the ability of making another actor acts as the first one's desires
Reward power	Source of power based on a firm's belief that another firm has the ability to mediate rewards and it will actually bring these rewards if the former complies	The belief that one actor has the ability of rewarding another actor (e.g., with money, higher privileges) if the second one acts according to the first one's desire
Coercive power	Source of power based on a firm's belief that another firm has the ability to punish the former if it fails to cooperate	The ability of an actor being able to punish another actor (e.g., by blocking him/her on the project) if the second one does something the first one disapproves

Table 2. Power relations dynamics extracted from SMS.

Dynamic	Power relations form	Source studies
Learning reference	Referent	S09 [3]
Technical leadership	Expert	S10 [15]
Control over development platform	Legalistic	S07 [16]
Role migration within the OSSECO	Reward	S02 [17], S10 [15]
Employment relation	Reward	S01 [18], S09 [3]
Conforming to stakeholders' requirements	Coercive	S06 [19]
Newcomers' contribution rejection	Coercive	S02 [17], S03 [20]

3 Discussion

The power forms and dynamics identified help to understand who are the ones that hold power within an OSSECO in different situations and how this power affects the relation between actors and artifacts. Therefore, it would be possible for OSSECO community members to make decisions according to their objective within the ecosystem depending on their goals and needs. It would also make it possible to understand why previous decisions or movements happened within an OSSECO based on the relations that led to them.

The *referent* power relations form appeared in the "Learning reference" power relations dynamic. In this dynamic, a project, an actor or the experience of contributing to an OSSECO itself would make an actor to play according to rules, desires or expected behaviors to be able to remain in touch with the knowledge and, therefore, learn [3]. The dynamic "Technical leadership" was identified and linked to the *expert* power relation form. In this dynamic, an actor, known by having a large technical skill in a specific technology, is seen by others as a reference. Therefore, other actors will play as the expert desires, so they can count on his/her assistance in their projects or in their problems [15]. The *legalistic* power relations form takes place through the "Control over development platform" dynamic. In this dynamic, an organization owns a specific platform and can decide how things are done within this platform because of such ownership [16].

The *reward* power relations form was identified in two power dynamics. "Role migration within the OSSECO", the actors would play as other actors who have the power to give them higher privileges within an OSSECO, and consequently, more power. This happens because having more privileges within an OSSECO means that the actor has the possibility of helping to make decisions about the ecosystem's evolution and because his/her contributions are more likely to be accepted [15,17]. "Employment relation", happens since the motivations for contributing with OSSECO have been changing and there are actors that contribute because of their work [3]. In this case, an organization employs an actor and he/she acts as the organization desires to keep his/her employment and to receive his/her payment.

When analyzing the *coercive* power relations form, two dynamics were found. "Conforming to stakeholders' requirements", usually happens when a project tends to guide their development within the OSSECO according to some specific stakeholders' requirements. This happens because there are some stakeholders whose requirements are considered as a priority in relation to others. Therefore, actors that control the projects would be afraid of, if not conforming to their stakeholders' requirements, being replaced by others who would [19]. "Newcomers' contributions rejection", happens when a newcomer tries to contribute to a new project and he/she has his/her contribution rejected because the project's owner do not know him/her yet. This occurs because the nearly hierarchical structures that tend to appear within an OSSECO [17] acts as a barrier, where the ones that guide the projects' decisions and development decide if a newcomer's contribution is accepted or not [20].

This work has some limitations as follows: (i) as power relations have not been deeply explored yet, it was necessary to add more terms related to interactions into the search string to minimize the risk of some information not being gathered; (ii) the power relations dynamics were identified by a researcher and evaluated by two experts, both with experience of more than 10 years conducting SMS (one of them is an OSS expert and the other one is a software ecosystem expert); and (iii) other power relations dynamics might not have been identified from the selected studies.

4 Final Remarks

In an OSSECO, interactions are fundamental for maintaining an ecosystem [12]. In this paper, we reported on a SMS that aimed at exploring the power relations within OSSECO and how they can affect the OSSECO development. In the end, 10 studies were selected and 7 power relation dynamics were found and categorized into 5 power relations forms. Moreover benefits and challenges of power relations within OSSECO context were summarized.

As a contribution to the research and the practice communities, power relation forms were adapted to the OSSECO context and power relations dynamics within an OSSECO were identified. They can be used to enhance contribution or to prevent OSSECO abandonment. As future work, an ongoing study is focused on interviewing OSSECO community members to try to extract more information about power relations within an OSSECO.

Acknowledgements. The authors thank to UNIRIO and FAPERJ (Proc. 211.583/2019) for the partial support.

References

1. AlMarzouq, M., Grover, V., Thatcher, J.B.: Taxing the development structure of open source communities: an information processing view. Decis. Support Syst. **80**, 27–41 (2015)
2. Franco-Bedoya, O., Ameller, D., Costal, D., Franch, X.: Open source software ecosystems: a systematic mapping. Inf. Softw. Technol. **91**, 160–185 (2017)

3. Gerosa, M., et al.: The shifting sands of motivation: revisiting what drives contributors in open source. In: IEEE/ACM 43rd International Conference on Software Engineering (ICSE) on Proceedings, pp. 1046–1058 (2021)
4. Foucault, M.: Discipline And Punish: the Birth of the Prison. Pantheon Books, New York (1977)
5. Telleria, J.: Power relations? What power relations? The de-politicising conceptualisation of development of the UNDP. Third World Q. **38**(9), 2143–2158 (2017)
6. Stehr, N., Adolf, M.: Knowledge/power/resistance. Society **55**, 193–198 (2018)
7. Leonidou, L., Aykol, B., Lindsay, V., Katsikeas, C., Talias, M.: Drivers and outcomes of exercised power in buyer-seller relationships: a meta-analysis (2014)
8. Costa, L., Fontão, A., Santos, R.: Investigating asset governance mechanisms in a proprietary software ecosystem. In: XVI Brazilian Symposium on Information Systems (SBSI 2020) on Proceedings, pp. 1–8. Association for Computing Machinery (2020). Article No. 25
9. Alves, C., Valença, G., Franch, X.: Exercising power in software ecosystems. IEEE Softw. **36**(3), 50–54 (2019)
10. Valença, G., Alves, C., Jansen, S.: Strategies for managing power relationships in software ecosystems. J. Syst. Softw. **144**, 478–500 (2018)
11. Kitchenham, B., Charters, S.: Guidelines for performing systematic literature reviews in software engineering. Staffordshire, UK (2007)
12. Liao, Z., Wang, N., Liu, S., Zhang, Y., Liu, H., Zhang, Q.: Identification-method research for open-source software ecosystems. Symmetry **11**, 182–199 (2019)
13. Teixeira, J., Robles, G., González-Barahona, J.M.: Lessons learned from applying social network analysis on an industrial Free/Libre/Open source software ecosystem. J. Internet Serv. Appl. **6**(1), 1–27 (2015). https://doi.org/10.1186/s13174-015-0028-2
14. Eckhardt, E., Kaats, E., Jansen, S., Alves, C.: The merits of a meritocracy in open source software ecosystems. In: 2014 European Conference on Software Architecture Workshops (ECSAW 2014) on Proceedings, pp. 1–6. Association for Computing Machinery, New York (2014)
15. Farias, V., Wiese, I., Santos, R.: What characterizes an influencer in software ecosystems? IEEE Softw. **36**(1), 42–47 (2019)
16. Plakidas, K., Stevanetic, S., Schall, D., Ionescu, T., Zdun, U.: How do software ecosystems evolve? A quantitative assessment of the R ecosystem. In: 20th International Systems and Software Product Line Conference (SPLC 2016) on Proceedings, pp. 89–98. Association for Computing Machinery, New York (2016)
17. Jergensen, C., Sarma, A., Wagstrom, P.: The onion patch: migration in open source ecosystems. In: 19th ACM SIGSOFT Symposium and the 13th European Conference on Foundations of Software Engineering (ESEC/FSE 2011) on Proceedings, pp. 70–80. Association for Computing Machinery, New York (2011)
18. Linåker, J., Runeson, P.: Public sector platforms going open: creating and growing an ecosystem with open collaborative development. In: 16th International Symposium on Open Collaboration (OpenSym 2020) on Proceedings, pp. 1–10. Association for Computing Machinery, New York (2020)
19. Linåker, J., Regnell, B., Damian, D.: A method for analyzing stakeholders' influence on an open source software ecosystem's requirement engineering process. Requirements Eng. **25**, 115–130 (2020)
20. Jensen, C., Scacchi, W.: Role migration and advancement processes in OSSD projects: a comparative case study. In: 29th International Conference on Software Engineering (ICSE 2007) on Proceedings, pp. 364–374 (2007)

When Player Communities Revolt Against the Developer: A Study of Pokémon GO and Diablo Immortal

Samuli Laato[1,2](✉) and Sampsa Rauti[1]

[1] Department of Computing, University of Turku, Turku, Finland
{sadala,sjprau}@utu.fi

[2] Gamification Group, Tampere University, Tampere, Finland

Abstract. Several popular contemporary online multiplayer games and franchises are developed and managed with the aid of multiple data sources. Despite the control and insight that the utilization of data brings to game design and business decisions, video game developers occasionally receive backlash from their player communities. Examples include the announcement of Diablo Immortal at BlizzCon 2018, and the #HearUsNiantic campaign among Pokémon GO players in August 2021. In this article we analyze these two examples and demonstrate the importance of understanding player behavior more broadly than what can be derived from quantitative in-game data. In both the analyzed cases, players' offline culture played a paramount role in the backlash. We argue that the primary reason for the observed backlash is that the players' lives have become intertwined with digital products, and hence, changing these products alters the players' lives as well.

Keywords: Game design · Game development · Video games · Game industry · Player culture · Player communities

1 Introduction

Video games are complex forms of art that combine elements of story-telling [13], visuals, audio, game mechanics and sometimes also pervasive elements [11] into digital artifacts. The variance in video games is enormous in terms of all the above mentioned aspects. The complexity of video games makes it difficult to predict player behavior, how well the games sell and how long players stay engaged with them [14]. Even with multiple data sources and analytics at their disposal, popular franchises still occasionally make decisions which make customers revolt and turn against the creator [6]. These situations are always unique, but can be mitigated by better understanding the customers [6].

Recently, player behavior modelling through data-driven approaches has gained significant traction [4]. This approach relies on automatically collecting logged data of player behavior and using statistical or machine learning methods to profile players and predict their future behavior as well as what they

X. Wang et al. (Eds.): ICSOB 2021, LNBIP 434, pp. 194–201, 2021.
https://doi.org/10.1007/978-3-030-91983-2_15

enjoy [4,14]. Besides player profiling, data-driven approaches can be used for, for example, procedural content creation [5], automatically tweaking game settings such as difficulty [15] and understanding player retention across multiple situations [14]. In the case of trying to predict player retention, the data can consist of, for example, players' monthly playtime, playtime of individual sessions, data on the situations where players quit individual play sessions and data on the situations leading to quitting playing more permanently [14].

The recent upswing in data-driven game development has also raised concerns, in particular pertaining to ethics and fairness [12]. Algorithmic design decisions may marginalize certain player subgroups and the use of inscrutable machine learning models to analyze player data introduces trust issues [12]. A recent study showed that there are tensions in implementing ethical game design, for example, it may sometimes compete with functionality [1]. In addition, there are several other potential blind spots in data-driven development. In this study we focus on the player communities surrounding online games and franchises. These communities can have various game-related activities and culture that, while function outside the game, are still connected to it [2,9]. For example, players may engage in conversations about specific game mechanics or gather together to play a game in a specific way that only makes sense in the community context [9]. As video games are constantly developed and updated, player communities are hence in constant danger of losing the ability to practise an activity they enjoy. This leads to situations where players may be prepared to vigorously contact developers and ask them to revert changes, or change the course of their business, in order to save the community surrounding the game or the franchise.

In this short paper, we look at situations where player communities have openly revolted against the developer and demanded that they change the course of their game development. We focus on two famous real-world examples where game design has been disrupted by the player community. Based on these examples, we argue that while data-driven development is effective in increasing player retention and boosting income, it is crucial to also account for the player communities that exist around video games and franchises.

2 Two Examples: Diablo Immortal Announcement and HearUsNiantic

2.1 Materials and Methods

We wanted to investigate cases where the playing community has revolted against game developers regarding their design decisions, with the consequence that the developer has shifted plans in response. To this end, we selected two recent and highly public cases from world renown franchises: Diablo and Pokémon. As our first example, we look at the announcement of Diablo Immortal in November 2018 and its aftermath, and as our second example we focus on the #HearUsNiantic hashtag in August 2021. Basic information about these cases is given in Table 1. Both these examples are from developers who are well-known from utilizing in-game data collection and business intelligence in their game development and design decisions.

Table 1. General information regarding the two cases discussed in this work

Case	Date	Developer	Game
Diablo Immortal announcement	November 2018	Blizzard entertainment	Diablo Immortal
HearUsNiantic	August 2021	Niantic	Pokémon GO

Methodologically this work follows the netnography research approach [7], meaning we conducted ethnographic observations online to get acquainted with the player communities, their sentiment, the actions of the developer, the retaliation by the community and the underlying reasons and critique given by the players for their actions. When going through the two examples, we used the developers' official sources[1,2] as the main source of evidence. Additionally, we observed posts and comments on the Blizzard official forums, and 3rd party online discussion forums including Reddit, Twitter, Discord and YouTube. These included, for example, videos of independent content creators (e.g. Quinn69, Rhykker, Mystic7) and posts on popular subreddits (e.g. r/pokemongo, and r/thesilphroad). The authors were both participants in the observed communities, and hence, conducted their observations first without collecting any notes or data. Upon writing this article we revisited the original data sources and made notes to support our analysis. Subsequently, from the community response, we derived recommendations for the developers on what caused the situation and how it could be avoided.

2.2 Announcement of Diablo Immortal

Description of Events. During a video game convention BlizzCon, Blizzard Entertainment hyped up and announced a new mobile game in the fan-favorite Diablo franchise for a hard core PC gamer audience. The event sparked controversy due to fans being heavily disappointed in the announcement, and the company seemingly not caring about the PC-focused audience. The announcement led to the production of multiple memes and heavy downvoting of all Diablo Immortal content across social media. For example, the announcement trailer on YouTube received hundreds of thousands dislikes during the first few days [10] which can still be seen in the video today as shown in Fig. 1. A line from

[1] For Diablo Immortal, https://news.blizzard.com/en-us/blizzcon/22653697/diablo-immortal-unveiled-at-blizzcon.

[2] For Pokémon GO, https://pokemongolive.com/post/sep-taskforce-updateaccessed September2021

.

the Blizzard representative: *"Don't you guys have phones?"* was interpreted on social media as condescending and even arrogant, while a line from one of the BlizzCon convention attendees: *"Is this an out-of-season April fools' joke?"* was treated as a symbolic representation of the gamer audience.

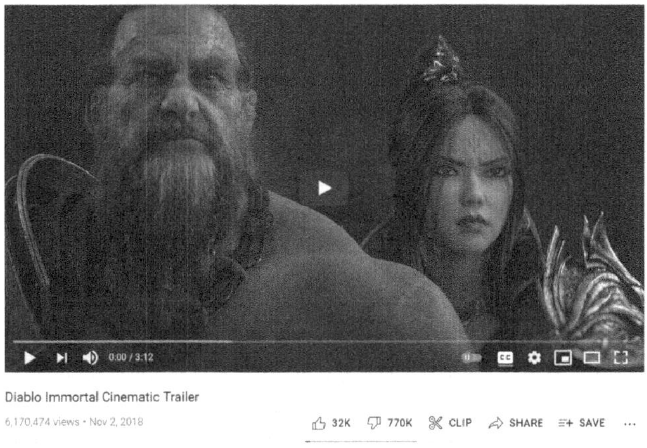

Fig. 1. Screenshot of the Diablo Immortal Announcement trailer on YouTube in September 2021. The downvotes following the announcement in 2018 can still be seen in the video at https://www.youtube.com/watch?v=RtSmAwpVHsA.

Following the announcement of Diablo Immortal in November 2018, Blizzard quickly delivered a statement that they were developing multiple Diablo franchise games and that Diablo Immortal was but one of many games in development, with the apparent aim of calming down the angered fans [10]. The next year at the same event, BlizzCon, Blizzard released a trailer for Diablo 4, a new PC game in the franchise, that was warmly welcomed by the audience.

Implications for Franchise Management. Diablo Immortal appears to be a part of the Activision-Blizzard business strategy to expand towards the mobile gaming market. Interestingly, recent academic literature suggests PC gamers have low intentions to switch to mobile gaming [3]. This data may have deterred Blizzard from announcing a mobile Diablo game to a primarily PC gamer audience. The community backlash forced Blizzard to consider new data points and shift their communication strategy.

The lessons learned from the announcement of Diablo Immortal pertain to the needs and desires of an existing playerbase. Also in the social media discussion, Diablo Immortal was treated as an example of what happens when a company forgets their existing audience. Despite being criticised for being subjective [7], netnographic participant-observation approaches offer a way forward for understanding and better catering the existing player communities.

2.3 #HearUsNiantic

Case Description. The Pokémon GO player community has repeatedly criticized the game developer Niantic about not listening to the community's concerns. This type of behavior is typically observed in situations where the players' social lives and daily activities are closely tied to the game [6]. Maybe the most notable example of Pokémon GO players revolting against the developer was the #HearUsNiantic campaign, which was the community's reaction to Niantic decreasing the PokéStop interaction distance from 80 m to 40 m. Originally, the interaction radius was increased to 80 m as a result of the COVID-19 pandemic. However, it was apparent to the community the change had many positive effects in addition to the social distancing. For instance, crossing dangerous roads or trespassing properties was often no longer necessary and disabled players could have an easier access to pokéstops.

In the wake of the commotion in social media, Niantic eventually reverted the pokéstop interaction radius back to 80 m. Moreover, Niantic set up a "task force" consisting of players and community representatives in order to continue the dialogue with players and better take into account any concerns about Pokémon GO. This response from Niantic indicates they acknowledge the importance of the opinions of the player communities that exist outside, but connected to, their game.

Implications for Game Development. In addition to the "Niantic task force", other ways to gain insight into player communities include player surveys and interviews, ethnographic observations and data, social media data, theoretical knowledge and history-based understanding of the game franchise. Understanding player communities can make a huge difference business wise, as it can open new opportunities to design for more engaging features and support player profiling in boosting player retention [14]. In the case of Pokémon GO, the fusion between the game and the real world has contributed to the players' lives being integrated to the game [9], meaning that changes to the game world influence the players' real world behavior and interactions [2,8].

In summary, as the data-based monetization approaches continue to evolve, they can affect game design in ways that can lead to strong criticism from players. For example, in Pokémon GO, players have to pay real money to obtain access to certain shiny pokémon, and at times, better events and prices are promised as a reward of active playing and using money. Sparrow et al. [1] discovered that video game developers are in fact often facing tensions between monetization approaches and ethics. While developers would want and be prepared to scaffold healthy player communities and behavior, business needs may get in way. Following the categorization of ethical considerations in data-driven game development by El-Nasr and Kleinman, video game developers may have to implement "monetization techniques that encourage irresponsible spending" [12].

3 Discussion

3.1 Recommendations for Practitioners

In both observed examples, the developers ultimately readjusted their course due to relentless community feedback. Blindly trusting modelled player behavior or business intelligence can backfire unless, for example in this case, the cultures and innate desires of the player community are acknowledged. Hence, quantitative data should not be the sole basis of decision making, and it is paramount to acknowledge the real world players communities and how players interact with the games in the real world. This can be particularly true in location-based games such as Pokémon GO that purposefully intertwine the game with the physical world [2,8,9], but also relevant in the Diablo franchise whose fanbase connect with one another beyond individual games through online communication as well as offline events.

Players can revolt for several reasons and sometimes developers are forced to make decisions that go against the wishes of players [6]. In these situations understanding the player communities can still help mitigate the damage. Hence, developers and franchise managers are encouraged to maintain active participation among player communities. This was in fact implemented by Niantic when establishing "the Niantic Task force". Quick reaction to community feedback is also important. This was shown by the positive responses of the player communities in both cases.

While developers have the capability to rapidly adjust to community responses, constantly staying alert and reacting can be consuming. Thus, it is important to use of a wide range of tools to understand players and their needs. This includes quantitative player profiling [4,14] and understanding the communities and cultures of various player demographics [7]. In addition, developers should carefully consider how they communicate their actions to the players [6].

3.2 Limitations and Future Work

In this work, we looked at a limited number of data sources. Hence, the analysis contains the risk of only acknowledging the mainstream opinions [12]. Furthermore, the authors conducted the majority of their observations as members of the player communities. This may have left us with blind spots. This study is also limited in scope, since we only looked at two examples. A more holistic study could reveal with greater certainty which game cultural factors are crucial in video game development and franchise management.

Future research agenda in this field should seek to identify the data and approaches needed to ensure video game developers stay on course with the wishes and desires of their players while simultaneously making financially profitable decisions. Yet, in the world of imperfect information, blindly trusting any singular data sources will ultimately always end in unintended consequences. The only way to mitigate the risks is to leverage multimodal data and be quick to react if things start to go wrong.

3.3 Conclusion

In this work, we revealed adverse consequences of focusing too much on quantitative data and ignoring online and offline player cultures. We looked at two examples where the players revolted against their developer: (1) the launch of Diablo immortal at Blizzcon 2018; and (2) the #hearUsNiantic social media campaign in 2021. In both cases the player communities by large were unhappy with the direction where the developers were taking the franchises, not because of the digital artifacts themselves, but because their social lives were tied to them.

References

1. Sparrow, L.A., Gibbs, M., Arnold, M.: The ethics of multiplayer game design and community management: industry perspectives and challenges. In: Proceedings of the 2021 CHI Conference on Human Factors in Computing Systems, pp. 1–13 (2021)
2. Bhattacharya, A., et al.: The pandemic as a catalyst for reimagining the foundations of location-based games. In: CHI PLAY. ACM (2021). https://doi.org/10.1145/3474707
3. Cai, X., Cebollada, J., Cortiñas, M.: From traditional gaming to mobile gaming: video game players' switching behaviour. Entertain. Comput. (2021)
4. Hooshyar, D., Yousefi, M., Lim, H.: Data-driven approaches to game player modeling: a systematic literature review. ACM Comput. Surv. **50**(6), 1–19 (2018)
5. Hooshyar, D., Yousefi, M., Wang, M., Lim, H.: A data-driven procedural-content-generation approach for educational games. J. Comput. Assist. Learn. **34**(6), 731–739 (2018)
6. Jabeen, F., Kaur, P., Talwar, S., Malodia, S., Dhir, A.: I love you, but you let me down! how hate and retaliation damage customer-brand relationship. Technol. Forecast. Soc. Change **174**, 121183 (2022)
7. Kozinets, R.V.: Netnography: Redefined, 2nd edn. Sage, New Delhi (2015)
8. Laato, S., Inaba, N., Hamari, J.: Convergence between the real and the augmented: experiences and perceptions in location-based games. Telemat. Inform. **65**, 101716 (2021)
9. Laato, S., Inaba, N., Paloheimo, M., Laajala, T.D.: Group polarisation among location-based game players: an analysis of use and attitudes towards game slang. Internet Res. **31**, 1695–1717 (2021)
10. McWhertor, M.: Blizzard responds to diablo: immortal backlash (2018). https://www.polygon.com/blizzcon/2018/11/3/18059222/diablo-immortal-blizzard-response-blizzcon
11. Santos, L.H.D.O., et al.: Promoting physical activity in Japanese older adults using a social pervasive game: randomized controlled trial. JMIR Serious Games **9**(1), e16458 (2021)
12. Seif El-Nasr, M., Kleinman, E.: Data-driven game development: ethical considerations. In: International Conference on the Foundations of Digital Games, pp. 1–10 (2020)
13. Smed, J.: Interactive storytelling: approaches, applications, and aspirations. Int. J. Virtual Commun. Soc. Netw. **6**(1), 22–34 (2014)

14. Viljanen, M., Airola, A., Heikkonen, J., Pahikkala, T.: Playtime measurement with survival analysis. IEEE Trans. Games **10**(2), 128–138 (2017)
15. Yin, H., Luo, L., Cai, W., Ong, Y.S., Zhong, J.: A data-driven approach for online adaptation of game difficulty. In: 2015 IEEE Conference on Computational Intelligence and Games (CIG), pp. 146–153. IEEE (2015)

Continuous Improvement

Design Principles for a Crowd-Based Prototype Validation Platform

Sebastian Gottschalk(✉), Muhammad Suffyan Aziz, Enes Yigitbas, and Gregor Engels

Software Innovation Lab, Paderborn University, Paderborn, Germany
{sebastian.gottschalk,enes.yigitbas,gregor.engels}@uni-paderborn.de

Abstract. One of the most critical aspects of developing successful products is the early feedback of potential customers. Here, customers can provide feedback iteratively on prototypes before the actual development of the product to save development resources on dissatisfying features. This feedback, in turn, could be collected using crowdsourcing. To gain knowledge about the design of software to support the iterative prototype development based on crowd feedback, this paper develops design principles for a crowd-based prototype validation platform. On this platform, developers can present their software prototypes in different forms and receive iterative feedback from a selected crowd of potential customers. The feedback is presented to the developer in an aggregated form to support his decision-making in further development. We conduct a design science study that builds the design principles based on an analysis of literature and software tools. We instantiate the design principles as a platform and evaluate them within an expert workshop. Our results show that the identified design principles support developing such software support for crowd-based prototype validation.

Keywords: Prototype validation platform · Design principles · Crowdsourcing · Lean development · UI prototyping

1 Introduction

The development of new software products is a cost- and resource-intensive task for a company [34]. In addition, the development is challenged by the fact that users want more and more solutions for their needs instead of just products [37]. Together with the rising number of available new products in the market, the chances of building products that the users do not use are tremendously increasing. Therefore, for sustainable software development, companies have to validate those uncertain user needs and proposed solutions before the actual development

This work was partially supported by the German Research Foundation (DFG) within the CRC "On-The-Fly Computing" (CRC 901, Project Number: 160364472SFB901) and the German Federal Ministry of Education and Research (BMBF) through Software Campus grant (Project Number: 01IS17046).

X. Wang et al. (Eds.): ICSOB 2021, LNBIP 434, pp. 205–220, 2021.
https://doi.org/10.1007/978-3-030-91983-2_16

of the product [19]. This is especially important in highly competitive markets like mobile ecosystems with millions of already developed apps.

To build products that fulfill the user needs, lean development [34] has been proposed as an essential technique. During the development, the company builds a Minimum Viable Product (MVP), tests it with potential users, and uses their feedback for iterative improvements. This, in turn, is similar to product discovery that aims to "quickly separate the good ideas from the bad to answer the question which products, features or services should be developed to fulfill the needs of the customer" [26]. UI prototypes based on images or clickable prototypes are often used to give users insights and feelings about the proposed product. For this, prototyping tools like Figma[1] or Adobe XD[2] can be used. However, one key challenge of those approaches is the access to users for validations [26].

The access to users can be solved by involving crowd workers in product development [38]. Here, crowdsourcing describes the outsourcing of value-creating activities from a company to a large undefined set of users by using an open call [18]. Based on this technique, different subcategories like crowd testing, crowd funding, crowd ideation, crowd logistic, crowd production, crowd promotion, and crowd support have been established in research [8]. Moreover, different platforms like KickStarter[3] for crowd funding or Amazon Mechanical Turk[4] for crowd working have been launched in practice. However, to the best of our knowledge, there is a gap in how to design platforms that support the prototype development based on the iterative feedback from a crowd of potential customers and, therefore, reduce uncertainties in product development. Consequently, this paper aims to gain abstracted design knowledge about such platform by answering the following research question (RQ): *How to design software for platforms that integrates crowdsourcing techniques in the iterative validation of prototypes?*

To answer the research question, we conducted a design science research (DSR) study [17] to develop a *Crowd-based Prototype Validation (CBPV) Platform*. For that, we have analyzed literature and tools in the areas of lean development, UI prototyping, and crowdsourcing to develop design principles (DPs) [13] for the platform. DPs, in turn, are used to represent abstracted design knowledge in a cross-domain transferable way. On this platform, developers can present their prototypes and receive iterative feedback from a selected crowd of potential users. The feedback is presented to the developer in an aggregated form to support his decision-making in further development. We have implemented the whole approach as a platform and evaluated it within an expert workshop. While we focus on mobile applications as one of the biggest areas for prototypes in this paper, the design principles bind the abstracted knowledge about the platform design so that the concept can be easily transferred to other areas.

The rest of the paper is structured as follows: Sect. 2 provides our research background in terms of lean development and design principles. Section 3 cov-

[1] Figma Tool: https://www.figma.com/.
[2] Adobe XD Tool: https://www.adobe.com/products/xd.html.
[3] Kickstarter Platform: https://www.kickstarter.com/.
[4] Amazon Mechanical Turk Platform: https://www.mturk.com/.

ers our research approach based on the DSR. Section 4 shows the derivation of the design requirements and their mapping to the design principles. Section 5 develops the platform by extracting concrete design features from the design requirements and their instantiation as a platform prototype. Section 6 shows our evaluation by explaining the evaluation setting and the received results. Finally, Sect. 7 concludes the paper and shows up the next design cycle.

2 Research Background

2.1 Lean Development and Co-creation of Software Products

Lean development is used to develop products that the customers want [34]. Using an iterative build-measure-learn cycle, the developer builds a minimum but viable product, measures the effect of the customer, and learns from their feedback. Here, it is important to prioritize the features with the most important assumptions [19]. While this technique can be used for every product, there are also approaches specific to software products. HYPEX [29] develops an iterative approach to evaluate new features by analyzing the gap between the expected and actual behavior. RIGHT [10] is similar to HYPEX but incorporates more of the business model into the development cycle. While both approaches focus on quantitive measurement, QCD [30] combines qualitative customer feedback with quantitative customer observations. For that, they propose the conduction of different experiments in addition to the implementation of the feature. While all approaches provide an iterative validation of products, none of the approaches focuses on prototype validation with the support of a crowd.

Co-creation of software products can be seen as the active participation of different stakeholders in software development [5]. One concept is crowdsourcing, where the opinion of crowd users that are unknown to the developer in advance are considered during the development [18]. Here, especially the directions of crowd testing and crowd ideation can be used by the developer [8]. While crowd testing tests software applications and websites, crowd ideation generates ideas for new strategies, products, services, processes, and activities. For these directions, there are also different approaches proposed in the literature. CrowdStudy [28] is a framework to let web developers test the usability of their interfaces with the crowd workers of Amazon Mechanical Turk. CrowdCrit [21] is a system for supporting designers in the validation of posters by allowing them to upload specific images and test them with the crowd of Amazon Mechanical Turk. ERICA [32] is a tool to use expert knowledge in the validation process of diverse crowd answers. Here, none of the approaches has a focus on prototypes.

2.2 Design Principles for Information Systems

Design science research aims to solve a class of problems by developing a solution to a specific problem and then generalize the gained knowledge [12]. One concept here is the usage of formulating the solution through design principles

(DPs). DPs, in turn, codify and capture design knowledge in a generalized way so that they can be transferred through the problem class [13]. There are two ways to derive DPs [25]. First, they can be created supportive by identifying knowledge sources, electing design requirements, and deriving design principles (used by us). Second, they can be created reflective by defining a problem, designing an IT artifact, and deriving the design principles. In both cases, the design principles need to be evaluated regarding DSR. In recent years, design principles for different software tools have been proposed. The Crowd-based Business Model Validation Systems [7] is a group of software that reduces uncertainties in the business model development using crowdsourcing. In [36], the DPs for an intrapreneurial platform to generate ideas are constructed. Moreover, in [33] generic DPs for crowd collaboration based on different incentives are derived. Here, none of those approaches focuses on the specialties of software prototypes.

3 Research Method

The CBPV platform is part of a larger research project supporting service providers in software ecosystems to build successful services both in terms of business model and product features. To develop the corresponding design principles, we use design science research (DSR) [15] to design an IT artifact that supports service providers in this challenge. For this, we follow the DSR methodology by Kuechler & Vashnavi [17] as shown in Fig. 1.

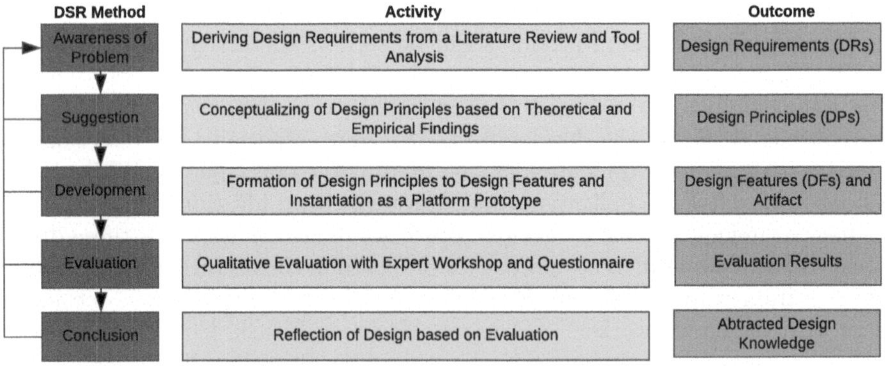

Fig. 1. Research method adopted from [17]

We base our DSR on the opportunity creation theory (OCT) [1] as kernel theory to stick in line with similar approaches like business model validation [7] or venture ideation [39] from digital entrepreneurship [27]. Concerning the concept of OCT, we conduct a non-systematic literature review and tool analysis on the topics of lean development, UI prototyping, and crowdsourcing to get an *Awareness of [the] Problem.* We analyze the literature with support of

Framework Analysis [35]. Here, we are getting familiar with the literature and tools (i.e., Familiarization), identifying important aspects for our platform (i.e., Identifying a Thematic Framework), indexing the content of the literature and tools according to the aspects (i.e., Indexing), building a storyline around those content (i.e., Charting), and, finally, deriving the design requirements (i.e., Mapping and Interpretation). In *Suggestion*, we conceptualize our design principles based on a mapping to the theoretical and empirical derived design requirements. After that, in *Development*, we form concrete design features out of the abstract design requirements and initiate them as an IT artifact in the form of a web-based platform prototype. As *Evaluation*, we provide a qualitative evaluation in the form of an expert workshop and subsequent questionnaire. In the online workshop with six experts from academics, we present the concept of the platform and the IT artifact to start a guided discussion about the problem we aim to solve, their opinions on the presented solution, and future improvements. In the subsequent questionnaire, we ask the experts to rate the effectiveness of the design principles and give them the chance to provide additional feedback missed in the workshop. By taking their input into account, we make a *Conclusion* in the form of abstracted design knowledge.

4 Design for CBPV Platform

This section shows our derived design requirements together with a mapping to the conceptualized design principles and the presentation of the overall design.

4.1 Derivation of Design Requirements

In the beginning, we need to derive the actual design requirements for our proposed solution based on the literature review and tool analysis.

Developers in the early stage of product development have high uncertainties regarding their product idea that can be reduced by testing the underlying assumptions directly with the market [2]. A large crowd of heterogeneous users can provide feedback on the assumptions by incorporating all perspectives of the products [22]. This, in turn, reduces the biases of the developer on the assumptions behind his idea [4]. Therefore, **DR1** ***Access to Heterogeneous Users:*** *The platform should enable developers to access a large number of heterogeneous potential users to validate their prototypes.*

In order to reduce the uncertainties, the developer can create Minimum Viable Products (MVPs) of their ideas, bring them to the market and learn from the feedback [34]. These MVPs can contain possible product features [34] and business model aspects [24], and the crowd can be used to test those ideas [8]. Here, the rapidness of the feedback is a critical factor for the developer [2]. Therefore, **DR2** ***Provision of Rapid Feedback:*** *The platform should enable a feedback mechanism to allow developers to rapidly receive feedback and capture user needs on their prototypes directly from the users.*

By developing a MVP, the developer could have different expectations of what should be evaluated by the user. Therefore, the provision of information is essential for the user to let them focus on specific parts [6]. This, in, turn also saves the scalability of the approach due to a reduced amount of inquiries and a higher quality of feedback [8]. This assistance is also implemented in Innocentive[5] to solve problems and Amazon Mechanical Turk to accomplish tasks. Therefore, **DR3** ***Assistance in Test Completion:*** *The platform should help users perform the tests by enabling developers to provide them with the essential information.*

Due to uncertain and changing user needs, more and more developers use iterative development approaches to adjust their products based on users' feedback [34]. This is not just for the product features but also for the business model that needs to be validated and adjusted to the market [24]. Here, both the feedback for the product features and the business model can be refined over time [30]. Therefore, **DR4** ***Iterative Conduction of Experiments:*** *The platform should enable an iterative refinement mechanism to enable developers to develop and adapt their prototype.*

Depending on the product's development stage, the prototype can have various forms like textual descriptions, images, or clickable mockups [20]. This diversity can also be used for different tasks of Amazon Mechanical Turk or representations of Figma. Moreover, those diversity leads also to different types of tests like questionnaires or split-tests [30]. This is also covered by the feedback mechanism of the prototyping tool UIGiants[6]. Therefore, **DR5** ***Diversity of Tasks:*** *The platform should facilitate different validation tests and types of feedback to help developers validate different assumptions related to the prototype.*

To ensure the quality of the feedback, the tasks must be just conducted by users of a relevant target group of the developer [23]. Conversely, users should see only tasks in which they are interested [16]. Amazon Mechanical Turk also uses two-sided filtering. Therefore, **DR6** ***Filtration between Tests and Users:*** *The platform should provide different filters for both developers and users.*

Depending on the number of individual user feedback, it can be a time-consuming and challenging activity to process them. Here, the feedback should be provided to the developer in an aggregated form for fast processing [11]. Moreover, appropriate visualizations should support the developers in interpreting the feedback [40]. Therefore, **DR7** ***Visualisation and Aggregation of Feedback:*** *The platform should aggregate and visualize the feedback results to help developers learn and make appropriate decisions.*

Developers usually have limited financial capacities for developing new products [34]. Especially startups have just limited financial but also development resources [3]. Here, the validation needs to be cheap enough so that the developer can use it in a regular manner. Therefore, **DR8** ***Cost-efficiency of Test Completion:*** *The platform should enable a cost-efficient validation to developers so that developers can validate their prototypes cheaply.*

[5] Innocentive Platform: https://www.innocentive.com/.
[6] UIGiants Platform: https://www.uigiants.com/.

Giving valuable feedback is a time-consuming activity, which should ideally be done regularly. Therefore, users should be offered extrinsic incentives like money or intrinsic incentives like fame [14]. While money is used as an extrinsic incentive by Amazon Mechanical Turk, intrinsic incentives like ratings and views are used by social media platforms like YouTube[7]. Therefore, **DR9 *Incentivization of Users:*** *The platform should provide incentives to crowd-workers to encourage their active participation.*

Providing valuable interactions between the developers and the users is the key task for the platform to stay successful. Good governance of those interactions will let the users stick much longer on the platform [9]. Here, governance in terms of policies, regulations, and accountability should be provided by the platform [31]. Therefore, **DR10 *Governance of Platform:*** *The platform should enable appropriate governance to ensure accountability and regulations.*

4.2 Conceptualizing of Design Principles

Out of the derived design requirements, we conceptualize our design principles for the CBPV platform. We analyze the design requirements and derive the extracted design principles as shown in Fig. 2.

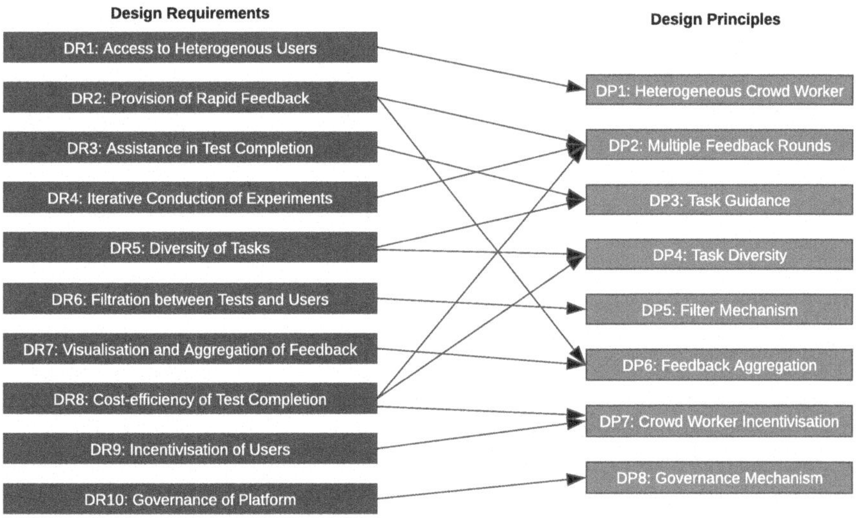

Fig. 2. Mapping from design requirements to design principles

The feedback of individual users is often biased by their past as well as their own experiences. By accessing the feedback of a heterogeneous crowd, this bias can be reduced, and the objectivity increases. This raises the chance to

[7] YouTube Platform: https://www.youtube.com/.

develop features that are used by the majority of the users. Therefore, **DP1** ***Heterogeneous Crowd Worker:*** *The CBPV platform should have access to a heterogeneous crowd so that developers can validate their prototypes.*

Prototypes can be created at various stages of the product development and can be continuously adapted to new requirements and feedback. Therefore, it is important that prototypes are presented iteratively over time, and appropriate feedback is collected. Therefore, **DP2** ***Multiple Feedback Rounds:*** *The CBPV platform should provide efficient and rapid multiple rounds of feedback mechanism to allow developers to refine their prototype iteratively.*

Based on the previously mentioned development phases, developers may have different requirements for the task to be performed. The users should be informed about those requirements in advance and be assisted in the execution. Therefore, **DP3** ***Task Guidance:*** *The CBPV platform should enable developers to provide necessary information to guide users in performing their tasks.*

The prototypes can be in different forms based on the tasks, such as textual descriptions, simple images, or clickable mockups. The same applies to feedback that is expected, for example, star ratings, field selections, or free text. Different types of prototypes and feedback should be supported. Therefore, **DP4** ***Task Diversity:*** *The CBPV platform should have support for (external) prototyping tools and allow the conduction of different tests.*

Based on the tasks, developers may have specific requirements for users, such as special skills and a certain age or gender. At the same time, users may also be interested in evaluating only prototypes in their area of interest, such as games or social media apps. Here, corresponding tasks should be filterable on both sides. Therefore, **DP5** ***Filter Mechanism:*** *The CBPV platform should provide two-sided filtration, so developers can shortlist crowd-workers and crowd-workers can shortlist tasks based upon their specific criteria.*

Developers can test a variety of prototypes with a potentially large number of users. To make it easier to keep track of the corresponding feedback, it should be provided in an aggregated form and supported by visualizations. Therefore, **DP6** ***Feedback Aggregation:*** *The CBPV platform should combine the users' feedback in aggregated form and visualize these results to help developers in decision making and learning.*

Crowd-working allows developers to access a large user base with corresponding feedback opportunities cost-effectively. To attract users to the platform in the long term and reward them for performing tasks, extrinsic incentives like money and intrinsic incentives like fame should be used. Therefore, **DP7** ***Crowd Worker Incentivization:*** *The CBPV platform should enable a cheap feedback mechanism for developers to afford the validation process and should also allow incentives for crowd workers whose feedback is selected by developers.*

Users often discard inadequately managed platforms because of their lower value creation. The creation of value can be improved through governance mechanisms such as reporting. For this reason, the platform owner should take care of the appropriate behavior of both the developers and the crowd workers. Therefore, **DP8** ***Governance Mechanism:*** *The CBPV platform should allow platform owners to take necessary action against users who misuse the platform.*

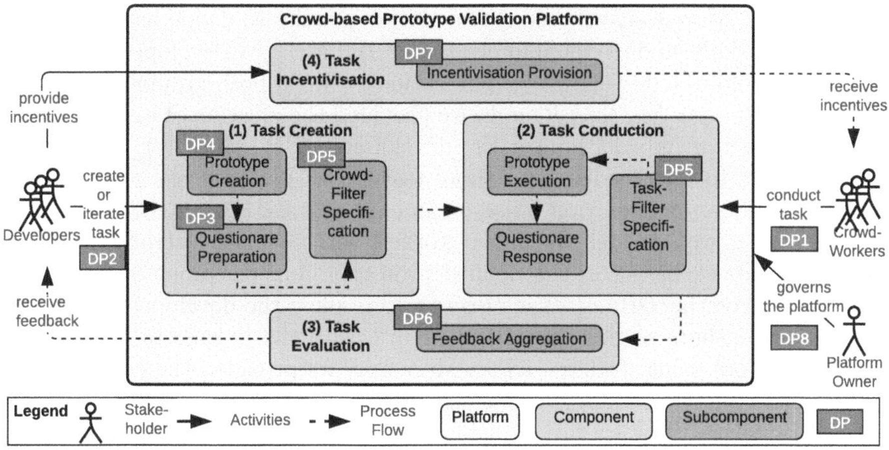

Fig. 3. Overall design of the platform

Out of those design principles, we develop an overall design for the *Crowd-based Prototype Validation Platform*, as shown in Fig. 3. It consists of the three roles of *Developer*, *Crowd-Worker*, and *Platform Owner* together with the four components of *(1) Task Creation*, *(2) Task Conduction*, *(3) Task Evaluation*, and *(4) Task Incentivisation*. First, the *Developer* starts the *(1) Task Creation* by creating the prototype, preparing the questionnaire, and specifying the crowd-filter. Next, the *Crowd-Worker* starts the *(2) Task Conduction* by specifying the task-filter, executing the prototype, and responding to the questionnaire. After enough feedback is collected, the *(3) Task Evaluation* aggregates those feedback. Here, the *Developer* can use the feedback for a new iteration or provides incentives through the *(4) Task Incentivisation*. Finally, the *Platform Owner* governs the whole platform by analyzing user reports and their tasks.

5 Development of the CBPV Platform

This section shows the development of our platform based on a formation of design features and their instantiation as an IT artifact.

5.1 Formation of Design Features

Our conceptualized design principles provide just abstracted design knowledge of how a CBPV platform should be developed for different areas. Therefore, before the implementation, we need to bind them to an application area and form concrete design features for the instantiation. In our case, we do that for the validation for mobile apps for mobile developers by potential early adopters.

For the *DP1 of Heterogenous Crowd Worker*, we developed user management with the feature to switch between the role of a developer and crowd worker (DF1). Moreover, we used crowd worker profiles to define basic information, existing skills, and personal interests (DF2). Lastly, we developed a message system that allows lightweight communication between both groups (DF3). For the *DP2 of Multiple Feedback Rounds*, we provided the creation of tasks with the most fundamental information for the developer (DF4). Moreover, we allowed crowd-workers to give feedback on those tasks (DF5). Lastly, we provided the instantiation of a new iteration based on an existing task (DF6). For the *DP3 of Task Guidance*, we provided the crowd workers with detailed instructions of the expected feedback based on the defined prototype and questions of the developer (DF7). For the *DP4 of Task Diversity*, we allow the developers to upload different screenshots of the app (DF8) or integrate the linkage to an external prototyping tool using iframes (DF9). Moreover, we provided the evaluation of a single prototype version or direct comparison of two versions with a split-test (DF10). Finally, with stars rating, field selections, and free text fields, we allow different types of feedback (DF11).

For the *DP5 of Filter Mechanism*, we provided corresponding selection criteria of crowd workers for every task based on their profiles (DF12). Moreover, we implemented a filter so that crowd workers can find tasks that they are interested in (DF13). For the *DF6 of Feedback Aggregation*, we combined the information of all aggregatable questions like stars ratings and selection fields in data visualization charts (DF14). Nevertheless, we also allowed the investigation of individual feedback details to analyze the relationships between the crowd worker answers (DF15). Lastly, we allowed crowd-workers the option to provide additional feedback for revealing unconsidered questions (DF16). For the *DP7 of Crowd Worker Incentivization*, we allowed the developer to provide crowd workers money for conducting the tasks (DF17). Moreover, we implemented a feature to publicly display a developer or crowd worker's trustworthiness (DF18). For the *DP8 of Governance Mechanism*, we provided an admin control panel with functionalities to manage users and tasks (DF19). Moreover, developers can report crowd workers or block them for their own tasks (DF20).

5.2 Instantiation of Platform Prototype

We initiated the CBPV platform as an artifact and implemented the formulated design features to evaluate our solution and the underlying design principles. Here, we initiated our platform based on state-of-the-art web technologies to allow a remote evaluation setting. For that, we used the Angular framework as frontend, ASP.NET core as backend, and PostgreSQL for the database. Moreover, we realized the connection between both with a REST API to allow a simple extension of functionality and transfer to other systems.

Two screens of our implemented platform are shown in Fig. 4. Here, we have the *Task Creation* with the features of defining a feedback questionnaire (DF11) and choosing the crowd worker selection criteria (DF12). Moreover, we have the *Task Evaluation* with the features of aggregated feedback visualization (DF14), individual answer analysis (DF15), reviewing additional comments (DF16), and rating crowd workers (DF18).

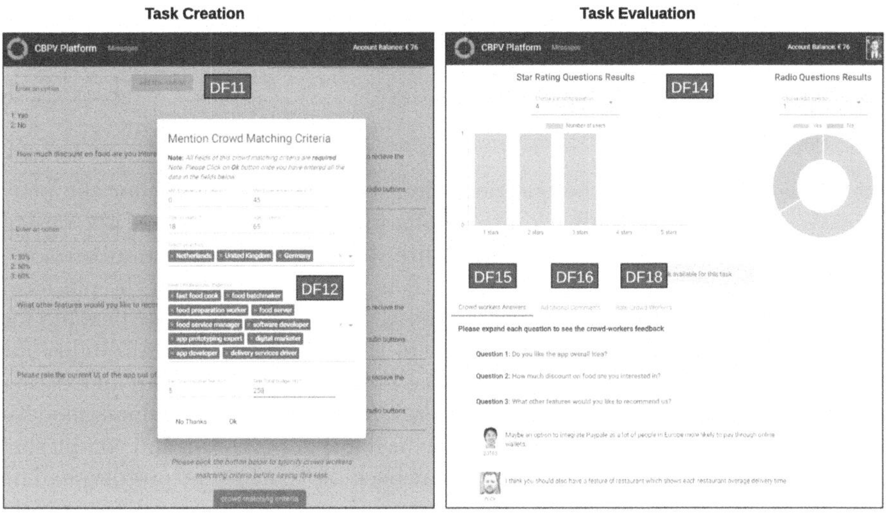

Fig. 4. Screenshots with mapped DFs of the platform

6 Evaluation of the CBPV Platform

This section shows the evaluation of our platform. For that, we explain our evaluation setting together with the gained results. Moreover, we discuss the threats to validity and implications together with pointing out future improvements.

6.1 Setting

Due to the ongoing pandemic, we decided on an online setting to evaluate our design principles and the overall concept together with pointing out future improvements. For that, we invited six experts with an academic background and multi-year experience in one of the areas of lean Development, UI prototyping, or crowdsourcing to an online workshop. Moreover, after the workshop, we sent them a follow-up questionnaire to collect additional feedback.

For the workshop, we scheduled a two-hour meeting using Microsoft Teams and recorded the whole session for later analysis. Inside the meeting, we conducted the following three steps: First, we gave a small presentation about the aim of the platform on the application scenario of mobile app developers and presented our design principles. Second, we gave a live demonstration of the platform prototype. Third, we managed a guided discussion through the experts based on the topic of the overall idea, the proposed solution, and future improvements, together with the ability to provide additional feedback. For the questionnaire, we provided the experts the given presentation slides and access to the platform prototype. Moreover, we created a questionnaire on Google Forms where experts could rate the design principles on a scale and give suggestions for further improvements. Moreover, we provided again the option for feedback on the overall idea, the proposed solution, and future improvements to receive additional thoughts from the experts after the meeting.

6.2 Results

Out of the workshop and the questionnaire, we received feedback for the platform. We divided those feedback into results for the overall idea and the design principles. We grouped the results for future research in a separate subsection.

For the overall idea, the experts gave their feedback mainly on the platform prototype. To summarize, the experts liked the overall idea and its benefits for saving development resources. Here, some of them liked the generalizability for different stages of product development (e.g., using screenshots from an existing app) and also related fields (e.g., validate revenue streams of a business model). Last, the platform prototype provides easy usability for creating and conducting tasks. Nevertheless, there is also some drawback on the current prototype. The majority of the experts said that building up a community is a challenging task, and it is currently not completely clear which groups can be developers and crowd workers on the platform. Moreover, some of them saw challenges in the manual matching of crowd workers and tasks, missing social network functionalities like trending prototypes, and intellectual property (IP) violations.

For the design principles, we based the results mainly on the answers to the questionnaires. Here, we directly ask the experts for the effectiveness of the design principles on a scale from 1 to 5. The rating of all design principles can be seen in Table 1. Here, the majority of the design principles (D2, DP4, DP5, DP6, DP8) have a mean of at least four and can be seen as effective in terms of the evaluation. Nevertheless, some design principles (DP1, DP3, DP7) have lower means and that is why they should be further investigated. *DP1 of Heterogeneous Crowd* can be explained with comments of challenges of community building and that it might make sense to consider a mix of experts and non-experts for better feedback. *DP3 of Task Guidance* can be connected to comments that too much guidance can hinder the occurrence of unexpected feedback. *DP7 of Crowd Worker Incentivisation* can be explained by comments

Table 1. Results for the effectiveness of the design principles (Scale: 1 to 5)

	DP1	DP2	DP3	DP4	DP5	DP6	DP7	DP8
Participant 1	4	4	4	4	4	3	3	4
Participant 2	2	5	5	4	4	3	4	4
Participant 3	3	5	5	4	5	5	3	4
Participant 4	5	4	2	5	5	4	4	5
Participant 5	3	4	1	4	3	5	3	5
Participant 6	4	4	3	3	4	4	4	3
Mean	**3.5**	**4.3**	**3.3**	**4**	**4.2**	**4**	**3.5**	**4.2**

on the contradictions between incentivization using money and receiving cheap feedback.

6.3 Discussion and Implications

Out of the evaluation, we got some results that we want to discuss and draw our implications on. We divided those into the Overall Idea and the Design Principles. For the *Overall Idea*, we saw the interest of the experts both in the concept and the prototype of the platform. Here, the experts' feedback got mostly in the direction of challenges that can be solved by providing new and replacing old features. Therefore, one implication is to modularize the architecture of our prototype so that it can be extended more simply in upcoming design cycles. For the *Design Principles*, we received concrete feedback from the expert on what problems they have with them and what could be improved. For *DP1 of Heterogenous Crowd*, experts and external crowd workers could be added to the principle. *DP3 of Task Guidance* could be reframed with the level of guidance that should be given and the aspect that guidance should also be used during the task creation. *DP4 of Task Diversity* could be split into prototype diversity and feedback diversity to improve the support of different development stages and related fields. *DP7 of Crowd Worker Incentivisation* could be extended with a design principle on task affordability. Finally, new design principles for machine learning integration and IP theft dealing could be added. Here, the change of those design principles also implies additional evaluation through design cycles.

6.4 Threats to Validity

We discuss our threats to validity according to Yin [41], who divides between Constructs Validity, Internal Validity, External Validity, and Reliability. In order to *Construct Validity*, we clarify the goal and purpose to the experts and provide an additional questionnaire with a renewed clarification. Nevertheless, there can be misunderstandings on that purpose. A threat to *Internal Validity* is the non-systematic literature review. While we cover different areas and use a technique like snowballing to reduce that threat, we can not completely ensure to missed relevant literature. A threat of *External Validity* is the limited number of experts that all have an academic background. Here, we cover experts with different knowledge backgrounds but can not ensure that the results are the same in a different setting. For *Reliability*, we record the whole expert workshop for further analysis. While this increases our results out of the workshop, it could harm the experts from giving negative feedback.

6.5 Future Improvements

From the expert workshop and the follow-up questionnaire, we derived future improvements for the overall solutions and their abstraction into design principles. We divided them into the topic of Task Diversity, Machine Learning

Integration, External Platform Integration, and IP Theft Dealing. For the *Task Diversity*, we currently allow just screen uploads or the usage of external tools for the prototypes and fives star rating, field selections, and free texts for the feedback. In the future, additional diversity of prototypes (e.g., textual ideas, internal prototyping tool) and feedback (e.g., ordered lists, image markers) could be implemented. Moreover, deeper integration of prototypes and feedback (e.g., different questions for different images, click analysis) could be provided. For the *Machine Learning Integration*, we currently support just manual matching and static suggestions. In the future, machine learning could provide additional support like an automatic matching of task and crowd workers, the suggestions of fitting questions, and the recognition of patterns in given feedback. For the *External Platform Integration*, the crowd workers currently need to register on the platform manually. In the future, integration of external platforms could be used for the authentication of the crowd workers or the conduction of the tasks. For the *IP Theft Dealing*, the worker can currently see all tasks that fit their profile. In the future, we could let sign those crowd-workers an NDA from the developers, or they could allow just preselected crowd workers.

7 Conclusion and Future Work

To develop successful products, early feedback from users is essential for the developers. This feedback, in turn, could be provided by crowd workers, but there is currently a lack of knowledge on how to handle those feedback. Therefore, we analyzed existing literature and tools to develop design principles for a Crowd-based Prototype Validation (CBPV) platform. We instantiated the design principles as a platform and evaluated them using an expert workshop. The evaluation shows the applicability of the design principles, which, therefore, can be used to design new and extends existing platforms.

Our future work is twofold and deals with the modularization of the architecture and the conduction of additional design cycles. First, we want to modularize our platform architecture so that existing features could be simply replaced and new features could be easily added. This should allow a flexible extension of the platform. Second, we want to improve our design principles by conducting additional design cycles. Based on the modularized architecture, we add future functionalities like task diversity, machine learning integration, external platform integration, or IP theft dealing as proposed as future improvements.

References

1. Alvarez, S.A., Barney, J.B., Anderson, P.: Forming and exploiting opportunities: the implications of discovery and creation processes for entrepreneurial and organizational research. Organ. Sci. **24**(1), 301–317 (2013)
2. Blank, S.: Why the lean start-up changes everything. Harv. Bus. Rev. **91**, 63–72 (2013)
3. Blank, S.G., Dorf, B.: The Startup Owner's Manual: The Step-By-Step Guide for Building a Great Company, 1st edn. K&S Ranch Press, Pescadero (2012)

4. Burmeister, K., Schade, C.: Are entrepreneurs' decisions more biased? An experimental investigation of the susceptibility to status quo bias. J. Bus. Ventur. **22**(3), 340–362 (2007)
5. Ceccagnoli, M., Forman, C., Huang, P., Wu, D.J.: Cocreation of value in a platform ecosystem! The case of enterprise software. MIS Q. **36**(1), 263 (2012)
6. Chen, K.T., Chu, W.T., Larson, M., Ooi, W.T. (eds.): Proceedings of CrowdMM 2012. ACM (2012)
7. Dellermann, D., Lipusch, N., Ebel, P.: Developing design principles for a crowd-based business model validation system. In: Maedche, A., vom Brocke, J., Hevner, A. (eds.) DESRIST 2017. LNCS, vol. 10243, pp. 163–178. Springer, Cham (2017). https://doi.org/10.1007/978-3-319-59144-5_10
8. Durward, D., Blohm, I., Leimeister, J.M.: Crowd work. Bus. Inf. Syst. Eng. **58**(4), 281–286 (2016)
9. Evans, D.S., Schmalensee, R.: Matchmakers: The New Economics of Multisided Platforms. Harvard Business Review Press, Boston (2016)
10. Fagerholm, F., Sanchez Guinea, A., Mäenpää, H., Münch, J.: The RIGHT model for continuous experimentation. J. Syst. Softw. **123**, 292–305 (2017)
11. Geiger, D., Seedorf, S., Schulze, T., Nickerson, R.C., Schader, M.: Managing the crowd: towards a taxonomy of crowdsourcing processes. In: AMCIS 2011 Proceedings - All Submissions. AIS (2011)
12. Gregor, S., Hevner, A.R.: Positioning and presenting design science research for maximum impact. MIS Q. **37**(2), 337–355 (2013)
13. Gregor, S., Kruse, L., Seidel, S.: Research perspectives: the anatomy of a design principle. J. Assoc. Inf. Syst. **21**, 1622–1652 (2020)
14. Hammon, L., Hippner, H.: Crowdsourcing. Bus. Inf. Syst. Eng. **4**(3), 163–166 (2012)
15. Hevner, A.R., March, S.T., Park, J., Ram, S.: Design science in information systems research. MIS Q. **28**, 75–105 (2004)
16. Kittur, A., Chi, E.H., Suh, B.: Crowdsourcing user studies with mechanical turk. In: Czerwinski, M., Lund, A., Tan, D. (eds.) Proceeding of CHI 2008, p. 453. ACM (2008)
17. Kuechler, B., Vaishnavi, V.: On theory development in design science research: anatomy of a research project. Eur. J. Inf. Syst. **17**(5), 489–504 (2008)
18. Leimeister, J.M.: Crowdsourcing. Control. Manag. **56**(6), 388–392 (2012)
19. Lindgren, E., Münch, J.: Raising the odds of success: the current state of experimentation in product development. Inf. Softw. Technol. **77**, 80–91 (2016)
20. Linsey, J.S., Clauss, E.F., Kurtoglu, T., Murphy, J.T., Wood, K.L., Markman, A.B.: An experimental study of group idea generation techniques: understanding the roles of idea representation and viewing methods. J. Mech. Des. **133**(3), 031008 (2011)
21. Luther, K., et al.: Structuring, aggregating, and evaluating crowdsourced design critique. In: Proceedings of the 18th ACM Conference on Computer Supported Cooperative Work and Social Computing, pp. 473–485. ACM (2015)
22. Maalej, W., Nayebi, M., Johann, T., Ruhe, G.: Toward data-driven requirements engineering. IEEE Softw. **33**(1), 48–54 (2016)
23. Mao, K., Yang, Y., Wang, Q., Jia, Y., Harman, M.: Developer recommendation for crowdsourced software development tasks. In: 2015 IEEE Symposium on Service-Oriented System Engineering, pp. 347–356. IEEE (2015)
24. McGrath, R.G.: Business models: a discovery driven approach. Long Range Plan. **43**, 247–261 (2010)

25. Möller, F., Guggenberger, T.M., Otto, B.: Towards a method for design principle development in information systems. In: Hofmann, S., Müller, O., Rossi, M. (eds.) DESRIST 2020. LNCS, vol. 12388, pp. 208–220. Springer, Cham (2020). https://doi.org/10.1007/978-3-030-64823-7_20
26. Münch, J., Trieflinger, S., Heisler, B.: Product discovery - building the right things: insights from a grey literature review. In: Proceedings of ICE/ITMC, pp. 1–8. IEEE (2020)
27. Nambisan, S.: Digital entrepreneurship: toward a digital technology perspective of entrepreneurship. Entrep. Theory Pract. **41**(6), 1029–1055 (2017)
28. Nebeling, M., Speicher, M., Norrie, M.C.: CrowdStudy. In: Proceedings EICS, p. 255. ACM (2013)
29. Olsson, H.H., Bosch, J.: The HYPEX model: from opinions to data-driven software development. In: Bosch, J. (ed.) Continuous Software Engineering, pp. 155–164. Springer, Cham (2014). https://doi.org/10.1007/978-3-319-11283-1_13
30. Olsson, H.H., Bosch, J.: Towards continuous customer validation: a conceptual model for combining qualitative customer feedback with quantitative customer observation. In: Fernandes, J.M., Machado, R.J., Wnuk, K. (eds.) ICSOB 2015. LNBIP, vol. 210, pp. 154–166. Springer, Cham (2015). https://doi.org/10.1007/978-3-319-19593-3_13
31. Parker, G., van Alstyne, M., Choudary, S.P.: Platform Revolution: How Networked Markets Are Transforming the Economy and How to Make Them Work for You. W.W. Norton & Company, New York (2016)
32. Quoc Viet Hung, N., Chi Thang, D., Weidlich, M., Aberer, K.: ERICA. In: Proceedings of the 38th International ACM SIGIR Conference on Research and Development in Information Retrieval, pp. 1037–1038. ACM (2015)
33. Reibenspiess, V., Drechsler, K., Eckhardt, A., Wagner, H.T.: Tapping into the wealth of employees' ideas: design principles for a digital intrapreneurship platform. Inf. Manag. 103287 (2020)
34. Ries, E.: The Lean Startup: How Today's Entrepreneurs Use Continuous Innovation to Create Radically Successful Businesses. Crown Business, New York (2014)
35. Srivastava, A., Thomson, S.B.: Framework analysis: a qualitative methodology for applied policy research. J. Admin. Gov. **4**, 72–79 (2009)
36. Tavanapour, N., Bittner, E.A.C.: Towards supportive mechanisms for crowd collaboration – design guidelines for platform developers. In: Zaphiris, P., Ioannou, A. (eds.) HCII 2019. LNCS, vol. 11591, pp. 353–372. Springer, Cham (2019). https://doi.org/10.1007/978-3-030-21817-1_27
37. Teece, D.J.: Business models, business strategy and innovation. Long Range Plan. **43**(2–3), 172–194 (2010)
38. Tran, A., Hasan, S.U., Park, J.Y.: Crowd participation pattern in the phases of a product development process that utilizes crowdsourcing. Ind. Eng. Manag. Syst. **11**(3), 266–275 (2012)
39. Vogel, P.: From venture idea to venture opportunity. Entrep. Theory Pract. **41**(6), 943–971 (2017)
40. Xu, A., Huang, S.W., Bailey, B.: Voyant: generating structured feedback on visual designs using a crowd of non-experts. In: ACM Conference on Computer Supported Cooperative Work & Social Computing, pp. 1433–1444. ACM (2014)
41. Yin, R.K.: Case Study Research: Design and Methods. Applied Social Research Methods Series, vol. 5, 4th edn. Sage, Los Angeles (2009)

What Are Critical Success Factors of DevOps Projects? A Systematic Literature Review

Nasreen Azad(✉) and Sami Hyrynsalmi

Software Engineering, LUT University, Lappeenranta, Lahti, Finland
{nasren.azad,sami.hyrynsalmi}@lut.fi

Abstract. DevOps is a software development and operation practice, and a recent addition to a large family of different kinds of software process models. The model was born as it was observed that information systems operations and information system developments are closely integrated activities for the success of any organization. Thus, DevOps methods are an addition for the companies to improve overall performance in their software development process and operations. DevOps fills the gap between the development and operations teams and maintains the collaboration among information technology professionals for delivering the software applications. Due to its recent emergence, there are relatively little research done, at least when compared to the other software process models, on DevOps and its successful usage. Previously, some empirical research studies have been conducted on the success factors of DevOps, but a synthesis of these findings is needed. This paper aims to find out various critical success factors of DevOps projects that have been discussed in prior research by following a systematic literature review. Based on our extensive keyword search and after applying inclusion/exclusion criteria, we have included 30 research articles in this paper. The identified critical success factors were categorized into technical, organizational and social and cultural dimensions. Finally, this study offers a comprehensive framework depicting how the critical success factors impact or drive DevOps success.

Keywords: DevOps · Development and operation · Success factors · Barriers · Literature review

1 Introduction

To compete in a highly-volatile market, it is necessary for an organization to release a software that is both effective and has the capability to sustain in the competition [19]. For customers, it is important to have new features with an efficient software delivery [13]. As the software business has matured over the years, also the requirements for speed and efficiency have changed [23]. As a response to the changing business environment, also the software development life-cycles and the development processes have been evolving.

X. Wang et al. (Eds.): ICSOB 2021, LNBIP 434, pp. 221–237, 2021.
https://doi.org/10.1007/978-3-030-91983-2_17

In software development, Agile Software Development Methods are a set of practices that helps to improve the effectiveness of the software development of the organizations, teams, and professionals. The purpose of agile practices is to discover the user requirements and develop solutions through collaboration with cross functional teams and end users [29]. Agile practices have some limitations and create complexity while scaling agile development framework [36]. In contrast, DevOps is the combined process of 'development' and 'operations', which is used for the software development to speed up the delivery process with efficiency [41].

DevOps is a widely used development strategy that helps to minimize software development costs through implementation and adoption. The aim of DevOps is to provide continuous development and continuous delivery for the software development process [39]. DevOps allows to make collaboration with development and operations teams within the organization and provide an effective delivery process for software development.

Critical success factors is a management literature concept, which dates back to the beginning of the 1960s [17]. While there is a vast literature on the critical factors and their role, they can be briefly defined as *"the few key areas of activity in which favorable results are absolutely necessary for a particular manager to reach his goals"* [8, p. 4]. There are various critical success factors for DevOps projects, which have been discussed in prior empirical studies. In recent years, literature review articles were published which described DevOps concept, DevOps adoption, DevOps Implementation, DevOPs specific use, DevOps implementation with agile, and DevOps challenges, benefits and success factors [3,20,22,26,33,46]. However, we did not find any literature review that proposed a synthesized framework which could provide a clear, comprehensive idea about the critical success factors of DevOps projects. This is the potential research gap that will be addressed in this paper.

Therefore, we aim to provide a better understanding of the critical success factors of DevOps projects by identifying how those success factors impact DevOps implementation and its success. We will use the extant academic literature as a starting point for this inquiry. We will focus on identifying various success factors of DevOps and categorize them in this paper. That is, this study aims to answer the following research question:

RQ What are the critical success factors, as reported on the extant research literature, of DevOps projects?

For this study, we limit the scope only to the research literature—that is, we exclude gray literature—and put emphasis on studies reporting empirically acquired results. The rationale of this is to focus on verified and peer-reviewed information in this study.

The remainder of this paper is structured as follows. Section 2 presents the research process utilized in this study as well as the systematic literature review method used to gather the primary studies. It is followed by the results in Sect. 3 and discussion in Sect. 4. Finally, Sect. 5 concludes the study.

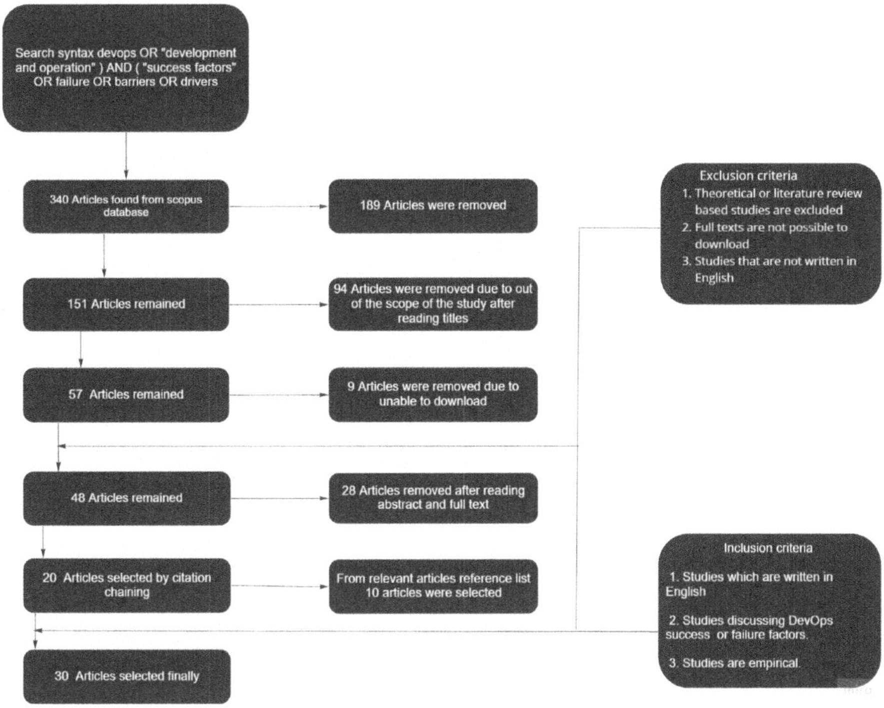

Fig. 1. The SLR process used in this study to collect the primary studies for analysis.

2 Research Process

For answering the presented research question, a systematic literature review (SLR) approach was followed to collect the primary studies done in the topic. SLR has a specific purpose to address a focused theme and detailed research presentation. SLR has predefined steps which differentiate it from unstructured literature reviews [27].

We have followed the methodology by Kitchenham and Charters [27] for searching the research articles. To perform the search properly, we identified suitable keywords. After the search, we got the initial list of articles. Various criteria and parameters were then applied to filter out irrelevant articles. After that, we finalized the final list of articles which guided us to answer the research question adequately. The overall SLR process has been shown in Fig. 1.

2.1 Search Terms and Strategy

The most important step for an SLR is to define and select the search protocol. After setting the research question of this study, it was decided to utilize search terms and queries into publication databases in order to guarantee the largest number of relevant studies published in the theme. Utilizing a manual search strategy for selected publication venues could have biased the study heavily towards issues discussed in those venues. After this decision, a set of relevant keywords to be used in the searches were analyzed. We tested several different alternatives and found that the keywords of *DevOps*, *Development and Operation*, *Success factors*, *Failures*, *Drivers*, and *Barriers* bring the largest, yet still relevant set of hits in different databases. We used the logical connections 'AND' and 'OR' to create a usable search string.

In the phase of defining the search protocol, different publication databases were considered. Finally, we decided to use only the Scopus database as it already indexes most of the venues used by the computing discipline scholars. Using some other databases, such as IEEE Xplore[1], did not bring a significant number of new hits to be included.

Finally, we retrieved the primary studies from Scopus database to identify the articles using the following search string:

```
TITLE-ABS-KEY ( ( devops OR "development and operation" ) AND
( "success factors" OR failure OR barriers OR drivers ) )
```

2.2 Exclusion and Inclusion Criteria

The first part of conducting the review is to define inclusion and exclusion criteria [27]. The following exclusion and inclusion criteria were applied to extract the final list of articles.

The inclusion criteria are:

1. Studies discussing DevOps success or failure factors.
2. Studies are empirical.
3. Studies which are written in English.

The exclusion criteria are

1. Theoretical or literature review based studies are excluded.
2. Full texts were not possible to acquire by using any media.
3. Studies that are not written in English

2.3 Selection of the Final List of Articles and Analysis

Initially, we have found 340 articles in the Scopus database with the search terms. The searches were done at the beginning of August 2021. At first, we looked at the title of each article and excluded the articles which were clearly not relevant for answering our research question. After excluding the articles based on title, we were left with 151 articles. Then we looked at the abstract of these 151 articles and we found 57 articles were relevant for our study. Among

[1] As of October 2021, IEEE Xplore return 65 articles with the mentioned search term. Out of those, 50 were present in the set of search results returned from Scopus. The remaining 15 documents contained, e.g., a keynote address, editorial commentaries, notes from a plenary talk and a tutorial summary. By using the exclusion and inclusion criteria discussed in Subsect. 2.2, none of these 15 documents would have been included into the further steps of this study.

these 57 articles, 9 articles were not possible to acquire when this study was carried out. Therefore, we downloaded 48 articles. Among these 48 articles, 28 articles were excluded after reading the full text. Then we used citation chaining (also known as snowballing) and found 10 more relevant articles. Finally, we could consider including 30 relevant papers for this study.

After the final list of the relevant primary studies found for this research was created, a researcher read through all articles. We used an unstructured model for extracting the data from the primary studies; that is, the researchers listed all success factors listed in the article without pre-existing codes or categories. In addition, general details regarding the study were recorded. Examples of extracted data from these included studies are shown in Appendix (Table 3). A second researcher agreed and verified the created coding. After all studies were went through, the researchers started categorizing the first-level codes into larger hierarchies. Finally, a three-tiered model was created, wherein the first level are the factors as they were given in the primary studies. The second level combines the factors into commonly understood logical groups. The third level categorizes the second level codes into large, remarkably differentiating perspectives. Both researchers agreed with the end result.

3 Results

Altogether 30 relevant primary studies were found and nearly a hundred different factors were identified. The selected articles are referred together with the identified factors in Table 1. The selected articles are given in Table 2. DevOps critical success factors were classified into ten groups which form three major categories. The major categories are *Technical*, *Organizational*, and *Social and cultural*. All categories are discussed below.

Table 1. Categorization of factors. In parenthesis, following a critical success factor, there are examples of individual success and failure factors (i.e., first-level codes in our coding) belonging into this category as well as the primary studies proposing them.

Categories	Critical success factor (success and failure factors)
Technical	*Performance Engineering* (Performance engineering complexity [7], Performance measurement [45], Performance regressions effects [11], Lightweight approaches for performance engineering [7],Software release [9] Seamless upgrades [12])
	Integration (Smooth integration with existing tools [7], Integrated solution for the combined system [24],Limited mechanism for quality feedback [10], AISD and a closer integration of ISD with IS should be maximized [21], Integrate the challenges of operations and support, Continuous integration process [12], Continuous integration and deployment [3],Continuous integration [25] Continuous integration [40] Implement continuous integration [15])
	Build and Test automation (Test automation improvement [38], Drive change management [1], Verification (soundness) [6], Specific tools to automate building [30], Automatic testing techniques [3],Development and test automation [9],Automation [40], Process automation [49] Automation [48], Lack of process automation [16])
	Infrastructure (Deployment and infrastructure provisioning [30], Infrastructure [12], Design a common infrastructure [3], Accommodate legacy systems [3])
	DevOps as a Service and its associated challenges [44]

(*continued*)

Table 1. (*continued*)

Categories	Critical success factor (success and failure factors)
Organizational	*Intra-organizational collaboration or communication* (Collaboration between dev and ops [16], Misalignment among departments [15], Inflexibility of communication processes [15], Communication structures [42], Miscommunication between development and operations [15], Help from cross-organizational team [15]) *Organizational Hierarchy* (Willingness to accept requests from superiors [42], Absence of a lead person [5], Attempt matrix organization and transparency [3], Seeking immediate manager's approval for team task in defense to local superiors [42], Collaboration between departments that boosts communication and employee welfare [38]). *Strategic Planning* (Continuous delivery [15,35,48], Keep to the sequencing of the DevOps approach [3], Internal DevOps event [3], Demonstrating Lean leadership behavior [3], Plan next improvement [3], Clearer goal [50], Deployment risk by Identified tooling obstacle [34], Company pressure, Reluctant to warn about non-feasible deadlines [42], Reluctance to discuss failure [42], Dissimilar development [38], Production environments [38], System Quality and development [35], Use system orchestration [3], Real-time feedback [3], Limited mechanism for quality feedback [10], DevOps security pipeline [3], Reduce the time to market [15], Emphasizing the silos [16], Clear role setting [50])
Social and Cultural	*Team Dynamics* (Team and process efficiency [16], Reluctant to reveal a lack of understanding [42], Reluctant to expose problems [42], Reluctance to voice criticism or propose alternatives to perceived directives from superiors [42], Mutuality, Reciprocity, Trust, commitment among teams [45],Fear of changes [47], Blaming team mates [47] Efficient collaboration [48], Understanding and respect for each other and their respective organizations [28], Shared responsibilities [34], Improved collaboration [34], Common ways of working [34], Team roles [12], Team coordination [12],team collaboration [32], cross functional team integration [49] Team experience Source code control [12]) *Cultural shift* (Emphasize Culture than tools [3], Cross-functional team [3], Established skilled DevOps teams [3], Change in organizational culture [31],Isolation in teams [47] Getting quick response time to business demands [15], Organization and employees culture [15], Cultural norms, values mutual respect, understanding, trust among teams [28], Cultural impacts [34], Collaboration culture,diversity and knowledge absorption [50])

3.1 Organizational Success Factors

Organizational success factors are an important category for DevOps success. After reviewing the studies, we have found three subcategories for organizational success factors. These include intra-organizational collaboration or communication, organizational hierarchy and strategic planning.

Intra-organizational Collaboration or Communication. According to Diaz et al. [15,16], the collaboration between Dev and Ops teams, misalignment among departments and inflexibility of communication processes are the factors that might impact the success of DevOps practices. Riungu et al. [38] claim that collaboration between departments boosts communication and employee welfare. They also state that the production environment has a role in intra-organizational communication. According to Akbar et al. [3], real-time feedback is crucial for the successful implementation of DevOps practices. According to Chen [10], mechanisms for quality feedback is essential for DevOps use and can impact collaboration.

Organizational Hierarchy. Another subcategory of organizational success factors is the organizational hierarchy. In [42], the authors found that willingness

Table 2. The publications included into this systematic review.

&	Authors	Year	Title
1	Abdelkebir et al. [1]	(2017)	"An agile framework for ITS management In organizations: A case study based on DevOps"
2	Akbar et al. [3]	(2020)	"Identification and prioritization of DevOps success factors using fuzzy-AHP approach"
3	Alnamlah et al. [5]	(2021)	"The necessity of a lead person to monitor development stages of the DevOps pipeline"
4	Ben Mesmia et al. [6]	(2021)	"DevOps workflow verification and duration prediction using non-Markovian stochastic Petri nets"
5	Bezemer et al. [7]	(2019)	"How is performance addressed in DevOps?"
6	Callanan et al. [9]	(2016)	"DevOps: making it easy to do the right thing"
7	Chen [10]	(2019)	"Improving the software logging practices in DevOps"
8	Chen [11]	(2020)	"Performance regression detection in DevOps"
9	Claps et al. [12]	(2015)	"On the journey to continuous deployment: Technical and social challenges along the way"
10	Dıaz et al. [14]	(2018)	"DevOps in practice: an exploratory case study"
11	Dıaz et al. [15]	(2019)	"Devops in practice-a preliminary analysis of two multinational companies"
12	Dıaz et al. [16]	(2021)	"Why are many businesses instilling a DevOps culture into their organization?"
13	Hüttermann et al. [21]	(2019)	"Devops: Walking the shadowy bridge from development success to information systems success"
14	Júnior et al. [24]	(2021)	"From a Scrum Reference Ontology to the Integration of Applications for Data-Driven Software Development"
15	Karamitsos et al. [25]	(2020)	"Applying DevOps practices of continuous automation for machine learning"
16	Kolfschoten et al. [28]	(2010)	"Collaboration 'engineerability"'
17	Luz et al. [30]	(2018)	"Building a collaborative culture: a grounded theory of well succeeded devops adoption in practice"
18	Marnewick et al. [31]	(2020)	"DevOps and organisational performance: the fallacy of chasing maturity"
19	Mohan et al. [32]	(2016)	"Secdevops: Is it a marketing buzzword?-mapping research on security in devops"
20	Nybom et al. [34]	(2016)	"On the impact of mixing responsibilities between devs and ops"
21	Olszewska et al. [35]	(2015)	"DevOps meets formal modelling in high-criticality complex systems"
22	Riungu-Kalliosaari et al. [38]	(2016)	"DevOps adoption benefits and challenges in practice: a case study"
23	Salameh [40]	(2019)	"The Impact of DevOps Automation, Controls, and Visibility Practices on Software Continuous Deployment and Delivery"
24	Šmite et al. [42]	(2021)	"Overcoming cultural barriers to being agile in distributed teams"
25	Trihinas et al. [44]	(2018)	"Devops as a service: Pushing the boundaries of microservice adoption"
26	Tsanos et al. [45]	(2014)	"Developing a conceptual model for examining the supply chain relationships between behavioural antecedents of collaboration, integration and performance"
27	Wahaballa et al. [47]	(2015)	"Toward unified DevOps model"
28	Wettinger et al. [48]	(2014)	"Devopslang-bridging the gap between development and operations"
29	Wiedemann et al. [49]	(2020)	"Understanding how DevOps aligns development and operations: a tripartite model of intra-IT alignment"
30	Yoon et al. [50]	(2017)	"Typology and success factors of collaboration for sustainable growth in the IT service industry"

to accept requests from superiors is a key organizational success factor. They also found that seeking immediate manager's approval for team tasks and communication plays a vital role in team progress. Alnamla et al. [5] state that when there is an absence of a lead person in the team then the efficiency of the team decreases. According to Diaz et al. [16], emphasizing the silos is also an essential factor that determines success.

Strategic Planning. Strategic planning is an integral part of a successful system. It is very important that there should be an initiative, resources, budget, integration with strategic IT and business plans that align with the company objectives [1]. According to several studies [9,15,18,25,35,47,48], continuous delivery and continuous development have become important practices for software development, therefore these should be taken into account for strategic planning. They also found that DevOps practices for continuous delivery and continuous development promote fast and frequent delivery of changing features and ensures the quality of the product. Akbar et al. [3] stated that there should be a continuous sequencing of DevOps approaches. They have also found that internal DevOps events are necessary to introduce DevOps to the employees and empower practitioners to share their work, problems and collaboration with peers. This helps the employees to accomplish clear goals that help to plan for future improvement with lean leadership. According to both Šmite et al. [42] and Riungu et al. [38], issues such as company pressure, reluctance to non-feasible deadlines, and reluctance to discuss failures and dissimilar development must be considered during strategic planning. Furthermore, system orchestration [3], change management [3], reduce the time to market [1,42] are also important to consider while doing strategic planning for the organization.

3.2 Social and Cultural Success Factors

Social and cultural factors are among the most important factors for DevOps critical success. Under these social and cultural categories, we have found two subcategories named 'team dynamics' and 'cultural shift'. We will explain these factors below.

Team Dynamics. From the results of our literature review, we have found that team dynamics play a vital role in DevOps success. According to Diaz et al. [16,32] team and process efficiency have some patterns that impacts on the organizational and cultural perspective for DevOps usage. Šmite et al. [42] suggested that reluctance to reveal a lack of understanding in asking questions impacts team efficiency. They also claimed that offshore teams (Sweden and India) with DevOps practices might be reluctant to voice criticism or propose alternatives to perceived directives from superiors. Akbar et al. [3] found some factors that influence the DevOps practices in software organizations. Cross-functional teams and established skilled DevOps teams impact the DevOps success. Tsanos et al. [45] and Kolfschoten et al. [28] explained that mutuality, trust, commitment and mutual respect among teams impact the team efficiency for DevOps. Yoon et al. [50] conducted a survey on Korean IT organizations and found that clear role setting, methods for solving common issues in teams are critical for team dynamics. Wettinger et al. [48] state that efficient collaboration in teams has a positive impact on team dynamics. Kolfschoten et al. [28] found that understanding and respect for each other and their respective organizations speed up teams efficiency. Nybom et al. [34] conducted a survey on 14 engineers of an organization and found that several benefits such as improved collaboration, trust, smoother workflow, shared responsibilities, and common ways of work the team's efficiency. According to Claps et al. [12], team roles, teams coordination, team experience, source code control impacts on the success of DevOps.

Cultural Shift. After reviewing the literature, we have identified that cultural shift is another important component for DevOps critical success factors. According to Riungu et al. [38], cultural shift impacts on DevOps adoption which is bigger than the technical or processes issues. A lead architect was interviewed by the authors and found that the company should work towards a common goal to achieve the overall objectives of the project. Akbar et al. [3] stated that companies should emphasize culture rather than tools that will help the task execution [6]. Diaz et al. [15] conducted an interview of Stakeholders of 11 (multinational) software-intensive companies and found that organization and employees culture impacts the success of an organization. Finally, cultural norms [28] and understanding of culture [34] are important factors.

3.3 Technical Success Factors

Technical success factors are another important factor category. Under these factors, we have found five subcategories named 'Performance engineering', 'Integration', 'Build and test automation', 'Infrastructure', and 'DevOps as a service'. These are discussed below.

Performance Engineering. Bezemer et al. [7] described how performance can be addressed in industrial DevOps projects. According to them the complexity of performance engineering approaches is one major barrier to DevOps success. Therefore, they suggested that performance engineering approaches need to be lightweight. They also suggested integrating performance engineering approaches with the tools of the DevOps pipeline. In the context of DevOps, the adoption of performance engineering practices is low. This is because the performance engineering approaches are not designed for DevOps contexts. The existing tools and approaches which are used for DevOps settings do not integrate properly with existing performance engineering processes. Thus, performance engineering researchers could ensure that their tools integrate properly with the existing DevOps pipelines. According to Bezmer et al. [7], integrated solutions may help to improve estimations, allocate teams and manage team productivity and project performance. According to Chen [11], performance regression often slips to operation while using DevOps. Thus, techniques are needed to detect performance regression at the source code level.

Integration. According to Junior et al. [24], integrated solutions for the combined process of DevOps help for DevOps success. In [21], the authors state that AISD (Agile information system development) and a closer integration of ISD with IS should be maximized for success. According to Claps et al. [12], continuous integration process and challenges of operations and support may impact DevOps success.

Build and Test Automation. According to Riungu et al. [38], test automation, automatic testing technique improvement can affect the success of DevOps. Furthermore, verification of soundness [6], specific tools for automation [6], automation techniques [48], building and process automation [16] may impact DevOps success.

Infrastructure. According to Claps et al. [12], infrastructure is vital for software process integration. Infrastructure helps in continuous development and solves problems regarding hardware and software issues. The infrastructure allows software products to be deployed when it is needed. According to Luz et al. [30], development and infrastructure provisioning are needed for better execution of DevOps practices.

DevOps as a Service. Microservices are an integral part of DevOps culture. The DevOps team works together and manages the life cycle of the application and goes through continuous releases. DevOps as a service platform thus facilitates software teams in respect of microservices [44].

4 Discussion

4.1 Key Findings and Observations

This study sets forth a research question to identify the critical success factors presented in the extant research literature for a successful DevOps project. After reviewing 30 primary studies and analyzing them, we identified 10 critical success factors. The factors were divided into three main categories.

In addition, we summarize our key observations into the following three points:

Firstly, the identified ten factors are logically categorized into technical, organizational as well as social and cultural groups. When compared to similar studies done with agile or plan-driven methods (c.f. [2,4,43]), the role of technically-oriented factors is overemphasized. Yet, this might indicate a major characterizing difference of technologies between DevOps and more traditional software development process models.

Secondly, while DevOps is a relatively young software process model, there is already remarkable research literature built on it. Whereas it is clearly smaller than the extant literature addressing e.g., Agile methods, it is emerging swiftly. Furthermore, the extant literature is already suggesting critical

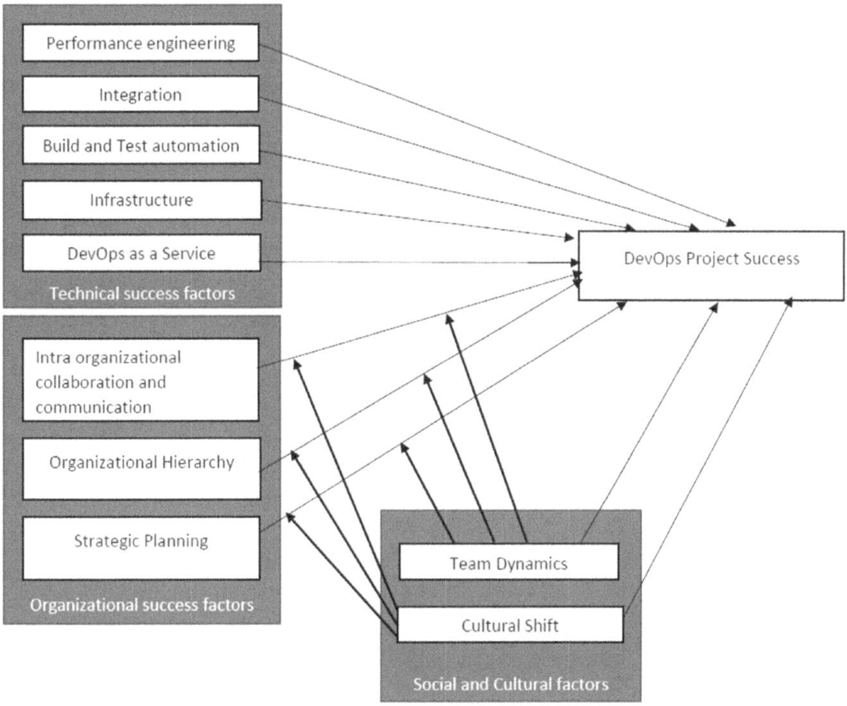

Fig. 2. The synthesized framework of critical success factors

success factors and drives to identify them (cf. [3]), there is a clear lack of a comprehensive model addressing all factors and their relationships. In addition, the critical success factors literature on DevOps is fragmented on addressing the phenomenon through narrowly defined lenses. There are only a few studies using a broader view of the phenomenon.

Thirdly, some of the critical success factors often seen in other areas such as the personal competencies, training, and top management support were not present among the primary studies addressed. There are several possible explanations for their absence ranging from their mitigated role (e.g., top management support might not be important at all after the prerequisites for DevOps have been set as was found in the project cost estimates [37]) to the extant research being too heavily focused on DevOps specific characteristics. Further research is needed to address this.

4.2 A Synthesized Critical Success Factor Model

To address the lack of a comprehensive model of the critical success factors of DevOps, we have developed a synthesized model from our findings. The first version of the model is shown in Fig. 2. The model is built on top of the identified factors and categories.

In this model, we suggest that technical factors and organizational factors (intra-organizational collaboration, organization hierarchy, and strategic planning) would directly impact DevOps success. The social and cultural factors (team dynamics and cultural shift) would moderate the effects of organizational factors on DevOps success. In addition, social and cultural factors might also impact DevOps success directly.

However, we note that the actual relationships can be explored in future research by collecting empirical data from organizations that use DevOps. Furthermore, as discussed previously, might be that not all important critical success factors have been already identified and the model might need to be updated after the field has matured more.

4.3 Future Research Avenues

From our literature review, we have identified several fruitful avenues for future work in this domain. First, our synthesized framework can be used as the guiding framework to investigate the important critical success factors in the future. For example, our framework could help build research models to answer possible research questions such as "What are the most important technical factors?", "What are the most important organizational factors?", and "What are the most important social and cultural factors?". Empirical data can be collected to investigate the factors and structural equation modeling techniques can be used to test the research models to answer the described research questions.

Second, we observed that prior research lack using theoretical frameworks when investigating DevOps success. The organizational and social factors can be tied together with theories from organizational behavior and communication. Therefore, future research can focus on theory-guided approach to investigate DevOps success. Third, opportunities exist in developing scales for measuring DevOps success as well as many of the factors identified in our literature review. Fourth, this systematic literature study provides only an academic view on the phenomenon. A gray literature review would provide an alternative, a more practitioner-focused view on the topic subject.

4.4 Limitations

Naturally, there are certain limitations related to this research which worth noting. First, several papers found in the search used the term 'DevOps' in their keywords (either manually defined by the authors or automatically by the publication database) but the paper actually does not touch the issue at all. Therefore, the initial search returned a large number of false positives which were later excluded in different phases. While we followed a strict protocol in removing a study, still some relevant studies might not have been included in the final list.

Second, for selection of primary articles researcher bias might have an impact on the selection process. The inclusion criteria might have been interpreted falsely. To mitigate this risk of false inclusion criteria, the authors performed the abstract filtering independently. For the full-text filtering stage, the authors

Table 3. Examples of the selected primary studies and extracted data

Authors	Method	Context	Theory	Critical success factors
Bezemer et al. [7]	Survey method	Participants industry sectors	No theory	Performance engineering complexity, Lightweight approaches for performance engineering, Smooth integration with existing tools of Devops
Alnamla et al. [5]	Survey	Not available	No theory	Absence of a lead person (failure factor)
Diaz et al. [16]	Semi-structured interviews, survey, Observation, Workshops	Stakeholders of 30 multinational software-intensive companies	Constructivism model	Cultural and organizational perspective, Emphasizing the silos, Lack of collaboration between dev & ops, Team and process efficiency, Lack of process automation
Diaz et al. [15]	Case study, interviews	Study on +20 software-intensive companies who use DevOps.	No theory	Misalignment among departments, Inflexibility of communication processes
Šmite et al. [42]	Group interviews, workshops	Devops offshore teams between India and Sweden	No theory	Reluctance to warn about non-feasible deadlines, Willingness to accept requests from superiors, Seeking immediate manager's approval for team task in defense to local superiors, Reluctant to reveal a lack of understanding in asking questions, Reluctant to expose problems at earliest convenience, Reluctance to discuss failure, Reluctance to voice criticism or propose alternatives to perceived directives from superiors
Huttermann et al. [21]	Multi-staged Qualitative research, multiple-case study	Two major IT-related enterprises	Information system success model	AISD and a closer integration of ISD with IS should be maximized

went through the texts carefully and made decisions regarding unclear articles. After considering the inclusion and exclusion criteria the articles were included.

Third, we have listed many success factors in this paper, but we did not do prioritization among those factors. Therefore, in future studies we will prioritize these success factors.

Fourth, we used only the Scopus database for searching the articles. This was justified decisions as during the search term testing, the other databases did not bring a remarkable number, if any, of new studies when compared to using only Scopus. However, some relevant studies might have been excluded due to this selection.

5 Conclusions

We conducted a systematic literature review on critical success factors, reported on the extant literature of the DevOps project. We have listed down the success factors which may influence the success of DevOps operations and classified them. We proposed a view of DevOps success factors by synthesizing the findings based on extracted data from the literature. We have categorized the factors into the technical, organizationak, and social & cultural factors. The proposed framework provides a comprehensive view of critical success factors and how they impact the success of DevOps practices in organizations.

References

1. Abdelkebir, S.A.H.I.D., Maleh, Y., Belaissaoui, M.: An agile framework for its management in organizations: a case study based on devops. In: Proceedings of the 2nd International Conference on Computing and Wireless Communication Systems, pp. 1–8 (2017)
2. Ahimbisibwe, A., Cavana, R.Y., Daellenbach, U.: A contingency fit model of critical success factors for software development projects: a comparison of agile and traditional plan-based methodologies. J. Enterp. Inf. Manag. **28**(1), 7–33 (2015). https://doi.org/10.1108/JEIM-08-2013-0060
3. Akbar, M.A., Mahmood, S., Shafiq, M., Alsanad, A., Alsanad, A.A.A., Gumaei, A.: Identification and prioritization of devops success factors using fuzzy-ahp approach. Soft Comput. 1–25 (2020)
4. Aldahmash, A., Gravell, A.M., Howard, Y.: A review on the critical success factors of agile software development. In: Stolfa, J., Stolfa, S., O'Connor, R.V., Messnarz, R. (eds.) EuroSPI 2017. CCIS, vol. 748, pp. 504–512. Springer, Cham (2017). https://doi.org/10.1007/978-3-319-64218-5_41 ISBN 978-3-319-64218-5
5. Alnamlah, B., Alshathry, S., Alkassim, N., Jamail, N.S.M.: The necessity of a lead person to monitor development stages of the devops pipeline. Indones. J. Electr. Eng. Comput. Sci. **21**(01), 348 (2021). https://doi.org/10.11591/ijeecs.v21.i1.pp348-353
6. Ben Mesmia, W., Escheikh, M., Barkaoui, K.: Devops workflow verification and duration prediction using non-markovian stochastic petri nets. J. Softw. Evolut. Process **33**(3), e2329 (2021)
7. Bezemer, C.P., et al.: How is performance addressed in devops? In: Proceedings of the 2019 ACM/SPEC International Conference on Performance Engineering, pp. 45–50 (2019)
8. Bullen, C.V., Rockart, J.F.: A primer on critical success factors. Working papers 1220–81. Report (Alfred P. Sloan School of Management. Center for Information Systems Research); no. 69, Massachusetts Institute of Technology (MIT), Sloan School of Management (1981). https://EconPapers.repec.org/RePEc:mit:sloanp:1988
9. Callanan, M., Spillane, A.: Devops: making it easy to do the right thing. IEEE Softw. **33**(3), 53–59 (2016)
10. Chen, B.: Improving the software logging practices in devops. In: 2019 IEEE/ACM 41st International Conference on Software Engineering: Companion Proceedings (ICSE-Companion), pp. 194–197. IEEE (2019)

11. Chen, J.: Performance regression detection in devops. In: 2020 IEEE/ACM 42nd International Conference on Software Engineering: Companion Proceedings (ICSE-Companion), pp. 206–209. IEEE (2020)
12. Claps, G.G., Svensson, R.B., Aurum, A.: On the journey to continuous deployment: technical and social challenges along the way. Inf. Softw. Technol. **57**, 21–31 (2015)
13. Colomo-Palacios, R., Fernandes, E., Soto-Acosta, P., Larrucea, X.: A case analysis of enabling continuous software deployment through knowledge management. Int. J. Inf. Manag. **40**, 186–189 (2018)
14. Díaz, J., Almaraz, R., Pérez, J., Garbajosa, J.: Devops in practice: an exploratory case study. In: Proceedings of the 19th International Conference on Agile Software Development: Companion, pp. 1–3 (2018)
15. Díaz, J., Perez, J.E., Yague, A., Villegas, A., de Antona, A.: DevOps in practice – a preliminary analysis of two multinational companies. In: Franch, X., Männistö, T., Martínez-Fernández, S. (eds.) PROFES 2019. LNCS, vol. 11915, pp. 323–330. Springer, Cham (2019). https://doi.org/10.1007/978-3-030-35333-9_23
16. Díaz, J., López-Fernández, D., Pérez, J., González-Prieto, Á.: Why are many businesses instilling a devops culture into their organization? Empir. Softw. Eng. **26**(2), 1–50 (2021)
17. Dickinson, R.A., Ferguson, C.R., Sircar, S.: Critical success factors and small business. Am. J. Small Bus. **8**(3), 49–57 (1984). https://doi.org/10.1177/104225878400800309
18. Dyck, A., Penners, R., Lichter, H.: Towards definitions for release engineering and devops. In: 2015 IEEE/ACM 3rd International Workshop on Release Engineering, p. 3. IEEE (2015)
19. Erich, F.M., Amrit, C., Daneva, M.: A qualitative study of devops usage in practice. J. Softw. Evolut. Process **29**(6), e1885 (2017)
20. Hussain, W., Clear, T., MacDonell, S.: Emerging trends for global devops: a new zealand perspective. In: 2017 IEEE 12th International Conference on Global Software Engineering (ICGSE), pp. 21–30. IEEE (2017)
21. Hüttermann, M., Rosenkranz, C.: Devops: walking the shadowy bridge from development success to information systems success. In: European Conference on Information Systems: Human Values Crisis in a Digitalizing World. ECIS 2021 Research Papers (2019)
22. Jabbari, R., Bin Ali, N., Petersen, K., Tanveer, B.: What is devops? A systematic mapping study on definitions and practices. In: Proceedings of the Scientific Workshop Proceedings of XP2016, pp. 1–11 (2016)
23. Järvinen, J., Huomo, T., Mikkonen, T., Tyrväinen, P.: From agile software development to mercury business. In: Lassenius, C., Smolander, K. (eds.) ICSOB 2014. LNBIP, vol. 182, pp. 58–71. Springer, Cham (2014). https://doi.org/10.1007/978-3-319-08738-2_5
24. Júnior, P.S.S., Barcellos, M.P., de Almeida Falbo, R., Almeida, J.P.A.: From a scrum reference ontology to the integration of applications for data-driven software development. Inf. Softw. Technol. **136**, 106570 (2021)
25. Karamitsos, I., Albarhami, S., Apostolopoulos, C.: Applying devops practices of continuous automation for machine learning. Information **11**(7), 363 (2020)
26. Kerzazi, N., Adams, B.: Who needs release and devops engineers, and why? In: Proceedings of the International Workshop on Continuous Software Evolution and Delivery, pp. 77–83 (2016)
27. Kitchenham, B.A., Charters, S.: Guidelines for performing systematic literature reviews in software engineering. version 2.3. EBSE Technical Report EBSE-2007-01, Keele University, Keele, Staffs, United Kingdom, July 2007

28. Kolfschoten, G.L., de Vreede, G.J., Briggs, R.O., Sol, H.G.: Collaboration engineerability. Group Decis. Negot. **19**(3), 301–321 (2010)
29. Krawatzeck, R., Dinter, B.: Agile business intelligence: collection and classification of agile business intelligence actions by means of a catalog and a selection guide. Inf. Syst. Manag. **32**(3), 177–191 (2015)
30. Luz, W.P., Pinto, G., Bonifácio, R.: Building a collaborative culture: a grounded theory of well succeeded devops adoption in practice. In: Proceedings of the 12th ACM/IEEE International Symposium on Empirical Software Engineering and Measurement, pp. 1–10 (2018)
31. Marnewick, C., Langerman, J.: Devops and organisational performance: the fallacy of chasing maturity. IEEE Software (2020)
32. Mohan, V., Othmane, L.B.: Secdevops: is it a marketing buzzword?-mapping research on security in devops. In: 2016 11th International Conference on Availability, Reliability and Security (ARES), pp. 542–547. IEEE (2016)
33. Muñoz, M., Negrete, M., Mejía, J.: Proposal to avoid issues in the DevOps implementation: a systematic literature review. In: Rocha, Á., Adeli, H., Reis, L.P., Costanzo, S. (eds.) WorldCIST'19 2019. AISC, vol. 930, pp. 666–677. Springer, Cham (2019). https://doi.org/10.1007/978-3-030-16181-1_63
34. Nybom, K., Smeds, J., Porres, I.: On the impact of mixing responsibilities between devs and ops. In: Sharp, H., Hall, T. (eds.) XP 2016. LNBIP, vol. 251, pp. 131–143. Springer, Cham (2016). https://doi.org/10.1007/978-3-319-33515-5_11
35. Olszewska, M., Waldén, M.: Devops meets formal modelling in high-criticality complex systems. In: Proceedings of the 1st International Workshop on Quality-aware DevOps, pp. 7–12 (2015)
36. Petersen, K., Wohlin, C.: A comparison of issues and advantages in agile and incremental development between state of the art and an industrial case. J. Syst. Softw. **82**(9), 1479–1490 (2009)
37. Rahikkala, J., Hyrynsalmi, S., Leppänen, V., Porres, I.: The role of organisational phenomena in software cost estimation: an empirical study of supporting and hindering factors. e-Inform. Softw. Eng. J. **12**(1), 167–198 (2018). https://doi.org/10.5277/e-Inf180101
38. Riungu-Kalliosaari, L., Mäkinen, S., Lwakatare, L.E., Tiihonen, J., Männistö, T.: DevOps adoption benefits and challenges in practice: a case study. In: Abrahamsson, P., Jedlitschka, A., Nguyen Duc, A., Felderer, M., Amasaki, S., Mikkonen, T. (eds.) PROFES 2016. LNCS, vol. 10027, pp. 590–597. Springer, Cham (2016). https://doi.org/10.1007/978-3-319-49094-6_44
39. Sacks, M.: DevOps principles for successful web sites. In: Pro Website Development and Operations, pp. 1–14. Apress, Berkeley, CA (2012). https://doi.org/10.1007/978-1-4302-3970-3_1
40. Salameh, H.: The impact of devops automation, controls, and visibility practices on software continuous deployment and delivery. In: Proceedings of the 2nd International Conference on Research in Management and Economics, September 2019
41. Sebastian, I.M., Ross, J.W., Beath, C., Mocker, M., Moloney, K.G., Fonstad, N.O.: How big old companies navigate digital transformation. In: Strategic Information Management, pp. 133–150. Routledge (2020)
42. Šmite, D., Moe, N.B., Gonzalez-Huerta, J.: Overcoming cultural barriers to being agile in distributed teams. Inf. Softw. Technol. **138**, 106612 (2021)
43. Tam, C., da Costa Moura, E.J., Oliveira, T., Varajão, J.: The factors influencing the success of on-going agile software development projects. Int. J. Proj. Manag. **38**(3), 165–176 (2020). https://doi.org/10.1016/j.ijproman.2020.02.001

44. Trihinas, D., Tryfonos, A., Dikaiakos, M.D., Pallis, G.: Devops as a service: pushing the boundaries of microservice adoption. IEEE Internet Comput. **22**(3), 65–71 (2018)
45. Tsanos, C.S., Zografos, K.G., Harrison, A.: Developing a conceptual model for examining the supply chain relationships between behavioural antecedents of collaboration, integration and performance. Int. J. Logist. Manag. **25**(3), 418–462 (2014)
46. Van Belzen, M., DeKruiff, D., Trienekens, J.J.: Success factors of collaboration in the context of devops. In: Proceedings of the 12th IADIS International Conference Information Systems 2019, IS 2019, pp. 26–34 (2019)
47. Wahaballa, A., Wahballa, O., Abdellatief, M., Xiong, H., Qin, Z.: Toward unified devops model. In: 2015 6th IEEE international conference on software engineering and service science (ICSESS), pp. 211–214. IEEE (2015)
48. Wettinger, J., Breitenbücher, U., Leymann, F.: DevOpSlang – bridging the gap between development and operations. In: Villari, M., Zimmermann, W., Lau, K.-K. (eds.) ESOCC 2014. LNCS, vol. 8745, pp. 108–122. Springer, Heidelberg (2014). https://doi.org/10.1007/978-3-662-44879-3_8
49. Wiedemann, A., Wiesche, M., Gewald, H., Krcmar, H.: Understanding how devops aligns development and operations: a tripartite model of intra-it alignment. Eur. J. Inf. Syst. **29**(5), 458–473 (2020)
50. Yoon, C., Lee, K., Yoon, B., Toulan, O.: Typology and success factors of collaboration for sustainable growth in the it service industry. Sustainability **9**(11) (2017)

Towards Federated Learning: A Case Study in the Telecommunication Domain

Hongyi Zhang[1(✉)], Anas Dakkak[2], David Issa Mattos[1], Jan Bosch[1], and Helena Holmström Olsson[3]

[1] Chalmers University of Technology, Hörselgången 11, 412 96 Göteborg, Sweden
{hongyiz,davidis,jan.bosch}@chalmers.se
[2] Ericsson AB, Torshamnsgatan 21, 164 83 Stockholm, Sweden
anas.dakkak@ericsson.com
[3] Malmö University, Östra Varvsgatan 11, 205 06 Malmö, Sweden
helena.holmstrom.olsson@mau.se

Abstract. Federated Learning, as a distributed learning technique, has emerged with the improvement of the performance of IoT and edge devices. The emergence of this learning method alters the situation in which data must be centrally uploaded to the cloud for processing and maximizes the utilization of edge devices' computing and storage capabilities. The learning approach eliminates the need to upload large amounts of local data and reduces data transfer latency with local data processing. Since the Federated Learning technique does not require centralized data for model training, it is better suited to edge learning scenarios in which nodes have limited data. However, despite the fact that Federated Learning has significant benefits, we discovered that companies struggle with integrating Federated Learning components into their systems. In this paper, we present case study research that describes reasons why companies anticipate Federated Learning as an applicable technique. Secondly, we summarize the services that a complete Federated Learning system needs to support in industrial scenarios and then identify the key challenges for industries to adopt and transition to Federated Learning. Finally, based on our empirical findings, we suggest five criteria for companies implementing reliable Federated Learning systems.

Keywords: Federated learning · Machine learning · Case study

1 Introduction

Machine learning has steadily altered the way we live, learn, and work, with significant advances in speech, image, and text recognition, as well as language translation [1]. Large corporations like Google, Facebook, and Apple collect massive amounts of training data from users in order to build large-scale deep learning networks. However, while the utility of deep learning is clear, the training data it employs can have major privacy implications: images and videos of millions of people are collected centrally and stored indefinitely by major organizations, and individuals have little influence over how the data is used. Secondly,

X. Wang et al. (Eds.): ICSOB 2021, LNBIP 434, pp. 238–253, 2021.
https://doi.org/10.1007/978-3-030-91983-2_18

images and videos are likely to contain sensitive information such as faces, license plates, computer screens, and other people's conversations [2]. Large companies have a monopoly on "big data" and they could reap enormous economic gains as a result.

It is known that as the amount of training data increases, the diversity and performance of the models trained by machine learning will become better [3]. However, in many fields, the sharing of personal data is not allowed by regulations, such as GDPR [4]. Those regulations have put forward clear requirements for privacy provisions, further improving the protection of personal information. Therefore, researchers in related industries can only analyze and mine data sets belonging to their own organizations. If a single organization (e.g. a particular medical clinic) does not have a very large amount of data and includes insufficient diversity, then by performing machine learning on such a dataset, researchers may end up with a less generalized model. In this case, the limitations of data privacy and confidentiality clearly affect the effectiveness of machine learning.

On the other hand, with billions of edge devices connected worldwide, these devices are able to generate large amounts of data. In traditional cloud computing architectures, these data need to be centrally transferred to a cloud infrastructure for processing. The traditional method may increase the network load and cause transmission congestion and delays in the data processing. In order to solve those challenges, a new learning concept, Federated Learning, has emerged. Federated Learning refers to the provision of computing and storage services close to the source of things or data.

Although the concept of Federated Learning has significant benefits, it is sometimes hard for industries and companies to build reliable Federated Learning systems [5]. The contribution of this paper is threefold. We provide a case study in the context of a world-leading company with cutting edge technology and advanced practices. The study identifies the reasons why our case company considers Federated Learning as an applicable technique. Furthermore, based on our results, we summarize the services that a complete Federated Learning system needs to support in industrial scenarios and identify the challenges that industries are attempting to solve when adopting and transitioning to Federated Learning. Finally, we suggest 5 criteria for companies who want to implement reliable Federated Learning systems.

This paper is structured as follows. Section 2 presents the background of this study. In Sect. 3, we describe the research method we applied as our basic principle when searching and collecting data. In Sect. 4, we summarize the results from the interviews. In Sect. 5, we outline the challenges and the criteria when realizing Federated Learning components into industrial systems. Finally, we conclude the paper in Sect. 6.

2 Background

Due to the rapid development of the computation capability of edge devices, the integration of edge devices and machine learning has become more than a hypothesis. Due to its characteristics, Federated Learning is proposed to improve traditional Machine Learning approaches, as it enables edge devices to collaboratively learn a shared Machine Learning model. The theory of Federated Learning has been explored in [6,7]. Its major objective is to learn a global statistical model from numerous edge devices.

With the concept first applied by Google in 2017 [8], there have been several Federated Learning architectures, frameworks and solutions proposed to solve real-world applications. In a Federated Learning system, multiple devices work together in a collaborative manner to train predictive models. Federal learning can be built on edge devices (e.g., smart phones, video surveillance devices, etc.). Each edge node trains the machine learning model locally and independently, and the global model is optimized and merged by a central server (e.g., aggregation server). In the whole federation process, the privacy data does not leave the data owner and does not need to be shared with other nodes, which solves the problems of privacy and data security. In summary, the advantage of applying Federated Learning is conspicuous. Due to the mechanism of model training and data distribution, a Federated Learning system is a privacy-preserving Machine Learning approach. It is capable to utilize local computation resources, ease the computation pressure of the central server and provide rapid model evolution due to the local training fashion

Because of the local training fashion, it is capable of utilizing local compute resources, easing the computation load of central servers and providing rapid model evolution [9].

3 Research Methodology

The goals of this study were to explore the benefits for industries implementing Federated Learning and identify the issues that industries are attempting to solve when adopting and transitioning their machine learning components to Federated Learning. These goals were translated into the following research questions:

RQ1. What are the reasons that companies considers Federated Learning as an applicable technique?
RQ2. What kinds of services a Federated Learning system needs to support in the production environments?
RQ3. What are the main challenges and limitations when deploying Federated Learning components into embedded systems?

To answer these research questions, we designed the research in collaboration with Ericsson AB. This study built on a 6-month (Jan 2021–July 2021) case study and applied a case study approach [10]. In this paper, we chose a qualitative case study research approach since it allowed us to look at the current situation with a number of people from a given domain and understand a phenomenon in the industrial context in which it arises [11,12]. In particular, case studies are considered appropriate for examining real-life contexts, such as software development and technique evolution, where controlling the context is not possible [13] and where there is a desire to access the interpretations and expectations of people so that a particular context can be richly understood [10]. Therefore, the high interdependence between the industrial context, the benefits of implementing Federated Learning (RQ1), required services (RQ2) and the faced challenges (RQ3) makes the case study a suitable choice.

3.1 Data Collection and Analysis

We collected data primarily through semi-structured interviews with practitioners who design or use machine learning applications, who involve heavily in data engineering, or who are otherwise machine learning experts [14]. The average interview length was around an hour. All of the interviews were recorded, transcribed, and shared via the case company's internal network.

Based on our interview protocol, we first asked participants to provide an overview of their domain and the specifics related to the telecom industry. Then, we asked participants to provide their view regarding the machine learning projects they were currently involved in, the challenges they faced and the issues that the case company are attempting to solve when adopting and transitioning their machine learning components to Federated Learning. Finally, we asked the participants what they considered the key requirements for building a reliable Federated Learning system.

In addition to the interviews, we collected internal materials to support some of the interviews in addition to conducting interviews. These documents were either shared by participants or were available on the internal network as training, resources, or publications. The use of multiple data sources seeks to present a more comprehensive picture and improve the accuracy of this research [15].

The obtained data were processed using inductive thematic coding technique [12,16]. The authors acquainted themselves with the data by reading and transcribing the interviews in the first phase. During the interviews, at least two authors were present and took notes. After conducting all interviews, the contents were transcribed by the authors. In the second phase, the authors developed the initial set of codes by emphasizing significant observations in relation to the study's specified objectives. The initial set of codes were individually created by three of the authors and then combined later. The authors identified the primary themes in the third phase: machine learning applications, barriers for the industry to implement Federated Learning components and move toward Federated Learning. The authors reviewed these themes in connection to the retrieved codes and the entire data in the fourth phase. The authors defined and named the themes in the context of the appropriate material in the fifth phase. The final part entails the creation of the report, which includes the selection of data and quotes, reflection on current issues and the summary of methods that help companies step towards Federated Learning.

3.2 Case Company

In this research, we worked in close collaboration with Ericsson. Ericsson is one of the most well-known ICT (Information and Communication Technology) suppliers to service providers. They help clients get the most out of connectivity by creating game-changing technology and services that are easy to use, adapt, and scale in a fully connected world. Due to large-scale and distributed customers, Ericsson is also seeking a way to deliver reliable service quality to their customers. Since the company has board experience and tries to investigate the possibility of implementing Federated Learning, we chose it as our case company and try to identify the issues for companies to deploy Federated Learning into an industrial context.

3.3 Use Cases and Participants

During the research, we studied three different use cases within Ericsson. As we listed in Table 1, use case A refers to data collection and analysis. This field is critical for machine learning as well as Federated Learning since the quality and efficiency of the data collection procedure has a huge impact on final model performance [17]. Use case B refers to system architecture design and operation. Since Federated Learning is a distributed system, infrastructure design requires experience and careful consideration. Use case C refers to machine learning project design, development and operation, which is highly relevant to our topic and the experience from those practitioners is valuable for constructing a Federated Learning system. In total, we interviewed 10 participants in 9 interviews. Participants were gathered through industry contacts and were selected based on their relevance to the use cases involved in this study. All participants were experienced architects, senior developers, team leaders and development managers with at least eight years of experience, and most were also very experienced in data engineering and machine learning application development. To maintain confidentiality, we referred to the participants using labels P1 to P9, reflecting the interview numbers. As there are several participants in a single interview, we give the label suffixes, such as P7-1, P7-2. A summary of participants is listed in Table 1.

3.4 Threats to Validity

The findings, like any case study, is primarily applicable to the domain and situations that were studied in this research [18]. The insights and results however, can be applicable and relevant also beyond the specific case at hand. Furthermore, while the empirical results are subjective because they represent the experiences of the chosen individuals, the possible scope of the results and their applicability is enlarged due to the extensive experience of the professional participants.

Table 1. Overview of the interviewees

Participant ID	Role	Use Case	Experience (Years)
P1	Global Data Domain Expert	A	30
P2	Data and Analytic Manager	A	25
P3	Analytic System Architect	B	13
P4	Analytic System Architect	B	14
P5	Data and Analytic Technical Driver	A	8
P6	New Products Operations Director	B	25
P7-1	Machine Learning Project Manager	C	30
P7-2	AI Systems Developer	C	18
P8	Customer data collection expert	A	28
P9	Head of Automation and AI	C	17

As for the construct validity, both the authors and participants in this case study have extensive machine learning, Federated Learning, and data engineering experience. Furthermore, if structures with special nomenclature within the industries or in academia were not understood, the authors with experience in both could translate and demonstrate them. As a result, the presence of dangers in the construct validity is not recognized.

In order to prevent threats to the validity of the conclusions, we took a number of steps during the study. The first stage was to eliminate bias created by individuals who had a similar point of view. To assist eliminate any personal prejudice, participants from various roles in different project teams were invited. The second stage was to gather data in the form of documentation to supplement the information gained through interviews, which also helped to avoid bias from being created by just collecting data in one format. Finally, direct participant comment on the developing data was obtained to assist validate the findings.

4 Empirical Findings: Towards Federated Learning

4.1 Benefits of Implementing Federated Learning

As we observed in most of the companies, maintaining qualified service has become more and more expensive with the exponentially increased number of customers. One of the participants stated that their clients prefer to focus more on their own strengths while leaving service monitoring and maintenance to their device supplier.

> *"Customers want to focus on their strengths, such as marketing, bundling, and selling. Ericsson will track SLA (Service Level Agreement) to ensure that this network meets these KPIs and maintains SLA at these levels".*
> —Interview P6, New Products Operations Director

However, with the trend of this situation, the challenge appeared. In order to maintain and monitor a wide variety of equipment and traffic devices, companies may need to put more resources on products maintenance and troubleshooting, which turns out to be inefficient and inapplicable.

> *"It is not wise or feasible to have more people pumped in to monitor these types of systems as traffic density rises. As a result, AI assistance is required."*—Interview P2, Data and Analytics Manager

Our case company is a pioneer in the use of machine learning techniques in its products. As additional improvements in performance and network optimization are required for new demands from industrial applications, machine learning may help reduce complexity, meet new technologies and case requirements, improve network performance and allow for network automation.

> *"We use machine learning in every aspect of a telecommunication network you can think of, from the different use cases to the functions of creating a mobile network."*—P7-1, Machine Learning System Project Manager

When it comes to Machine learning, data has become crucial to model performance and service quality. In general, the addition of large amounts of reliable data in industrial applications will significantly improve the learning quality and prediction accuracy of machine learning. As described by the participants:

> *"Customer issue: When it comes to machine learning, the right data is like food to humans."*—P7-1, Machine Learning System Project Manager

Nevertheless, the development of machine learning techniques also raises concerns about data privacy leaks when significant amounts of customer data are transferred. With the improvement of regulations and the importance of privacy protection, more constraints have been recognized:

> *We also recognize the growing number of constraints on data movement, such as those imposed not only by data sovereignty concerns, correct? So, Norway, data stays in Norway, India said, our data stays here, and so on. Again, more constrained geographies."*—P5, Data and Analytic Technical Driver

In order to tackle those challenges, industries are trying to seeking a way to both avoid large data transmission but continuously provide stable service. One of our participants stated that with commonly applied learning strategies, such as centralized learning, it is almost impossible to make a quick response to large-scaled distributed customers when the characteristic of data has been dramatically changed.

> *"It's nearly impossible to respond quickly to large-scale customer changes without a Federated setting."*—P9, Head of Automation and AI

4.2 Transition to Federated Learning

Federated Learning can be a potential solution to those challenges due to its characteristics. Even though our participants agreed on the increasing interest in developing Federated Learning components into an industrial context, there are also issues that prevent companies adopt and transiting traditional learning strategies to Federated Learning.

> *"We need to think about how we can bring data out in a clever way, and I believe federated learning can help. Not only from radio base stations but also from the center."*—P8, Customer Data Collection Expert

One of the problems is a systematic distributed management system. Especially when industries are trying to collect data and monitor service performance from millions of network elements, it will become expensive and painful to discover the error. The situation may become more crucial if an additional function is added to edge devices, such as model training and validation.

> *"We don't have anything in place to quickly identify, for this one network element out of the million missed one file or wasn't available. It's extremely expensive because it requires people to manually check the edge to see what is going on."*—P3, Analytic System Architect

In addition, the system architecture is another important issue that has to be considered. Since in most of the scenarios, centralized data collection architecture is still the major data pipeline and support for current machine learning model development, as described by one of the participants, different levels of closeness to the source can be gradually applied when trying to transit current learning strategy to fully Federated Learning.

> *"The challenges I see are that there are different levels of closeness to the source, the different levels may result in different costs of management and transmission efficiency"*—P4, Analytic System Architect

The technique to guarantee model performance is another key issue. The models may require more capacity for generalization and automated learning iteration due to varied data features to accommodate rapidly changing customer environments and decrease the risk of poor service.

> *"It's critical for us to not only ensure model performance when it comes to the inference phase in Federated Learning but also to point out what's causing the degradation if any, especially if you've made certain data or network configuration changes in some nodes without informing the supplier."*—P9, Head of Automation and AI

Even though there are many other steps to be taken in order before a company transit to fully Federated Learning, our participants mentioned that it's a good time to consider now what kind of case studies it needs to be used and how these types of capabilities can be moved to a network.

> *"When introducing federated learning, you need to think large, but you probably also need to identify these small steps because these are the most valuable steps."*—P6, New Products Operations Director

There are three problems stated by one of our participants that we have to consider before moving towards and migrating Federated Learning components into embedded systems:

> *"What is the migration story there? How do you go about introducing this new capability? What type of use cases is suitable for Federated Learning?"* —P6, New Products Operations Director

In summary, as we observed from the interviews from our case company, although the federated learning idea has considerable benefits, the creation of a trustworthy and relevant federated learning system is often problematic for them and may encounter different kinds of challenges. In this context, in the following section, we concluded the challenges and concerns that the industry is trying to resolve when adopting and migrating to federated learning.

5 Discussion

5.1 Benefits

From the empirical data, we identify that there are two major reasons which drive our case company to explore Federated Learning. One reason is the data privacy. As mentioned by our participants, Federated Learning may be one of the optimal solution to solve data silos and avoid privacy leakage. Since our case company has large amount of customers, the way of effectively integrating and analysing data that are scattered in various places is one of their biggest challenges. In the Federated Learning, as the data doesn't leave the edge and the analysts do not have direct access to the data, so the various data-related problems mentioned above are resolved. The value contained in the data can be exploited more effectively by the companies while still ensuring the data security of their customers.

Another reason is that companies may be able to respond to customers more quickly. Since Federated Learning can improve data collection and model training efficiency, the learning strategy can assist companies in implementing real-time functions to consume fresh customer data and adapt to environment changes, resulting in better service quality and enhanced model performance for their customers.

5.2 Learning Services

When conducting Federated Learning in actual production environment, we must consider not only the coupling and stability of the system, but also the business requirements with multiple data sources. Therefore, in order to cope with complex business requirements for each component of the system, we need to find a balance between flexibility and convenience. As mentioned by one of our participants:

> *"For Federated Learning, a complete training service should support functional features such as pre-checking, mid-term fault tolerance, full-cycle monitoring, and traceability of the results."*—P9, Head of Automation and AI

According to our empirical results, in Fig. 1 we have summarized the services that a complete Federated Learning system needs to support in industrial scenarios.

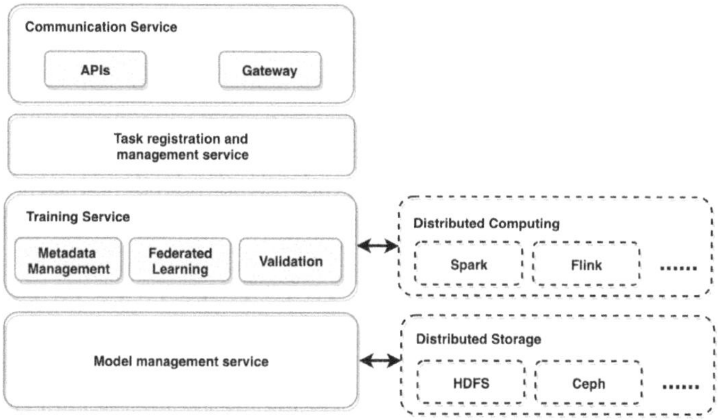

Fig. 1. Services that a complete Federated Learning system needs to support

Communication services: Since communication is required between the end customers, we must provide a gateway service to handle service routing and expose the API interfaces to the outside world in order to reveal as little information about our services to the other side as possible and to conveniently invoke training services. All queries from external systems will be routed through the gateway service for processing.

Task registration and management service: Task registration and management should be implemented to assure the service's high availability. The service information will be registered to the server when the service is started. When a training request is sent to the gateway, the gateway will retrieve the server's available computing resources and finish the service invocation using the defined load balancing policy.

Training Service: This service includes a metadata management component, Federated Learning component, and a validation component. The metadata management component will be in charge of keeping track of the progress of each training task, as well as the operating status and configuration parameters. In contrast, the Federated Learning component is used to conduct the numerous functions required during the distributed model training process. The validation component will be in charge of validating the configuration settings we submit as well as controlling model quality and performance.

Model management service: When the training task is finished, the training service provides the trained model information to the model management service, which then completes the distributed persistent storing, grouping, and other processes.

5.3 Challenges

Based on our empirical results, we derive the challenges for industries stepping towards Federated Learning. Figure 2 illustrates five challenges and problems which a typical system may encounter, including components failures, inefficient communication, unstable model performance, large-scaled end customers and incomplete system security.

Challenge 1 - Components Failures. There are three main components in a typical Federated Learning system, including an aggregation server, communication links and remote edge devices. The architecture applied in current systems may often lead to significant bottlenecks and inevitable single-point failure. The problem can destroy system service stability and largely influence user experience. Furthermore, due to a large amount of communication, the link between servers and edge devices may be fully occupied or disconnected which results in unexpected information drop. Nevertheless, local edge devices may suffer problems of non-reachable server, program-stuck, high latency responses, etc.

> *"From the customer's perspective, nobody wants to hear what's going on in their network in terms of failures and crashes."*—P3, Analytic System Architect

Based on the characteristic of the Federated Learning technique, the problem of how to guarantee continuous federated model training and global model deployment to the edge is highly important to a service-sensitive industrial Federated Learning system. System robustness and fault tolerance issues are significantly more prevalent than in traditional distributed system environments.

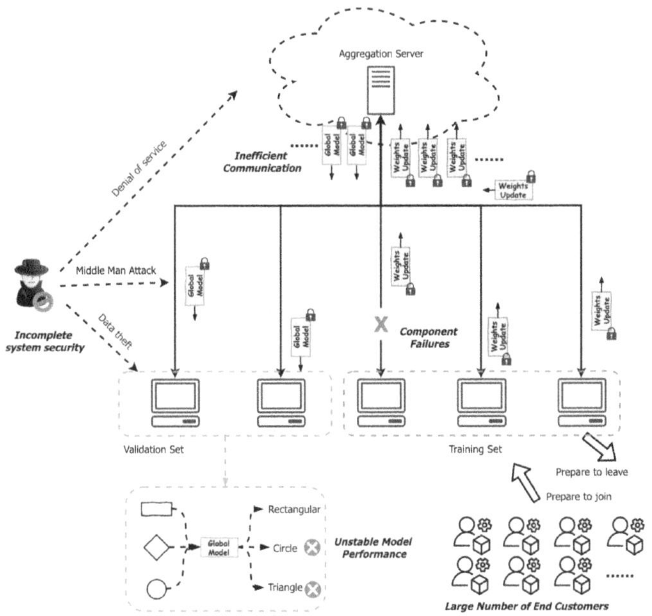

Fig. 2. Problems and challenges for Federated Learning to be implemented into service-sensitive systems.

Challenge 2 - Inefficient Communication. Federated Learning highly relies on a fast network and frequent communication of weight updates, either between peers or servers. However, the network situation for different devices may differ a lot. Since distributed edge devices need to frequently communicate to a central server in order to update model gradients and deploy fresh global models, the bottleneck and high bandwidth occupation at aggregation servers are inevitable issues. Imagining hundreds and thousands of edge devices needs to constantly keep the connection to the servers, communication resources must be constrained due to frequent model updating and global model deployment. As mentioned by one of our participants:

> *"Efficiency is one of the key features. We want to reduce the cost such as bandwidth utilization but still be able to improve service quality"*—P2, Data and Analytic Manager

Although there are some of the research [6,19] related to communication-efficient Federated Learning systems, the problems of how to reduce the communication round in real industrial scenarios, how to efficiently utilize network resources while maintaining or even improving model prediction performance still need to be searched and verified.

Challenge 3 - Unstable Model Performance. For a traditional Machine Learning approach, the main goal of the system is to provide an accurate prediction or classification based on existing user data sets.

> *"Model performance is crucial for Federated Learning. If we cannot guarantee a sustainable model performance, we then have no reason to adopt it."*—P5, Data and Analytic Technical Driver

Similar to Federated Learning techniques, this challenge is the most critical one and also an important metric to evaluate a Federated Learning system. However, in the real world system, data collected from edge devices are non-IID and sometimes are unbalanced [5]. This is due to the different scenarios and environment edge devices exposed. The problem of how to keep or even improve model prediction performance compared to the traditional centralized model training approach, how to ensure the model can perform well on all the edge devices, what is the benchmark tool of evaluating Federated Learning systems are still tricky and need to be verified in different real-world application scenarios as we have described before.

Challenge 4 - Large Number of End Customers. As we described before, the Federated Learning system can be considered as Machine Learning clusters with a distributed configuration.

> *"We do have a huge number of customers. With Federated Learning, the way how to properly manage them and handle connections is a question."* —P4, Analytic System Architect

Normally, the system contains numerous edge nodes which may frequently leave and join. In order to achieve system scalability, the mechanism of how to handle device joining in, how to schedule device utilization and how to deal with device leaving without influencing system service still need to be researched and algorithms can be designed.

Challenge 5 - Incomplete System Security. One of the main advantages of Federated Learning techniques is to prevent the transmission of sensitive user data. This is also the main reason why this technique has broad potential in various application domains. A privacy-preserving system is a big approach to Machine Learning system research.

> *"In the future, even with Federated Learning, We still have to explore a comprehensive approach in complying with applicable privacy regulations and legislation to handle the security and privacy aspects of our products."* —P6, New Product Operations Director

The question of how to avoid data leakage from global shared weights becomes essential. Therefore, a secured Federated System needs to protect not only local user data but also the transmission data from being damaged or leaked and forbidding illegal modification, access or usage of system programs, weight updates and global models. With the increasing attention and focus on AI-powered industrial solutions, security issues are more essential to the service provider.

5.4 Criteria for a Reliable Federated Learning System

Based on the issues mentioned by our participants that companies need to consider when implementing Federated Learning, we interpret those challenges to five criteria for a reliable Federated Learning system, including service availability for model training and improvements, efficient model training and sharing, accuracy assurance on the edge, scalable Federated Learning architecture and secured connection between edge and cloud. Those criteria are critical for effective and successful implementation of Federated Learning in embedded systems.

Service Availability for Model Training and Improvements. Availability means the durability of the system and likely to keep operating for a long period of time. As we described before, customers always need a reliable system service that guarantees continuous model training and deployment (Challenge 1), which is the foundation of model performance improvements. The problem is crucial in a Federated Learning system since most of the learning is real-time and fast-evolving. A reliable Federated Learning system needs to have a fault-dealing mechanism in order to guarantee service availability once a fault occurs. For example, the interaction between local edge devices and model aggregation server may suffer high latency, accidentally connection drop, server stuck due to high concurrence computation, etc.

Efficient Model Training and Sharing. Efficiency signifies low resource utilization (CPU, Memory, Disk usage), low communication round and bandwidth occupation. This criterion relates to low-cost model training on the edge and efficient communication between edge and server during weight updating and model deploying procedure (Challenge 2). Furthermore, the way to split training devices is also an important approach to save computing resources. A reliable Federated Learning system should consume fewer resources, less bandwidth and communication utilization while still keeping an acceptable model performance.

Accuracy Assurance on the Edge. Accuracy is another important criterion. The system has to guarantee model performance and has the mechanisms to evaluate models on all edge devices (Challenge 3). Because the main purpose of the machine learning approach is to provide an accurate model for the corresponding application scenario, a reliable Federated Learning system should achieve, guarantee a satisfying model performance on all edge devices and be applied in the real-world industrial environment.

Scalable Federated Learning Architecture. Scalability refers to the ability to handle an increasing number of tasks by joining more edge devices to the Federated Learning systems (Challenge 4). Due to the highly distributed devices, a reliable Federated Learning system should be able to locate, find and accept asynchronous join of different types of edge devices and can be extended and cooperate with other learning clusters.

Secured Connection Between Edge and Cloud. Secured connection implies system data and model safety during local data collection, weights updating and global model aggregation. As described in Challenge 5, industrial systems may still need to face numerous kinds of malicious attacks. A reliable Federated Learning system should protect data collected at the edge devices, secure interaction between local edge devices and aggregation servers and guarantee the integrity of Machine Learning model transactions.

6 Conclusions

In this paper, we present a cutting-edge case study that identifies issues that industries are attempting to solve when dealing with Machine Learning cases, as well as the reasons why they anticipate Federated Learning as an applicable technique. Based on our findings, we summarize the services that a complete Federated Learning system needs to support in industrial scenarios. Furthermore, we highlight the issues that industries are attempting to address when adopting and transitioning their machine learning components to Federated Learning, including components failures, inefficient communication, unstable model performance, large-scaled end customers and incomplete system security. In addition, we suggest five critical criteria for designing and operating a dependable industrial Federated Learning system. In the future, we intend to validate our findings in industry cases and investigate solutions to the problems identified in this paper.

Acknowledgements. This work was partially supported by the Wallenberg Artificial Intelligence, Autonomous Systems and Software Program (WASP) funded by the Knut and Alice Wallenberg Foundation, the Software Center and the Chalmers AI Research Center. The authors would also like to express their gratitude for all the interviewees and the support provided by Ericsson.

References

1. Bishop, C.M.: Pattern Recognition and Machine Learning. Springer, Heidelberg (2006)
2. Shultz, D.: When your voice betrays you (2015)
3. Sun, C., Shrivastava, A., Singh, S., Gupta, A.: Revisiting unreasonable effectiveness of data in deep learning era. In: Proceedings of the IEEE International Conference on Computer Vision, pp. 843–852 (2017)

4. Goddard, M.: The eu general data protection regulation (gdpr): European regulation that has a global impact. Int. J. Mark. Res. **59**(6), 703–705 (2017)
5. Bonawitz, K., et al.: Towards federated learning at scale: System design. arXiv preprint arXiv:1902.01046 (2019)
6. Konečnỳ, J., McMahan, H.B., Yu, F.X., Richtárik, P., Suresh, A.T., Bacon, D.: Federated learning: Strategies for improving communication efficiency. arXiv preprint arXiv:1610.05492 (2016)
7. McMahan, H.B., Moore, E., Ramage, D., Hampson, S., et al.: Communication-efficient learning of deep networks from decentralized data. arXiv preprint arXiv:1602.05629 (2016)
8. Yang, T., et al.: Applied federated learning: Improving google keyboard query suggestions. arXiv preprint arXiv:1812.02903 (2018)
9. Zhang, C., Xie, Y., Bai, H., Yu, B., Li, W., Gao, Y.: A survey on federated learning. Knowl.-Based Syst. **216**, 106775 (2021)
10. Walsham, G.: Interpretive case studies in is research: nature and method. Eur. J. Inf. Syst. **4**(2), 74–81 (1995)
11. Yin, R.K.: Case Study Research and Applications: Design and Methods. Sage publications, Thousand Oaks (2017)
12. Maxwell, J.A.: Qualitative Research Design: An Interactive Approach, vol. 41. Sage publications, Thousand Oaks (2012)
13. Sgier, L.: Qualitative data analysis. An Initiat. Gebert Ruf Stift **19**, 19–21 (2012)
14. Runeson, P., Host, M., Rainer, A., Regnell, B.: Case Study Research in Software Engineering: Guidelines and Examples. John Wiley & Sons, Hoboken (2012)
15. Runeson, P., Höst, M.: Guidelines for conducting and reporting case study research in software engineering. Empir. Softw. Eng. **14**(2), 131–164 (2009)
16. Rivas, C.: Coding and analysing qualitative data. Res. Soc. Cult. **3**(2012), 367–392 (2012)
17. Roh, Y., Heo, G., Whang, S.E.: A survey on data collection for machine learning: a big data - AI integration perspective. IEEE Trans. Knowl. Data Eng. **33**(4), 1328–1347, 08 Oct 2019
18. Braun, V., Clarke, V.: Using thematic analysis in psychology. Qual. Res. Psychol. **3**(2), 77–101 (2006)
19. Chen, Y., Sun, X., Jin, Y.: Communication-efficient federated deep learning with asynchronous model update and temporally weighted aggregation. arXiv preprint arXiv:1903.07424 (2019)

Author Index

The manufacturer's authorised representative in the EU is Springer
Nature Customer Service Centre GmbH, Europaplatz 3, 69115 Heidelberg,
Germany. If you have any concerns regarding our products, please
contact ProductSafety@springernature.com

Printed and bound by CPI Group (UK) Ltd, Croydon, CR0 4YY
02/10/2026
02227135-0003